GENDERING WELFARE STATES

GENDERING
WELFARE STATES

edited by
Diane Sainsbury

SAGE Modern Politics Series Volume 35
Sponsored by the European Consortium for
Political Research/ECPR

SAGE Publications
London · Thousand Oaks · New Delhi

First published 1994

 SAGE Publications Ltd
6 Bonhill Street
London EC2A 4PU

   SAGE Publications Inc
   2455 Teller Road
   Thousand Oaks, California 91320

   SAGE Publications India Pvt Ltd
   32, M-Block Market
   Greater Kailash – I
   New Delhi 110 048

British Library Cataloguing in Publication data

A catalogue record for this book is available from
the British Library.

   ISBN 0–8039–7852–9
   ISBN 0–8039–7853–7 (pbk)

Library of Congress catalog card number 94–068453

Typeset by Type Study, Scarborough
Printed in Great Britain by Biddles Ltd, Guildford,
Surrey

Contents

Acknowledgements

The chapters of this book were originally a set of papers presented and discussed at the ECPR workshop on Welfare States and Gender at the Leiden Joint Sessions of Workshops in 1993. Since this volume is a product of the workshop and the revised papers owe much to the lively exchange of ideas during our discussions, the editor and authors would like to express their gratitude to those participants whose papers are not included here: Jane Bayes (California State University, Northridge), Amy Mazur (Indiana University, Indianapolis), Jantine Oldersma (University of Leiden), Ilona Ostner (University of Bremen), Clare Ungerson (University of Kent, Canterbury) and Celia Valiente (Juan March Institute, Madrid). We would also like to thank Peter Mair, editor of the Sage Modern Politics Series, for his assistance and encouragement with this project. Thanks are also due to Robert Brewster for his bitter humour and budding secretarial skills in helping to produce the final manuscript for publication.

Contributors

Michael Bittman, Senior Lecturer in Sociology at the University of New South Wales, Sydney. He is author of *Juggling Time: How Australian Families Use Time*.

Anette Borchorst, Associate Professor of Political Science, University of Aarhus, Denmark. She has contributed chapters to *Women and the State* (1987) and *Gender and Caring* (1990). Her most recent publication is 'The Scandinavian welfare states – patriarchal, gender neutral or woman-friendly?', *International Journal of Contemporary Sociology* (1994).

Lois Bryson, Professor of Sociology at the University of Newcastle, Australia, has written extensively on gender inequality. Her most recent book is *Welfare and the State: Who Benefits?* (1992).

Jet Bussemaker, Lecturer in Women's Studies, Department of Political Science and Public Administration, Free University, Amsterdam. Her most recent publications in English are 'Equality, autonomy and feminist politics', in *Equality and Gender Principles* (1991) and 'Feminism and the welfare state: on individualism in the Netherlands', in *History of European Ideas* (1992).

Mary Daly, Researcher at the Department of Social and Political Science, the European University Institute, Florence, Italy. She has published widely on gender-related and poverty issues, and is author of *Women and Poverty* (1989). Her latest publication is 'A matter of dependency? The gender dimension of British income maintenance provision', *Sociology* (1994).

Sue Donath, Researcher in the Households Research Unit, Department of Economics, University of Melbourne. Her research focuses on the economic importance of unpaid work.

Siv Gustafsson, Professor of Economics, University of Amsterdam. Among her many publications are 'Equal opportunity policies in Sweden', in *Sex Discrimination and Equal Opportunity* (1984); 'The labor force participation and earnings of lone parents', in *Lone-Parent Families: The Economic Challenge* (1990); and 'Separate taxation and married women's labor supply', *Journal of Population Economics* (1992).

Barbara Hobson, Associate Professor of Social Policy, University of Stockholm, Sweden. She is author of *Uneasy Virtue: the Politics of Prostitution and the American Reform Tradition* (1987, 1990). Among her most recent publications is 'Feminist strategies and gendered discourses in welfare states', in *Mothers of a New World: Gender and Origins of Welfare States in Western Europe and North America* (1993). She is also co-editor of a new journal, *Social Politics: International Studies of Gender, State and Society*.

Kees van Kersbergen, Lecturer in Political Science, Free University, Amsterdam. His most recent publications include 'Trends in contemporary class structuration. A six-nation comparison', in *Changing Classes; Stratification and Mobility in Post-Industrial Societies* (1993) and 'The distinctiveness of Christian democracy', in *Christian Democracy in Europe* (1994).

Toni Makkai, Research Fellow, Sociology Program, Research School of Social Science, Australian National University, Canberra. She is co-author of *Drugs in Australian Society: Patterns, Attitudes and Policies* (1991) and *Raising the Standard* (1993).

- **Traute Meyer**, Research Fellow at WZB, the Social Science Research Centre Berlin. Her publications include 'Unterm neuen Kleid der Freiheit das Korsett der Einheit. Auswirkungen der deutschen Vereinigung für Frauen in Ost und West' (1992) and 'Kinder, Kirche, Kapitalismus', in *Auf die Kitaplätzefertig, los* (1993).

Diane Sainsbury, Associate Professor of Political Science at the University of Stockholm. She is editor of *Democracy, State, and Justice* (1988) and a special issue on 'Party Strategies and Party-Voter Linkages' of the *European Journal of Political Research* (1990). Among her most recent publications are 'Dual welfare and sex segregation of access to social benefits', *Journal of Social Policy* (1993) and 'Social policy and the influence of familial ideology', in *Different Roles, Different Voices* (1994).

Kirsten Scheiwe, Researcher at the Mannheim Centre of European Social Research. Her publications include 'Costs and benefits of housework: winners and losers', in *Recht en Kritiek* (1991), 'EC law's unequal treatment of the family', *Social and Legal Studies* (1994) and *Männerzeiten und Frauenzeiten im Recht* (1993).

Alan Siaroff, Assistant Professor of Political Science, University of British Columbia, Canada. He is co-author of 'Parties and party government in advanced democracies', in *Canadian Political Parties* (1992).

List of Tables

List of Figures

1

Introduction

Diane Sainsbury

Feminist and mainstream theorizing and scholarship on welfare states have been informed by different research paradigms resulting in distinctive contributions. As yet there has been little effort to confront the two perspectives and to combine their insights in analysing welfare states and gender. Instead mainstream researchers have largely ignored feminist scholarship, and feminists have primarily engaged in a critique of mainstream analysis. The result has been an intellectual impasse which needs to be overcome.

The purpose of this volume is to gender welfare states – to incorporate gender into the comparative analysis of welfare states – by drawing on a broad spectrum of insights from *both* feminist and mainstream research. To place this endeavour in the context of the existing literature, it is useful to present briefly the contributions and shortcomings of mainstream and feminist perspectives and subsequently indicate how the essays here aim to move beyond the current state of research.

One of the main contributions of mainstream literature since the mid-1970s has been to devise welfare state typologies and models of social policy. Scholarly interest gravitated towards welfare states and understanding variations – and away from the welfare state and generalizations. The comparative perspective of mainstream scholarship was further enhanced as researchers formulated competing explanations of the emergence and growth of welfare states, which they tested through cross-national analysis. The mainstream research paradigm has focused on explanations related to economic development, social structure (particularly class relations and politics), and state institutional arrangements and capabilities.

A major shortcoming of mainstream analysis has been its neglect of gender. Although the mainstream project has generally been cast in gender-neutral terms, several of its analytical concepts and units of analysis have men as their point of departure. For example, in conceptualizing something so central as different bases of social entitlements, mainstream scholars have overlooked perhaps the most common basis of women's entitlement: rights derived via their husband. The units of analysis in the mainstream literature have been the individual or various collectives – classes, occupational groups, generations or households. Seldom have these gender-neutral units been broken down by sex. Using these sorts of units of analysis and concepts, mainstream empirical studies have often failed to generate much information about women.

As a result, mainstream comparative analysis tells us little about how women have fared in different welfare states or about dissimilar policy outcomes for women and men. Nor has the mainstream research paradigm considered one of the most interesting aspects of the development of welfare states: how women have been incorporated in the core policies of welfare states and the politics of their entitlement.

By contrast, the feminist research paradigm has sought to bring women and gender into the analysis of the welfare state. Among its most important contributions, feminist analysis has documented the inequalities between women and men as recipients of welfare state benefits. Feminist scholarship has also emphasized a different set of determinants shaping the nature of public provision of welfare: the interrelationships of the state, the market, and the family. Feminists have also pointed to the role of familial and gender ideologies in influencing state provision of benefits and services. Furthermore, by examining care and the human services sector, feminists have broadened the analytical focus of the welfare state research in comparison to mainstream analysis, which has tended to concentrate on social insurance schemes and income maintenance policies. In short, the feminist research paradigm has been infused by a critical spirit, seeking to redress gaps in mainstream research.

A weakness of early feminist studies was a generic view of the welfare state and a lack of attention to differences in state formation. The notion of the state as an expression of patriarchy tended to blind feminists to significant variations between specific states and to the possibility of variations that might be beneficial to women. Also influential was the fact that many studies were set in the context of a single country and initial comparisons focused on similar countries. Moreover, the specific context of the studies was often the Anglo-Saxon countries, and the experiences of these countries were interpreted in terms of universals. Gradually feminists have extended the horizons of their theorizing and comparisons, and in the process the welfare state has been superseded by welfare states.

What does the task of gendering welfare states and social policy regimes involve? And what strategies can and have been pursued to this end? Two general approaches to gendering welfare states are discernible in the literature. The first has been to problematize several basic concepts in the mainstream literature by inquiring how they are gendered. In effect, this approach seeks to utilize mainstream theories and conceptions, and when necessary to refashion them, so as to encompass both women and men (Orloff, 1993; O'Connor, 1993). The second approach argues that mainstream theories are fundamentally lacking. Because crucial elements are missing, alternative theories and models are required (Lewis and Ostner, 1991; Lewis, 1992a).

This volume grew out of a set of questions related to these two approaches. To what extent can current mainstream typologies and models of welfare states and social policy regimes be used in gendering welfare states? How must these analytical constructs be modified? Or must we come up with entirely new frameworks to study welfare states and gender? Finally, when gender is incorporated into the analysis, to what extent do welfare state types based on gender regimes coincide with or deviate from those resulting from mainstream typologies? The chapters here answer these questions in different ways. A number of authors have applied mainstream typologies and models analysing gender or policy areas of importance to women, while others have devised alternative frameworks.

In the next chapter Jet Bussemaker and Kees van Kersbergen call for a synthesis of mainstream and feminist theories. They first assess developments in mainstream research – concentrating on the power resources approach and Gøsta Esping-Andersen's theory of welfare state regimes. Subsequently they review feminist scholarship on the welfare state. In discussing how to combine the insights of both schools, Bussemaker and van Kersbergen focus on the Dutch case. They problematize and confront the dimensions of Esping-Andersen's typology – the quality of social rights as measured by de-commodification (eliminating dependence on the market), the pattern of stratification resulting from welfare state policies, and the nature of the state–market nexus – with reference to gender. Their discussion elucidates the sharp divergences in social policy outcomes for women and men in the Netherlands. These differences, they stress, can only be understood by examining the gendered division of labour in the family.

Anette Borchorst's point of departure is women's interests, which she utilizes in combination with Esping-Andersen's regime typology to assess women's situation in several West European welfare states. She analyses women's interests – defined as the range of their choices in connection with responsibilities in human care – in the social democratic and conservative welfare state regimes, focusing on the three Scandinavian countries and the continental countries which are members of the European Community. The final section of the chapter discusses the impact of the EC/EU on the women's options and the implications of the European integration process.

Siv Gustafsson applies Esping-Andersen's typology to an analysis of a policy area that has been neglected by mainstream research of welfare states. She examines childcare in the US, the Netherlands and Sweden, and finds that the patterns of provision fit quite well into Esping-Andersen's categorization of welfare state regimes – the liberal or residual, conservative or corporatist, and social democratic or institutional regimes. In the US mothers work and most parents rely on the market; in Sweden there is close to universal use of subsidized childcare and mothers have jobs; in the Netherlands there is little subsidized daycare for children and most mothers do not participate in the paid labour force. In explaining these variations she looks at the ideological legacies in each of the countries.

Mainstream comparative analysis has emphasized the welfare state as a means of assuring independence from the market, while many feminists have analysed how social policy both reflects and maintains women's economic dependence on men. Instead Traute Meyer explores women's independence from the family through the social welfare market – or their access to state employment, that is, their commodification through the state as employer. In assessing the emancipatory potential of welfare states, she compares the British and German welfare states as employers. This choice of countries is important because earlier research has tended to identify the positive effects of women's employment in the public sector as a distinctive feature of the Scandinavian welfare states or the social democratic welfare state regime (Hernes, 1987a; Esping-Andersen, 1990, chapter 6). Meyer's analysis indicates similar positive effects in the German case, which is typically viewed as a social transfer welfare state. The focus on a least likely case and her findings suggest that this may not be a defining property of social democratic welfare states but a feature shared by several other welfare states.

Of all the chapters, Alan Siaroff's offers the most comprehensive comparison by utilizing data from the 23 OECD countries. As distinct from earlier typologies and models which have been gender neutral or gender blind, he focuses on the 'work–welfare' trade-off for women in an effort to establish a gender-sensitive typology of welfare states. Initially he looks at female/male differences in unemployment, total employment, wages and positions in the job hierarchy in the 1980s to establish a measure of female work desirability. Subsequently he combines this measure with an analysis of social programmes benefiting women and families to produce a new typology of work and welfare incentives for women.

A major theme of Mary Daly's chapter is the importance of

gendering welfare state research by including both sexes. In contrast to mainstream analysis, which has concentrated on the experiences of men, and feminist scholarship, which has centred on women, she outlines a framework of analysis which encompasses both men and women. In doing this she moves beyond the preoccupation of mainstream analysis with the state–market nexus to state–market–family relationships, and she suggests ways to make gender part of a theoretical and empirical framework for studying variations between welfare states.

Lois Bryson, Michael Bittman and Sue Donath argue that a fundamental inadequacy of mainstream analysis has been to focus implicitly on men by placing paid work in a pivotal position. A more appropriate gender balance can be achieved by consideration of paid and unpaid work simultaneously. Using data from national time use studies for Finland and Australia, they find that the women have quite different patterns. Finnish women spend considerably more time in paid work and less in unpaid work than their Australian counterparts. Despite the considerable difference, the women's patterns of paid and unpaid labour are more similar to each other than they are to the patterns for men from their respective countries. The men's patterns do not show the divergence of the women's but are instead very similar. On the basis of these findings, they criticize common interpretations that the two countries represent entirely different types of welfare states and challenge the basis of current cross-national categorizations of welfare states.

The dimension of time is also central to Kirsten Scheiwe's examination of German pension insurance. As an alternative to mainstream welfare state analysis which is generally preoccupied with the distribution of income, she develops the notions of 'time politics' and 'gendered times' to analyse women's and men's access to pension benefits. Instead of focusing on behaviour in the form of time use and how policies may alter women's and men's time patterns, as in the previous chapter, she examines how social legislation privileges certain uses of time and disfavours others. Women are disadvantaged because of the twofold structure of the time models which are gendered as well as hierarchical, subordinating 'female times' to 'male times'. Her analysis reveals the interplay of gender stratification and the German pension system's maintenance of occupational differentials. She also compares the differences in pension benefits in terms of gender and class of the two coexisting pension systems since German reunification.

Drawing upon feminist criticisms of mainstream analysis, Diane Sainsbury initially identifies a number of dimensions of variation for analysing social policy. As a heuristic device, these dimensions are presented as contrasting ideal types: the breadwinner and individual models of social policy. She then applies the dimensions to a comparative analysis of women's and men's social rights in four countries – the UK, the US, the Netherlands and Sweden. Using mainstream typologies Sweden and the Netherlands often cluster together, whereas the two countries represent very different policy regimes when analysed in terms of the breadwinner and individual models. Her analysis also clarifies the limitations of the breadwinner model in studying welfare states and gender – especially with regard to women's entitlements.

Barbara Hobson discusses a range of feminist critical perspectives on policy regime theorizing and suggests alternative strategies for constructing social policy regimes which are sensitive to gender differences in social rights. She focuses on the situation of solo mothers, whose vulnerability makes them a litmus test group in assessing the quality of social rights in a country. This focus also allows her to explore cross-national differences in 'the logics of gender' in policy regimes, specifically the organization of paid and unpaid work. Using data from the Luxembourg Income Study, she analyses the income sources and poverty rates of solo mothers in five countries: Germany, the Netherlands, the UK, the US and Sweden. The conclusion sums up the difficulties in developing social policy regime models attuned to women's social rights.

In discussing the differing impact of the restructuring process in Eastern Europe on women and men, Toni Makkai speculates on the emergent types of social policy regimes in these countries. Her analysis begins with earlier scholarly efforts to place social policies under state socialism in a comparative and historical perspective. Among the distinguishing features of the state socialist model of social provision in the past were the high participation of women in the labour force, or their commodification, and the provision of social benefits and services via labour market performance. The current transition from a command to a market economy has three adverse effects on social provision. The emerging market economy is destroying the nexus between the enterprise and particular forms of social services critical to women's labour market participation; and it is undermining the commitment to full employment, and prompting the withdrawal of the state from social provision. In the process traditional patriarchal structures that dominated the private lives of citizens are now being extended to the public sphere within a market economy. These developments will result not in the de-commodification of women but in their pre-commodification and the emergence of welfare state regimes resembling those of continental Europe based on the principle of subsidiarity.

Although the authors employ a variety of analytical constructs and their focus of analysis often differs, several unifying themes unfold. First, a common concern is to integrate both paid and unpaid work into the analysis of welfare states. Second, several chapters call for a rethinking of Esping-Andersen's notion of de-commodification (and the related ideas of commodification and pre-commodification) when applied to both women and men. Third, despite a recent tendency towards convergence in feminist and mainstream scholarship, there is still a marked lack of systematic comparative research on gender and welfare states, which this book helps to rectify. Fourth, the empirical analysis of several chapters suggests how gender regimes both correspond to and differ from Esping-Andersen's welfare state regimes and other mainstream typologies. Fifth, and most importantly, because of their comparative thrust, the following chapters contribute to our understanding of how the division of labour among the sexes and gender ideologies shape social provision and, in turn, how social policies affect the life situations of women and men across welfare states.

2

Gender and Welfare States: Some Theoretical Reflections

Jet Bussemaker and Kees van Kersbergen

This chapter offers some reflections on how the gender perspective might productively be incorporated in mainstream welfare state theories and is based upon provisional answers to two questions that we think fruitfully disentangle the various aspects of the relationship between welfare state theories and research on gender.

The first question is why should we be concerned with 'gender' as an analytical and explanatory concept in the context of welfare state theories at all? To a large extent the answer to this question lies in our critical approach to mainstream welfare state theories – a body of literature which not only forms the central point of reference of the entire debate on the origins, growth and consequences of welfare state development but also, and more importantly, patterns the very way in which we construct the theoretical concepts that help us understand what the welfare state is all about (see Orloff, 1993).

We would like to point out, however, that the argument cannot merely be that mainstream theories have been gender blind. For true as this observation may be, it just tends to provoke the standard, but not necessarily unfair reply: so what? It is in the answer to the 'so what?' that a justification of attempting to gender mainstream welfare state theories is to be found.

Let us rephrase the 'so what?' by asking what it is that one hopes to unveil by incorporating the notion of gender into mainstream welfare state theory. The response to this question is less obvious than one might think, for the type of answer depends very much on whether one is primarily interested in analysing the conditions of male dominance in contemporary society or whether one is trying to understand the quantitative and qualitative evolution of the welfare state *per se*. In the former case, one is principally concerned with *the conditions under which and the extent to which social politics and policies affect gender relations*. In the latter case one deals with the reverse, namely with *the conditions under which and the extent to which gender relations affect social politics and policies*. To put it differently, both 'welfare state' and 'gender' are concepts that can alternately emerge as *explanandum* or *explanans*, depending upon the theoretical and empirical angle of the research. Our claim is that gendering mainstream welfare state theories will give us an improved comprehension of the variations in how different nations pursue and implement social policies. Moreover, concentrating on the gender dimension of social politics and policies will give us a better picture of what Gøsta Esping-Andersen (1987, 1990) has identified as welfare state regimes, the specific institutional configuration of market, state and family adopted by societies in the pursuit of work and welfare.

The main criticism of mainstream theories cannot be that they neglect women, but that they theoretically privilege social class and capitalist market relations in the frameworks employed to explain the development of social rights. As a result, the analysis of welfare state regimes appears to focus exclusively on how the relation between state and market patterns the institutional arrangements of social policy in advanced capitalist democracies. The extent to which a welfare state regime is actually dependent upon and perhaps even patterning gendered social relations that cannot easily be identified in terms of either political or economic power relations, is not really included in the theoretical dimensions that make up the typologies of mainstream welfare state theories. The issue is whether including the gender dimension does enhance our knowledge of welfare state types.

The second question relevant for disentangling the problem under consideration deals with how one could constructively incorporate the gender perspective in welfare state research. Until now, it seems that mainstream welfare state theories and feminist theories have largely evolved side by side without much cross-fertilization (Orloff, 1993). Ann Shola Orloff (1993) has rightly suggested that it might be fruitful to employ the conceptual framework of welfare state theories, amending it where necessary, using insights from research on gender relations and the state.

The method we choose for our attempt to incorporate the gender perspective in welfare state research can now be stipulated. First, we present an evaluation of mainstream welfare state research as it has evolved in the preceding decades. We particularly focus on the power resources approach and the influential theory of welfare state regimes. Second, we offer a review of the stages through which the concept of gender progressed to become what the American historian Joan Scott (1986) calls a useful analytical category of historical analysis. Third, we submit our thoughts on where and how two relatively separate research traditions can be productively synthesized by offering some illustrative examples from the Dutch case. The Dutch welfare state appears to be an intriguing and relevant case in this context, because it has traditionally puzzled both mainstream and feminist theorists, particularly with respect to its striking social policy paradoxes.

Mainstream welfare state theories

According to Esping-Andersen the central question with which the entire debate on the welfare state has been concerned is: 'whether, and under what conditions, the class divisions and social inequalities produced by capitalism can be undone by parliamentary democracy' (1990: 11). Social class and the possibility that politics can alter the outcomes of capitalist market relations by means of the extension of social rights have indeed been the central concepts of a research agenda of political sociology that can be traced back to the work of T. H. Marshall (1964). Marshall argued that citizenship consisted of civil, political and social rights that corresponded to successive phases in the history of capitalist democracies. Eighteenth-century civil rights established individual freedom, nineteenth-century political rights inaugurated political freedom, and twentieth-century social rights provided the foundation of social welfare, or – as one might say – of freedom from want. The social principle of citizenship embodied 'the whole range from the right to a modicum of economic welfare and security to the right to share to the full in the social heritage and to live the life of a civilized being according to the standards prevailing in the society' (Marshall, 1964: 72). *Civil* rights emerged as the rights of the individual to be free, particularly in the economic realm. *Political* rights are conceptualized as strengthened individual civil rights that both permitted groups to perform as legal individuals (as the recognition of the right of collective bargaining demonstrates) and established universal suffrage that 'treats the vote as the voice of the individual' (Marshall, 1964: 94). The development of *social* rights was mainly understood as the consequence of trying to make civil rights actually work, of removing the barriers that blocked the full and equal exercise of civil and political rights. Capitalist market relations, poverty and inadequate education tended to reduce these rights to mere formal capacities, a contradiction that created the necessity for social policy. The development of the welfare state on this account is the historical process in which members of a national community as citizens became inclusively entitled to the *material* promises of civil freedom and political equality. Marshall firmly believed that liberal and social democratic principles could come together in generating a better life for both the community and its citizens.

This belief was shared by numerous studies that appeared in the late 1970s and the 1980s, whose leading question was whether and to what extent *political* variables determine the variations in welfare state development, when economic or demographic variables had been controlled for. The best-established research agenda on the political determinants of the welfare state is found in those studies that can be grouped under the headings of the power resources approach or social democratic model (Hewitt, 1977; Cameron, 1978; Castles, 1978, 1985; Korpi, 1978, 1983; Stephens, 1979; Esping-Andersen, 1985a, 1985b, 1987; Shalev, 1983). The leading hypothesis of the model is that 'the bulk of the observable variation in welfare state emergence and growth in the western nations can be accounted for by the strength – especially in government – of social democratic labour movements' (Shalev, 1983: 316). Research strongly focused on the conditions under which democratic political intervention could reform and moderate the social consequences of capitalist market relations (Skocpol and Amenta, 1986: 140).

The more the mass of the population became organized as wage-earners within the social democratic movement (the mobilization of the resource of numbers), the higher the quality (universalism, solidarity, redistribution) of the welfare arrangements tended to be and, as a result, the higher the extent of equality. The distribution of power resources between the main social classes of capitalist society determined the success of political intervention in the economy and the extent of inequality (Korpi, 1978, 1983; Esping-Andersen, 1985a; Esping-Andersen and Korpi, 1984).

The social democratic power resources model has been criticized on many points (Esping-Andersen and van Kersbergen, 1992), the most important of which is the thesis that the linear relation between social democracy and the welfare state as the core of a *general causal theory* of welfare state development is inaccurate. The fact that the predominantly macro-comparative studies of welfare states frequently located significant exceptions to the leading thesis of the social democratic model underlies the increasingly critical approach to the power resources approach. The Netherlands has probably been one of the most troublesome cases for the model, not only because of the 'paradigmatically Dutch problem of high spending without social democratic dominance' (Shalev, 1983: 338), but also – as we will indicate below – because of other social policy paradoxes that are hard to account for within the social democratic paradigm.

Because theoretical progress is our present interest, the work of Esping-Andersen (1985b, 1987, 1990) is most relevant. He contributed two major theoretical innovations to the debate. First, there is the by now well-established insight that the social democratic welfare state is only one variety of a much richer world of welfare capitalism. Second, there is the pivotal thesis that high levels of spending are a poor indicator of welfare statism and do not tell much about the societal power relations upon which welfare state regimes are vested. According to Esping-Andersen, it is doubtful whether an operationalization of the welfare state in terms of social spending could clarify what is distinctive about welfare states at all, because looking at spending alone obscures the presence of a variety of welfare state *regimes* understood as the 'specific institutional arrangements adopted by societies in the pursuit of work and welfare' (Esping-Andersen, 1987: 6). His alternative consists of an analysis that goes beyond the theoretical framework of the social democratic model. It proposes to view cross-national variation in welfare state development as variation (a) in the quality of social rights; (b) in the resulting patterns of stratification; and (c) in the way in which state, market and family are interrelated.

On the basis of these dimensions Esping-Andersen identified three welfare state regime types, of which the social democratic welfare state is one variety. The characteristics of this latter regime concern universalism of social rights, de-commodification ('the degree to which individuals, or families, can uphold a socially acceptable standard of living independently of market participation': Esping-Andersen, 1990: 37), and the inclusion of the middle class. Such a welfare state regime is directed towards a high level of equality. Examples of this regime are the Scandinavian states.

The liberal model, on the other hand, is characterized by means-tested assistance, modest social insurance schemes and modest universal transfers. This model is historically characterized by the influence of liberal work ethics and the predominance of the market. In contrast to the social democratic regime the liberal regime typically upholds the commodity character of labour power to a large extent and limits the scope of social rights to the working class and 'the poor'. The liberal regime includes countries such as the United States, Canada, Australia and Britain.

Another cluster is composed of the conservative and corporatist statist regimes of continental Europe. De-commodification can certainly be an element of social policy in these nations. The distinguishing characteristic lies rather in the status-differentiating nature of social policy. Social rights are linked to class and status, and the capacity to reduce income inequality is small. Another key element of this regime is the commitment to the defence and maintenance of the traditional family and its functions. The family is a cornerstone of social policy. State provision of social services only comes in when the family fails to provide these services. The organizational structure of social security schemes mirrors the influence of corporatist legacies in nations such as Germany, Austria, France and Italy.

Esping-Andersen's analysis of welfare states is based on three dimensions (state–market relations, stratification and de-commodification) which produce the typology of welfare state regimes. Although regimes are defined in terms of the specific institutional configuration of market, state and family adopted by societies in the pursuit of work and welfare, one might raise some questions as to the consistency of the regime concept, particularly with respect to the theoretical status of the family. First, the regime approach is strongly biased towards an analysis of the extent to which states (the 'public') rather than markets (the 'private') provide welfare, and therefore analytically neglects the role of families (and women in particular) and semi-public and voluntary associations in the 'private' provision of care and welfare. Second, stratification is primarily defined in terms of the social inequalities that relate to the class structure of democratic capitalism and consequently tends to underrate the importance of other inequalities, notably those associated with the dimension of gender in our societies. Third, de-commodification deals with the manner in which social policies determine the extent to which wage labour is freed from the dictates of the market and tends to equate the level of economic autonomy with the economic independence of wage labour. As a result, the regime approach is strong in understanding the development of social rights attached to wage labour (the quality of social security schemes, for instance), but less convincing in the analysis of claims and rights based on needs (social assistance) and ambivalent in the study of claims and rights on the basis of gender (marriage, motherhood) (Orloff, 1993: 317). Moreover, how should one interpret active labour market policies for women: as commodification or as de-commodification?

The dimensions that structure the typology of welfare capitalism (state–market relations, de-commodification and stratification) are based on the assumptions that class cleavages are the root cause of the inequalities in capitalist market economies and that social policies almost exclusively focus on the regulation and modification of this type of social inequality. This indicates that the theory of welfare state regimes as well as its major explanatory categories (class, class divisions, class coalitions and the power resources of social classes) are still clearly based on the assumptions of the social democratic model.

The explanatory primacy attached to class and class divisions makes it difficult to consider in a theoretically convincing way other relevant inequalities as well as the relative and independent role of political actors other than social democracy in advancing the development of the welfare state. Because the typology of welfare state regimes is constructed on the basis of this set of assumptions it captures only a fragment of the relevant inequalities and power relations that shape the nature and variation of contemporary social politics and policies in Western societies. The point is that the assumptions taken from the social democratic model not only strongly influence and limit the potential content of the dimensions that make up the typology, but presuppose a distinct relationship between institutional arrangements providing welfare and the effect of these institutions on welfare.

The market dominance in the provision of welfare in the liberal regime implies a high degree of stratification and inequality and accordingly a low level of de-commodification. Characteristic of the stratification profile of the liberal welfare state regime is a 'curious mix of individual self-responsibility and dualisms: one group at the bottom primarily reliant on stigmatizing relief; one group in the middle predominantly the clients of social insurance; and, finally, one privileged group capable of deriving its main welfare from the market' (Esping-Andersen, 1990: 65). The liberal regime eludes a high level of de-commodification by relying on means-tested assistance for those who really fail to secure an income through the market. However, as long as social insurances mirror the employment histories of individual workers (contributions, performance) and do not moderate work incentives, public social insurances do not fundamentally change the commodity status of wage labour either.

State provision of welfare implies modest stratification and inequality and a high degree of de-commodification. The social democratic strategy with respect to stratification was aimed at solidarity and universalism, because 'it equalized status, benefits and responsibilities of citizenship, and because it helped build political coalitions' (Esping-Andersen, 1990: 68). De-commodification here means emancipation from market dependence, individual independence, maximization and institutionalization of social rights.

The ideal conservative regime aims at retaining traditional status relations through 'a myriad of status-differentiated social-insurance schemes – each with its peculiar rules, finances, and benefit structure; each tailored to exhibit its clientele's relative status position' (Esping-Andersen, 1990: 60). Conservatism has historically rejected commodification on moral grounds and developed several strategies to combat it, notably corporatism and etatism, both leading to moderate levels of de-commodification, particularly by safeguarding the family against the disruptive impact of the market.

Looking closely at the typology it becomes clear that in a

comparative perspective a nation's welfare state regime is not so much analytically identified by a specific *configuration* of market, state and family, but rather by the *dominance* of either the market or the state. In other words, it seems that the extent to which the state or the market is the dominant institution in a welfare state regime mainly determines the order of stratification and the level of de-commodification. As a result of this focus on these two institutions rather than on the specific configuration of all institutions, the theoretical status of the family in particular remains unclear. One tends to conclude that the family does not play any role in social policy in the liberal and social democratic welfare states and only an ambiguous role in the conservative cluster. For what in reality distinguishes the latter regime is that it does not fully rely on the market, but does not count on a highly interventionist state either. With respect to the family, the theory only argues that social policy enters when the family fails. The relevant question with respect to all regimes is, of course, what does the family do when it does not fail? In our view, this is one of the major problems in the regime concept. It does not precisely do what it says it does: analysing welfare states in terms of the configuration of market, state *and* family. In this respect one may conclude that the regime concept could benefit from an incorporation of the gender perspective.

Gender and welfare state theories

Where mainstream theories of welfare state development frequently neglect gender as an important category for the analysis of welfare facilities and states, until recently most research that has specifically focused on gender often lacked a comparative perspective (Koven and Michel, 1990; Bock and Thane, 1991; Skocpol and Ritter, 1991; Lewis, 1993) and has not sufficiently linked the gender dimension to the categories of analysis in mainstream theories on the welfare state (but see Orloff, 1993 and O'Connor, 1993).

The central focus on the gender dimensions of individual cases has already yielded a considerable number of interesting studies. However, there is a slight risk that the developing agenda of this research is reproducing a flaw of mainstream welfare state theories, both in terms of basic assumptions and methodologies and in terms of the choice of countries and comparisons (Sainsbury, 1991). An understandable, yet problematic preference to study the Nordic countries seems to be evolving (Siim, 1988; Hernes, 1984, 1987a; Simonen, 1990) and the Anglo-Saxon nations (Wilson, 1977; Fraser, 1989a; Pateman, 1988; Skocpol and Ritter, 1991; Gordon, 1990a; Lewis, 1983, 1991a), as a result of which nations such as Germany, the

Netherlands, Belgium and France tend to be treated in a step-motherly fashion.

At any rate, we seem to have arrived at a point in time where we can productively combine the results of 'gender-research on welfare' with the 'mainstream-often-gender-blind-research', without reiterating some of the inaccuracies of mainstream welfare state literature in particular.

In this context it seems appropriate to focus on some of the consequential insights into gender in relation to welfare and to start with the gender dimensions of social citizenship. Marshall's distinctions have provided many a researcher with a sound point of departure to reflect upon gender and welfare. Not only class but also gender must be understood as an element in the construction of citizenship. This implies that incorporating the notion of gender in the way we think about the welfare state helps correct the biased attention to the relationship between market and state of much of welfare state research. In what one might call the social policy tradition, the notion of social citizenship has been extended to women, focusing on the gender dimensions that interlink civil, political and social citizenship, and incorporating the family as a relevant category for understanding the development of the welfare state. Extending the idea of citizenship in the context of the relations between the family, the market and the state uncovered the fact that citizenship did not bear solely on the rights and duties in the private domain of economic activity and the public realm of democratic politics, but also on the private sphere of the family and the tasks of care. Studies in the social policy tradition have usually focused on the relation between care, gender and citizenship and have raised the critical question of whether and to what extent care, especially in the private sphere, tends to exclude people (women) from social citizenship or whether the responsibilities of care in practice effect a distinctive identity of citizenship? There appears to be some convergence around the thesis that in nations where the state effectively transfers the private duty to the public responsibility of care, the conditions for the development of a full civil, political and social citizenship of women are better fulfilled.

Although Esping-Andersen does not pay special attention to a public–private shift in the rights and duties of care, one could try to analyse this shift as a further element of de-commodification. One might then try to broaden the idea of de-commodification beyond the boundary of the degree to which individuals, or families, can uphold a socially acceptable standard of living independently of market participation. If one abandons the fixation on the relation between the market and the state and focuses on the relation between family and the state instead, de-commodification may then be taken to mean the degree to which individuals can uphold a socially acceptable standard of living independently of (unpaid) care responsibility in the family (O'Connor, 1993; Orloff, 1993). To the extent that the conception of family life is associated with matrimony, an important qualification with respect to the question of independence has to be added: independently of the marriage contract and its presupposition of the exchange between economic protection and obligation.

In this perspective, it is not surprising that the Nordic, social democratic type of welfare state has come to figure as *the* example of a welfare state regime which is to a considerable extent gender neutral and which allows women a substantial degree of independence *vis-á-vis* their spouses by stimulating female labour market participation by the provision of public childcare and parental leave.

The social policy approach obviously has its merits. However, the implied but unwarranted idolization of the social democratic model has not gone unnoticed (see Hernes, 1984, 1987a). Full citizenship implies equal rights, equal social participation and equal access to decision-making. Any attempt to integrate the gender perspective in mainstream welfare state theories, we might conclude here, does not simply or even primarily imply a more susceptible focus on the position of women as such, nor merely a more sensitive attention to the dependence of women on their spouses, but a theoretical account of the gendered character of various forms of dependency in relation to certain social domains. With regard to de-commodification, for instance, integrating the gender dimension not only entails an examination of social rights and social provision in terms of their effects on gender stratification, but would also have to include an evaluation of the gender dimensions which underlie the very meaning of social rights. Such an undertaking clearly would have definite consequences for the meaning of de-commodification. Julia O'Connor points out that the concept of de-commodification 'must be supplemented by the concept of personal autonomy or insulation from dependence, both personal dependence on family members and/or public dependence on the state agencies' (O'Connor, 1993: 515).

Despite the critical appraisals of social policy in Scandinavia, the Nordic rim does remain the central point of reference of the bulk of research on gender and welfare. The Scandinavian countries are not only commonly viewed as *prototypes* of what Hernes (1987a) has called 'women-friendly states', but also seem to function as some kind of *norm* for comparison in the debate of the gender dimension in welfare states.

There is a striking analogy here with the point we made in the preceding section with respect to Esping-Andersen's typology. There we concluded that Esping-Andersen's typology of welfare state regimes still bears the marks of the axiomatic structure of the social democratic model, which, in turn, not only influences the potential content of the dimensions that make up the typology, but, moreover, presupposes a distinct relation between the institutional arrangements providing welfare. It seems to us that something similar holds in the case of theories of gender and the welfare state. It appears that the assumptions that underlie the Scandinavian social democratic states determine the very idea of 'women-friendliness' and therefore the positive evaluation of the Nordic model.

Other countries that have attracted the attention of researchers interested in gender and the welfare state are nations from the liberal cluster, particularly the United States. The focus here was on the limited character of social rights, exemplified by the study of the relation between means-tested assistance and modest social insurance. From a gender perspective, the link between the two 'tracks' of social security were predominantly analysed in terms of a means-tested 'feminine' track and a 'masculine' social insurance track of social welfare. The taken-for-granted ideal of this type of welfare state seems to be the 'possessive individual', a person who does not belong to anyone but himself and is economically independent. As far as he (seldom she) is dependent on social security, he simply gets what he had already paid for in advance and is capable of upholding his identity as a rights-bearing individual. For those who do not comply with this ideal, there is the means-tested track of social security. People, mostly women, who have to rely on this kind of social security are being seen as dependent persons in their capacity as clients of welfare facilities: as welfarites.

Research on the two-track liberal model of the US has been of a historical and of a more theoretical nature. A fine example of the first category is Barbara Nelson's study of early social provisions in the United States, such as Workmen's Compensation and Mothers' Aid. The first was developed for the white northern men employed in heavy industry, and the second was originally designed for the white impoverished widows of men who were eligible for Workmen's Compensation. These programmes have given rise to a two-channel welfare state. The Workmen's Compensation established a channel that can be characterized as male, judicial, public and routinized, whereas Mothers' Aid can be typified as a channel which was female, administrative, private and non-routinized (Nelson, 1990: 133). Nelson not only shows the double standard of welfare provision, but also highlights the way in which welfare programmes support the social system of family life (breadwinner and caretaker) (see also Skocpol, 1992).

A more theoretical approach can be found in the work of Nancy Fraser (1989a), who tries to link the two-channel track with presuppositions of gender, corresponding to the identities of rights-bearing individuals (a masculine subsystem) and dependent clients of welfare states facilities (a feminine subsystem). Clients in this view are non-independent individuals, who are approached as members of households and objects of care.

This approach has been criticized by Orloff, who argues that it gives only half the story, because it misses the fact that many more women than the dependent clients (mainly needy mothers) are incorporated into the welfare state *directly* through their husbands, thus, technically, based on their *indirect* relationship to the labour market through marriage. Orloff proposes to replace the two-track approach in terms of different treatment of men and women by an approach that analytically distinguishes types of families or households. There are families that consist of a male breadwinner and an economically dependent wife (and children) and households that are almost entirely maintained by women who do (or can) not participate in the labour force and therefore make welfare claims on the basis of their status as mothers rather than wives (Orloff, 1993: 315).

Orloff's analytical alternative to the two-track approach is certainly helpful, but her proposal does not necessarily alter the characterization of the liberal welfare state regime with regard to gender. In both cases the gendered character of the liberal welfare state is to be found in the two-track system, which does seem to make a difference to gender (or households) and to the levels of stratification (high) and de-commodification (low) related to gender. It has struck us that the liberal regime is treated in many respects as the reverse of the social democratic type, which is characterized by a low level of stratification and a high degree of de-commodification and which tends to make less difference in the way men and women are capable of attaining the status of full social citizenship.

There is much less research available on the possible association between gender and welfare in nations such as Belgium, the Netherlands and Germany (but see for the latter nation Ostner, 1993). The Dutch welfare state is especially troublesome, because of this nation's striking paradoxes in social policy. These can be deciphered only by understanding how gender relations have patterned social policy and by appreciating the extraordinary extent to which the very fabric of the Dutch welfare state was erected on the foundation of a division of labour between paid work of men in the market, largely endowed with social rights, and unpaid labour of women, largely supplied by the derived and 'private' rights of their domestic and married status. Rather high levels of social provision and de-commodification go hand in hand with an extensive degree of dependence of female citizens. And an apparent weakening of stratification and hierarchy goes together with an emphasis on traditional family structures and morality.

The high level of social provision and de-commodification does not necessarily conflict with the traditional family structure. The influence of traditional family structures (together with a low labour market participation of women) can be explained by the high level of welfare provisions, together with high labour productivity. Commonsense explanations such as the late industrialization of the Netherlands, the broadly shared ideology of the traditional family or policy restrictions on the labour participation of women cannot explain the exceptionally low labour market participation of women. A better explanation concerns the thesis that the high level of national income and high labour productivity allowed, so to speak, to put ideology into practice (Plantenga, 1993: 193). The Netherlands could simply afford such a low rate of female labour participation as well as a relatively low rate of male participation. Childcare at home and own-home care, being luxury goods, could relatively easily be acquired (Pott-Buter, 1993: 231).

Apparently, the paradoxical Dutch welfare state is difficult to account for within the typological framework of distributional regimes in which the Netherlands stand out as an exception. We do not wish to be too harsh on the regime typology for failing to fully appreciate the characteristics of one single and – admittedly – peculiar nation. Yet the paradoxes of Dutch social policy do not necessarily turn the Netherlands into a truly exceptional case; in our view they point to a fundamental shortcoming in the conceptualization of a welfare state regime in terms of a nation's specific configuration of market, state and family, where the latter category has not yet assumed a proper place within the theoretical framework.

We claim that it is simply not sufficient to look at the relationship between market, state and family without explicitly theorizing the gender structure that in reality underlies and determines the very relationship between these institutions. For example, it is not incorrect to observe that the Dutch welfare state is characterized by social security schemes tailored to families. This fact, however, is in itself in need of further explanation and cannot be accounted for without referring to the 'breadwinner–caretaker' structure that underlies much of the social policy of the Netherlands. In sum, it is not enough solely to look at the position of women or to consider the structure of families when we develop or amend a typology of welfare state regimes. Instead, the manner in which basic assumptions about gender actually mould the very infrastructure of social policy has to be integrated into the theoretical framework. We want to illustrate this postulate by problematizing and confronting the dimensions of Esping-Andersen's typology with reference to the Dutch experience.

Gender and the Dutch welfare state: problems in the typology

The Dutch welfare state is characterized by a large degree of de-commodification, that is a de-commodification of wage labour workers, effectively insulating workers through the social security system from the constraints of the labour market. Generalizing Esping-Andersen's notion, one could claim that the Dutch welfare state also produces de-commodification of a different type, namely an insulation of divorced women from dependence on the financial support of their ex-husbands. This type of protection (both from the whip of the market and from the – financial – proximity of the former husband), however, does not come about via the relatively generous benefits of social security schemes but through means-tested social assistance. Social assistance, originally introduced in 1963–65 as a replacement of the old Poor Law of 1854, was never specifically intended for divorced women, but rather as the crowning glory of the welfare state. Nevertheless, currently close to 90 per cent of those who receive a benefit in virtue of the Social Assistance Act (*Bijstandswet, ABW*) are women (mainly single and divorced mothers).

It appears that the Dutch welfare state *is* characterized by the sizeable level of de-commodification for paid workers that is so typical of the social democratic regime. But at the same time social policy also shares some of the properties of a liberal two-track system, in which means-tested arrangements are mainly used by women under worse conditions than the social insurance schemes, which predominantly benefit men. Surely, this is a reflection of the divergent claims that men and women make on the welfare state. Men need and are entitled to social security benefits (or in the last resort, social assistance) if for whatever reason they cannot secure their means of income through the market. The social rights of women, on the other hand, are not primarily attached to economic performance and the status of wage-earner. On the contrary, the social rights of women are far more conditional on marital status, that is whether or not there is a husband who acts as the breadwinner of the household.

The Dutch welfare state also seems to have a fairly low level of stratification, if we look at the differences between male citizens in their capacity as workers. Social citizenship in the Netherlands is commonly viewed as relatively advanced. If we compare households, social stratification is rather low. But if we compare stratification patterns among male citizens with stratification among female citizens the picture changes dramatically. First of all, labour force participation of women in the Netherlands has traditionally been very low (Pott-Buter, 1993: 28). Secondly, there is still a huge discrepancy in the number of hours that men and women devote to paid work and, as a result, in the level of their respective economic independence. Many women work part time, 20 hours or less a week (around 25 per cent of the female labour force has a paid job of less than 15 hours), generating an income that is rarely sufficient to live on, and in many cases must be seen as a supplement to the wage of the husband. It is precisely this relevant information about the quality of welfare state regimes that is lost if one uncritically applies the regime concept.

If we take a slightly different perspective and look at the distribution of responsibilities and time spent on unpaid care, particularly in the private sphere, the pattern is again entirely different. A recent government report shows that women disproportionally carry the task of care-giving. In general, women devote approximately 26 hours a week to domestic work, while men only slightly more than 10 hours (SCP, 1993).

Paradoxically, then, the Dutch welfare state is characterized by a considerable degree of de-commodification of male wage-earners *and* a high level of stratification between men and women. Social rights are indeed highly advanced, but in a specific, gendered way. So the Dutch welfare system cannot be fully understood solely in terms of the notions of de-commodification and stratification as they are commonly employed in mainstream theories. Dutch social policy can only be understood when taking seriously the gendered identities that have historically been accorded to such groups as breadwinners and caretakers. The Dutch model is therefore based not so much on a strong notion of the family as such, as on the model of the breadwinner–caretaker.

If this point is appreciated, one can immediately see to what extent the distinction between such gendered identities had definite effects on how different groups have been defined as different objects of care in the postwar development of the welfare state. While social security benefits (child benefits included) predominantly had men as objects of policy, social services (such as social work and family supervision) had women as their objects. Child allowances, for instance, were basically seen as a component of the breadwinner's wages rather than as compensation for the caring activities of women. As a result, these allowances were paid to men. Services, on the other hand, were tailored to women in their capacity as wife and mother and were primarily meant to assist the woman in raising a happy family, in which she could figure as the ever-present, ever-caring wife and mother. Nevertheless, the social security schemes, too, clearly bear the marks of the gendered identities that underlie social policy in the Netherlands. It is only when we appreciate the fact that social security benefits in the Netherlands were designed to replace a family income that we can understand why the Dutch welfare state developed into one of the most generous welfare systems in the advanced capitalist world. Generosity of benefits, however, had much less to do with solidarity or social justice as commonly understood in the social democratic sense, than with the idea that a male breadwinner was to be enabled to maintain a decent life for himself and his family, under the assumption that women would not engage in wage labour. The dominance of the breadwinner–caretaker model in Dutch social policy must be understood in the context of a widely shared and strongly present ideology (also among social democrats and liberals) of family life in the nation's political history.

With respect to social citizenship, men and women were addressed differently. The different treatment of men and women with regard to social rights was not in any sense seen as discrimination or understood in terms of the inequality of power, but rather as an equitable approach to families and as a recognition of the natural differences in the talents and tasks of men and women. Although the women's movement has criticized this idea time and again since the 1970s, the conception of justice as family justice, presupposing the breadwinner–caretaker model, is still effectual.

In the moral context of the gendered breadwinner–caretaker model, stressing social citizenship in terms of the equal rights of men and women to personal autonomy, protection from the market and independence from the breadwinner, is frequently portrayed as a grave injustice and a threat to solidarity. Social services to help relieve women's caring tasks in the private sphere, especially in child care, are not seen as part and parcel of the welfare state. On the contrary, the absence of such facilities as an alternative for caring in the family are understood as an important blessing for the welfare state. Childcare facilities contradict the meaning of a happy family life and deny the specifically female talents of raising children. In terms of the traditional connotation of de-commodification, the argument is that the advanced qualities of the Dutch welfare state simply allow women to remain permanently de-commodified. Any positive change in the labour force participation of women would therefore entail a worsening of the quality of social policy.

Concluding remarks: problems and possibilities

The central concepts commonly used in mainstream research are not entirely suitable for fully grasping the relation between gender and welfare. The problem is that the attempt to understand the extent to which social policy potentially moderates the market dependency of wage-earners tends to neglect the economic dependence of house-wives on their breadwinner/husband. The theory of de-commodification is not well equipped to account for a transition from private dependency to state dependency. In sum, de-commodification is too fixated on the impact of wage labour and neglects the crucial role of unpaid caring work in the welfare state. If we want to integrate gender, the concept of de-commodification must be changed. An extension of the concept is difficult, because how do we designate the increasing labour market participation of women: as de-commodification or as commodification? Nor is a reformulation adequate, because it denies the gender dimensions underlying the concept. Orloff is very sceptical about attempts to supplement 'de-commodification' as a notion applicable only to (male) workers with an element of non-dependence for women, because it leaves the core concept of de-commodification intact and unreformed (Orloff, 1993). We need a new concept, such as personal autonomy (O'Connor, 1993; Bussemaker, 1991) or even a more general concept of independence (Orloff, 1993). Orloff's interesting alternative – to subsume de-commodification under a more generic concept of independence, related to the process of increasing individualization – might be a solution, although this is not necessarily a gender-neutral concept either. For that reason it is important to analyse independence as changing patterns of work and care, rights and needs between individuals, the state, the family and the market. This also means that the concept has to deal not only with economic independence, although this will be a very important part of it, but also with independence understood as the possibility of making choices and of insulation from emotional or psychological dependence. It strikes us that we should not try to extend the propositions of 'possessive individualism' and independence from men to women, but that we should rethink aspects of self-determination, independent judge-ment and psychological and economic independence as they interre-late (Bussemaker, 1993).

In the same way, the notion of stratification should not only refer to the degree of inequality of (male) workers, but also to the manner in which the relationships between men and women as well as between various racial and ethnic groups are stratified. We need a concept that not only encompasses the effects of capitalist market relations and economic performance but is also sensitive to societal differentiation and cultural pluralism.

The manner in which gender dimensions are embedded in the formulation and implementation of social policy as well as their effects must play a part in any attempt to integrate the gender perspective into mainstream theories. Thus, we can no longer focus only on the relation between the market, the state and the family; we have to incorporate the gender structures that interlink these different spheres into our framework of the comparative analysis of welfare state regimes. This means that we have to focus on the presuppositions of tasks and duties (formal and informal) of men and women. Unpaid care work is an important element – not only because such labour can be a reason for exclusion from social citizenship, but also because it must be viewed as an activity that is useful and valuable to society. Because of the increasing participation of women in the labour force in all welfare state regimes, caring work is becoming eroded. There are two solutions: creating more welfare facilities (such as childcare) or a redistribution of paid and unpaid work among men and women. But while women begin to look more like men in that they increasingly enter the labour market, men seem to refuse to look more like women, in that they do not take over care work to the same extent. The whole question of the gender dimensions that interlink the structure of the state, the market and the family is in fact the question of (gendered) social citizenship.

The points so far mentioned have theoretical and methodological implications for comparative research of welfare states. It is unlikely that the analytical and empirical distinction of types of welfare state regimes remains functional if we seriously integrate the gender dimension into our research. One of the main questions is whether the distinction between different welfare state regimes corresponds to different types of 'gender regimes' (Orloff, 1993). The Dutch case suggests that welfare state regimes and gender regimes do not necessarily coincide but that gender regimes have an extensive impact on a nation's specific configuration of work, care and welfare.

3

Welfare State Regimes, Women's Interests and the EC

Anette Borchorst

Scholarly interest in explaining welfare state variations has been considerable and has increased during the last decades. The main focus has been on state–market relations, and to a lesser extent on the family and its interplay with the other institutions. This research has offered valuable insights into why and how welfare state variations occur. However, mainstream research has largely ignored gender, whereas a number of feminist scholars have documented its importance in structuring welfare state policies. Yet there has not been much dialogue between the two paradigms, and mainstream authors rarely refer to the feminist literature. The position of this author is that mainstream research constitutes an important point of departure for understanding welfare state variations, and I find the lack of dialogue between the two traditions regrettable. An open-minded discussion of the effects upon and influence of class and gender on welfare state variations could indeed improve the explanatory power of each paradigm.

In this chapter I employ Gøsta Esping-Andersen's regime typology and the concept of women's interests to analyse the position of women *vis-à-vis* men in several West European welfare states. The first part of the chapter assesses the strengths and weaknesses of Esping-Andersen's typology, concentrating on the consequences of his neglect of gender. The second part deals with the feminist discussion of interest theory with the purpose of formulating a working definition of women's interests. The subsequent empirical analysis focuses on women's interests – defined by their possible choices connected to their responsibility for human care – in conservative and social democratic welfare state regimes. More specifically, I examine women's situation in the three Scandinavian countries and continental European countries which are members of the European Community. The final section considers the impact of the Community itself on women and their options.

Welfare state regimes and women

On the basis of historical and current studies, Gøsta Esping-Andersen has developed a theory to explain variations between different welfare states. A focal point of his work has been the rejection of the functionalist view that welfare states are merely a product of the industrial revolution. He concludes that politics matters and that 'the history of political class coalitions is the most decisive cause of welfare-state variations' (1990: 1).

In his recent book, Esping-Andersen (1990) clusters 18 Western welfare states into three different regimes. They have the following main characteristics:

> The *liberal regime* is dominated by means-tested benefits; modest universal cash transfers predominate, and some social insurance schemes exist. The sovereignty of the market is strongly emphasized. Examples of this regime are the United States, Canada and Australia.
>
> The *conservative regime* is characterized by status differentiation, and social rights are connected to status and class. Compulsory labour market insurances are common, and church and family play a crucial role. This regime is found in continental European countries such as Austria, France, Germany and Italy.
>
> The *social democratic regime* provides many universal benefits as social rights based on citizenship and financed by taxes. Benefits are relatively high, and the welfare state itself is extensive. Equality is a fundamental value. This regime is primarily found in Scandinavia.

A key question determining the clustering is whether state benefits are provided as citizens' rights or not. This is measured by the level of *de-commodification* of the labour force: 'The outstanding criteria for social rights must be the degree to which they permit people to make their living standards independent of pure market forces' (Esping-Andersen, 1990: 3). He concludes that the Scandinavian countries have the highest levels of de-commodification, and this has affected the power relations between the classes in these countries to the benefit of the working class.

Although Esping-Andersen's analysis has contributed significantly to the understanding of differences between welfare states, he largely ignores gender. When he notes differences in women's position within the regimes, he mainly describes them; he does not explain them, and his theoretical framework, which he has developed during the last 15 years, also lacks the gender dimension.

A cornerstone of his theory is the relation between state and market, whereas the family is more or less neglected in his analysis. He does suggest that the family should be included in the analysis (Esping-Andersen, 1990: 21), but it enters his research design through the back door, so to speak. This occurs when he incorporates the continental European countries and the Catholic social doctrine, which assigns the family a dominant role in the solution of social problems. Notwithstanding his correct observation that the family, the church and the community cannot 'play the game of the market if they are saddled with social responsibilities' (1990: 42), he fails to investigate the specific interplay of these institutions, and state and market in the liberal and social democratic regimes. Hence, he also excludes the hierarchical gender division of labour and the very different position of the sexes *vis-à-vis* family, state and market from his analysis. Nor does he pay much attention to the crucial difference of making individuals or families the basic unit of investigation. Thus de-commodification is concretized to refer to 'the degree to which individuals, or families, can uphold a socially acceptable standard of living independently of market participation' (1990: 37). However, it is crucial for the position of women, whether they are entitled to benefits as individuals or whether rights are tied to families, of which men are normally considered the head.

The dominant political ideologies of the three regimes differ substantially in their ideas on which mix between market, state and family is desirable. One indication of this is the considerable variations in the availability of public services for vulnerable persons, like small children, the sick and the elderly. Many feminist scholars have highlighted the major impact of public care on the position of women. If this dimension was added to Esping-Andersen's analytical framework, his conclusions on de-commodification would indeed need some modification. The liberal and especially the conservative regimes have contributed to the de-commodification of women, in the sense that they have actively supported a housewife–breadwinner family model. I will argue that the Scandinavian welfare states, especially the Swedish and the Danish, have conversely commodified women. Hence the process of de-commodification not only differs between regimes; it is also very different for men and women and is not determined by the same factors. Marriage tends for instance to have the opposite effect for men than for women. Married men often have a more permanent connection to the labour market than unmarried, whereas married women often adapt their labour market participation to their responsibility in the family, especially the care of children. Policies may work in the direction of supporting or altering this pattern.

Another aspect of Esping-Andersen's conceptualization of

de-commodification, which needs to be problematized, is the role of the public sector itself as an employer. Is this an indication of commodification or de-commodification? A crucial difference between the public and the private labour force is that public employment is mainly an outcome of political decisions, whereas the employment of the labour force in the private sector of the economy is determined by market forces. Subsequently public employees become independent of market forces but, if they are permanently employed, not in the same way as people receiving income transfers. This aspect also affects the sexes differently. The proportion of public employees in the Scandinavian countries is much higher for women than for men.

Esping-Andersen's theoretical neglect of gender is reinforced by his overwhelming empirical focus on income transfers like old age pensions, unemployment and sickness benefits. He does include services in a few sections in his latest book, but they are not dealt with in the central chapters on de-commodification. He argues that the focus on pensions is not due to the interest in them *per se*, but to 'the ways in which they elucidate how different nations arrive at their peculiar public–private sector mix' (1990: 2), but if he focuses on the private sector in terms of the family, an investigation of services would certainly become highly relevant. The exclusion of services, I would argue, probably has implications for his clusters, because there are considerable variations in expenditures on public services between countries (Andersen and Christiansen, 1991: 152–5). The Netherlands would for instance come much closer to the conservative regime than it is in Esping-Andersen's analysis. It is, however, not possible merely to add services to Esping-Andersen's research design, because it is not easily operationalized and measured according to his indicators of de-commodification.

Esping-Andersen's work has inspired many scholars and is often quoted, but also highly criticized. A basic question, which I shall not try to answer here, is whether it is actually possible to classify welfare states as he has done according to his typology. In this context I utilize Esping-Andersen's regimes as a point of departure for analysing the situation of women in several West European welfare states. In order to conceptualize the gender perspective further, I discuss the analytical value of the concept of interest.

Women's interests

The basic questions in the feminist discussion of interest theory are whether women have fundamentally different interests from those of men, and whether it is possible to make a distinction between women's objective and subjective interests. Can interests specific to women be determined either scientifically or politically, irrespective of what women themselves think? My focus is here on the Scandinavian debate, which was a follow-up and extension of an American debate on this issue.

Anna Jónasdóttir notes that since its origin the concept of interest has had two connected aspects, a form aspect and a content aspect (1988, 1991, 1994). She defines the *form aspect* as the need to be present or take part in the control of society's public affairs (1991: 157). The *content aspect* is related to the substantive values which are put into effect and distributed in society and their consequences for different groups of citizens (1991: 158). In opposition to most other feminist scholars engaged in the debate on the usefulness of the concept, Jónasdóttir believes that the form aspect is the more important, and that it can only be dealt with theoretically, whereas the content aspect relates to needs and wishes and is empirically more open. Thus, it cannot be the basis for the determination of objective interests. Differences in subjective gender interests may be a consequence of the difference in areas of responsibility for each sex, but this division of work is not absolute or biologically determined, except for childbearing. It is true that women are involved in biosocial reproduction and care of other people, but this involvement is a reflection of their social gender. Hence, the division of labour between the sexes is historically changeable and problematic as a basis for the determination of women's interests on a more objective level (1991: 160ff.).

Jónasdóttir suggests a theory of interests, in which she stresses the form aspect, concretized as the interest in the control of one's own choices. Thereby she connects the objective and subjective dimensions of the concept:

> 'Interest' always relates to some sort of *controlling attendance confronting conditions of choice* (more than what gains one receives from a choice, or an increased number of alternatives to choose between). This means either 'be/ing among' those creating alternatives, or knowing, by means of information, concrete thinking and clear vision, what one chooses and has to choose between. (Jónasdóttir, 1991: 169)

Beatrice Halsaa demonstrates that women rarely share common interests in the sense that they organize around the same concrete issues or agree on the same policy goals. However, this is not to say that gender is not a fundamental political category, when it comes to articulation of demands, actions to further these demands, or the formulation and implementation of public policies (1987: 43).

Halsaa criticizes Anna Jónasdóttir's restrictive understanding of the content aspect which, according to her, cannot be separated from the form aspect. She finds Jónasdóttir's solution to the difference between objective and subjective interests of women by focusing on choices, only formal or conceptual. Instead she argues that women's objective interests can be defined in substantial terms. The basis of women's objective interests is women's *principal work*, which is pregnancy, birth and breast-feeding, or what is connected to their biological sex. It is specific and common to women, and it is what makes sex a fundamental social category. Women's *actual work* consists of all tasks performed by women other than the principal work, but unlike the principal work, it can also be done by men.

I agree that biological motherhood characterizes women's lives fundamentally, and that it contributes to the limitation of women's choices. However it is problematic to link the interests of women so closely to biological sex, because in this way womanhood tends to become equated with motherhood. Differences between women which are partly an outcome of their own choices are obscured (Scott, 1988). Moreover a conceptualization based on women's principal work is highly controversial, as is evident throughout the history of women's organizations (Borchorst, 1989). Women's organizations are particularly interesting in this context because their point of departure is representation of women's interests, but according to Halsaa they reflect only the *subjective* articulation of interests. The consequence must be that women's interests cannot be determined politically, but must have a scientific point of departure.

One possible solution to the question of definition is a very broad conceptualization such as an interest in avoiding the oppression of women, but it is so broad that it is uninteresting, scientifically as well as politically. The form aspect in itself is not sufficient to justify the existence of specific women's interests either. There is, as Halsaa also states, no difference between women's and men's interests in gaining influence and being represented.

I believe like Halsaa that both the form and the content aspect should be included, but the determination of the concept should neither be so superficial nor so restricted that it is without use politically and scientifically. In my opinion, this might be solved by focusing, like Jónasdóttir, on women's *control of their choices* connected to their principal and actual work. The point of departure is women's reproductive abilities, and their biological sex, but not isolated from their social gender and responsibility for human reproduction. On the other hand, it is not possible, on the basis of objective interests, to concretize *what* solutions women should choose, for example whether they should engage in paid work or not, give birth to children or have abortions.

Throughout history, the biological and social division of work between the sexes has been intertwined, and as a consequence, women have had fewer options than men. Women's options have been restricted, independently of whether they actually gave birth or not, and the mere *ability* to have children has determined women's societal position fundamentally. Therefore, I do not accept Jónasdóttir's arguments that only biological motherhood is given, while social and political conditions change and thus cannot be the basis of objective interests. On the one hand, biology is not unchangeable, while on the other hand, the social division of work between the sexes has been amazingly continuous.

I find that the determination of the concept of objective interests on the basis of the control of choices is an acceptable compromise between Jónasdóttir's more pragmatic and Halsaa's radical solution. It is neither so superficial as to be meaningless, nor so narrow that it causes major political and scientific controversies.

The theory of women's interests does not in itself imply a denial of the existence of fundamental differences between women related to class and race. It simply states that across the differences they share the condition of being subordinate to men, and that their options, due to their special responsibility for human reproduction, are more restricted than those of men. However, the theory needs to be elaborated on the question of gender interests *vis-à-vis* other types of interests. The determination of the interests of men also remains open.

In the following discussion, I combine the two theoretical perspectives: variations between the regimes and women's possible choices connected to their responsibility for human care. Since my focus is on Western Europe, I look at only two regimes, the conservative and the social democratic. Finally I devote some effort to evaluating the effects of the European Community, because its influence on the policies of West European welfare states has been increasing.

Women's interests in the conservative regime

The balance between state, market and family in solving social problems in the conservative regime has its historical roots in Bismarck's social reforms of the 1880s. These reforms introduced a principle of mandatory social insurance for persons with labour market status, which has been a cornerstone in this regime ever since. Another cornerstone has been the social doctrine of the Catholic church, which has been formulated in a number of papal encyclicals (Leo XIII, 1942 [1891]; Pius XI, 1931 and John Paul II, 1981, 1991). These highlight a third way between liberalism and socialism in solving social problems, and they assign the family, the church and voluntary organizations a central role in this regard as a consequence of the *principle of subsidiarity*. According to this, the state should not engage in social problems before these other institutions have failed to solve the problems.

> In recent years the range of such intervention has vastly expanded, to the point of creating a new type of state, the so-called 'Welfare State'. This has happened in some countries in order to respond better to many needs and demands, by remedying forms of poverty and deprivation unworthy of the human person. However, excesses and abuses, especially in recent years, have provoked very harsh criticisms of the Welfare State, dubbed the 'Social Assistance State'. Malfunctions and defects in the Social Assistance State are the result of an inadequate understanding of the tasks proper to the State. Here again the *principle of subsidiarity* must be respected: a community of a higher order should not interfere in the internal life of a community of a lower order, depriving the latter of its functions, but rather should support it in case of need and help to coordinate its activity with the activities of the rest of the society, always with a view to the common good. (John Paul II, 1991: 69)

This quotation, which is from the most recent version of the social doctrine, reveals that the Holy See is highly critical of the welfare state of the social democratic regime type, substantiated by the principle of subsidiarity. The quote also illustrates that a distinct hierarchy between the societal arenas is entrenched in this principle, and that the Catholic social doctrine is highly opposed to public commitment to care for dependent persons. If the state or other institutions take over the responsibility, the encyclicals maintain that it will deprive the family of its functions and lead to an increase in bureaucracy (John Paul II, 1991: 69); instead the role of the state is to give directions, watch, stimulate and restrain (Pius XI, 1931: 41). The encyclicals also recommend social and family policies to support families in 'bringing up children and looking after the elderly' (John Paul II, 1991: 70), and they strongly favour a *family wage* which implies that: 'A workman's wages should be sufficient to enable him to support himself, his wife and his children' (John Paul II, 1991: 15). The Holy See has devoted much effort to condemning abortion as well as to limiting access to divorce and contraception, and mother-hood is praised as women's natural and holy vocation:

> Experience confirms that there must be a *social reevaluation of the mother's role*, of the toil connected with it, and of the need that children have for care, love and affection in order that they may develop into responsible, morally and religiously mature and psychologically stable persons. It will redound to the credit of society to make it possible for a mother – without inhibiting her freedom, without psychological or practical discrimination, and without penalizing her as compared to other

women – to devote herself to taking care of her children and educating
them in accordance with their needs, which vary with age. Having to
abandon these tasks in order to take up paid work outside the home is
wrong from the point of view of the good society and of the family when it
contradicts or hinders these primary goals of the mission of a mother.
(John Paul II, 1981: 46, 47)

According to this, women are intrinsically linked to human reproduction in the form of both principal and actual work, and the
encyclicals have directly sought to curtail women's options. At the
same time they seek to preserve a traditional and hierarchical
division of work between the sexes and married women's economic
dependence on their husbands.

The question is, then, how much political importance the social
doctrine has in the conservative regime today. It has indeed been the
ideological foundation for the Christian democratic parties, which
have been in government for long periods in many of the continental
European countries. At present there is, however, a certain political
distance between these parties and the church, except on issues like
abortion. In any event, abortion and divorce are legal in all EC
countries except Ireland.

The influence of the Catholic church is reflected in the lengthy
dominance of the housewife–breadwinner family model in the
conservative regime. It has been supported politically, among other
things by means of tax relief and child allowances and by very low
state involvement in provision of care of the sick, the elderly and
children. Hence the level of public services are clearly much lower in
the continental European countries than in Scandinavia (Andersen
and Christiansen, 1991). In childcare the difference relates specifically to the group of children aged 0–3, whereas the differences for
the children aged 3–6 are less pronounced (Borchorst, 1993).
Quantitative differences conceal considerable qualitative differences
in the content of childcare (European Commission's Childcare
Network, 1990).

The differences in married women's labour market participation
between the conservative and the social democratic regimes are
considerable, but there is a marked trend towards increased integration of mothers of small children into the labour market in all
countries within the conservative regime (OECD, 1990; European
Commission Network on Childcare, 1993).

So one can detect definite signs that the social doctrine of the
Catholic church is not decisive for the balance between state, market
and family or for the actual content of family and social policies in the
conservative regime. Neither do Catholics necessarily follow the
teachings of the church in their everyday practices. Hence Catholic

countries, such as Italy and Spain, at present have the lowest fertility rates in the West.

Familism is, however, strongly embedded in the conservative regime. The social rights of married women have been and are still tied to their husbands' social insurance, especially if they are housewives or work part-time in the labour market. Many married women do not have their own old age and sickness insurance, or their benefits are much more modest than men's, rendering them very vulnerable in case of divorce.

The question remains whether it is sufficient to operate with a single regime in continental Western Europe, or whether others should be added. I suggest, in line with several other authors in this volume, that the role of Catholicism is a factor of great importance for women's control of their options and for the balance between market, state and family. However, the influence of the Catholic church on the political culture varies considerably between the countries now included in this regime. Germany, for instance, is far more influenced by the social doctrine than France, and familism in the form of legislation directed towards families rather than individuals is also much more widespread in Germany than in France.

Women's interests and the social democratic regime

The social democratic regime is characterized by comprehensive welfare states modifying the market forces, and much less importance is ascribed to the family. The church has never obtained the same political influence as in Catholic countries, and today Denmark and Sweden in particular appear to be very secularized. The expansion of the welfare states in Sweden and Denmark occurred especially in the 1960s, but some of the basic principles embedded in the social democratic welfare states were shaped much earlier. Elements of universalism were introduced in the first part of the century. In this period the Bismarckian ideas also had a certain impact, but they never became predominant. Gradually these welfare states developed their distinct profiles, due, among other things, to political alliances between movements of peasants and workers, and ideas entrenched in the political culture.

When the agrarian family model was no longer predominant, the housewife–breadwinner family model became widespread in the social democratic regime as in the conservative, but in Sweden and Denmark it was prevalent only in the 1950s, and in Norway for a couple of decades longer. When family policy became a highly debated issue in Europe in the 1930s, initiated by the declining fertility rates, the Scandinavian countries headed towards qualitative provisions and improvement of the conditions of families with children. Initially the effects of the qualitative family policy were mainly ideological but, especially from the 1960s qualitative measures were enacted in Scandinavia.

The family wage has never played a major ideological and political role in Scandinavia. Wage gaps between the sexes persist in almost all occupational groups, but only during shorter periods have married men received higher wages, because they were family providers. Familism was prevalent in this regime in the beginning of the century, but it gradually disappeared partially due to an inter-Nordic effort to reduce familism in legislation. Benefits were often directed towards individuals or citizens rather than families. I disagree with Esping-Andersen, who interprets this as a reflection of liberalism (1990: 28). I find that it relates to the fact that egalitarian ideas also became related to gender, and that his evaluation is rooted in his neglect of gender relations as a power structure.

In the 1960s the social democratic parties, supported by other political parties, focused on equality between the classes and the sexes. Gender equality played a lesser role than class equality, and the political influence of women's organizations clearly was very restricted, compared to that of organized class interests. Yet gender equality has played a prominent role in shaping the policies of the Scandinavian countries ever since the 1960s. The dominant strategy to achieve gender equality, especially in Sweden and Denmark, was educating women and integrating them into the labour market, whereas changing the role of men played only a minor part.

In Scandinavia, abortion became fully legalized in the 1970s, and there is currently very little controversy over women's right to abortion in Denmark and Sweden. In Norway, where religion seems to play a far more important role, abortion is still a controversial issue.

The extensive commitment to human care in Denmark and Sweden contributed to the high workforce participation rate for mothers with small children in these countries. Denmark undoubtedly holds the record for provision of public childcare facilities; Sweden has the longest and best leave arrangements for fathers and mothers after the birth of a child and in relation to sickness and other special needs of the child. In Norway, the entry of women into the labour market on a large scale started in the 1980s, but with no major expansion in publicly provided daycare (Leira, 1989). Subsequently, this area has to some extent challenged the idea that Scandinavia forms a single regime.

Evaluations by feminist scholars of the effects of the Scandinavian welfare states are, however, ambivalent. A positive interpretation of the development in Scandinavia is that a partnership between women and the welfare state was established (Borchorst and Siim, 1987). The gender hierarchy was not dissolved, but women's options were extended, and they became more economically independent. Another interpretation is that the Scandinavian welfare states have the potential to be woman-friendly states, defined as states that enable women ' to have a natural relationship to their children, their work, and public life', and which do 'not force harder choices on women than on men' (Hernes, 1987a: 15). Hence this definition also stresses the enhancement of women's options.

A number of feminist scholars have characterized the development during the past 20–30 years more negatively, including some of the scholars quoted above. One interprets the development as a change from direct and personal to indirect and structural oppression (Holter, 1984); others see it as a shift from family to state patriarchy (Borchorst and Siim, 1987), from private to public dependence (Hernes, 1987a), or as a modernization of the gender system (SOU, 1990). It is assumed that gender relations have changed, but not to the benefit of women. A more precise interpretation may be that the effects of these welfare states on women's possible choices have been ambiguous (Siim, 1993a; Borchorst, 1994). I find that women's control of their choices has been extended in the social democratic regime during the last 25 to 30 years compared to the conservative regime. Their options have also been improved, in comparison with previous periods. Though it is difficult for a Danish mother of small children to choose to be at home and take care of her children, her possible choices are better than those of a Dutch mother of small children, who, by and large, cannot choose to work outside the home. The integration of women into the labour market did not dissolve the gender hierarchy, but the economic independence they gained has enhanced their options, and women have been empowered in terms of societal influence at a broader level. Some effects may become more noticeable in the longer run; I would for instance suggest that the role of men as fathers is changing in Scandinavia. Fathers have become more involved in the upbringing of their children than their own fathers were. This will create and has created new issues of gender conflict, but it also lessens the irreconcilability between motherhood and paid work.

It can be questioned whether the social democratic regime is becoming eroded as a result of internal as well as external pressure. The Scandinavian welfare states are undergoing a process of restructuring, and they face economic and political challenges. Some of the domestic criticism corresponds to the assessment of the welfare state by the Holy See, which was quoted above. The assertion is that welfare states take away the initiative of individuals. There may be an element of truth in this criticism, but it is crucial that suggestions for alterations are premissed on explicit statements of the desired outcome in terms of gender relations, as is the case in the papal encyclicals. In the restructuring process, the distribution of political power in terms of gender and class might turn out to be decisive. Are decisions which shape the future of the welfare state taken by political bodies with an equal gender representation, or are they heavily dominated by men? Women may not agree on the best solutions for tackling the relation between production and reproduction or the balance between market, state and family, but they often share the interest of getting these issues on the political agenda.

The EC and women's options

The welfare regimes of Western Europe have increasingly been influenced by the supranational level. The European Community will probably be even more decisive in the future. So far the impact on social and family policies of the European Community has been modest. Social policy has definitely not been at the core of the integration process: the role of the *social dimension* has been minor, and it was not ratified by Britain in the Maastricht Treaty. But it is highly likely that services and income transfers in the member states will be affected both directly through directives and recommendations on social and family policies, and indirectly through the effects of the political and economic union and the single market. The question here is: what impact does the Community have on the situation of women and their options, and is one regime model going to be nurtured more than others?

The EC was formed by leading Christian democrats from the conservative regime, and the overwhelming number of the present member states belong to this regime. Britain is the only country with liberal elements, but it is not included in the liberal regime by Esping-Andersen because it also has elements from the other regimes. At present Denmark is the only Scandinavian (and Nordic) country which is a member of the EC, and therefore the only member state which belongs to the social democratic regime. It could be anticipated that EC regulations would be heavily influenced by the social doctrine, and that a strong emphasis was given to the family and to principles embedded in the conservative regime. The principle of subsidiarity has truly become a guiding element of EC policies; it is often referred to and was incorporated in the text of the Maastricht Treaty. Until now it has mainly been related to the national versus the supranational level, but it remains very unclear how the principle will be implemented in practice.

In some areas, EC regulations have rejected central elements of the social doctrine. One example is that equal pay and not the family wage has been an explicit objective of the Community. Article 119 of the Treaty of Rome, on equal pay, was introduced as a result of French employers' fear of losing competitive advantages, because France was the only member country which had equal pay. This was followed up by a directive in 1975, and the European Court has ordered some member states to strengthen the national legislation on equal pay. Directives of 1978 and 1986 on equal treatment in social insurance schemes have also aimed at achieving parity between women and men in social insurance schemes. A 1976 directive on equal treatment in the labour market prohibited discrimination on the basis of sex, and the general policy of the Community has been to support the integration of women into the labour market. The contradictions between family life and working life have also been dealt with, but this has mainly been in the form of very general statements without much effect. In 1992 childcare provision was included in EC policies. It was originally suggested that this should be in the form of a directive, which is binding for the member states, but due to resistance in the Council it was passed as a recommendation, which has much less effect. A directive, which calls on the national states to provide 14 weeks of paid maternity leave with the right to draw benefits, was passed in 1993.

On this basis it has been stressed that the equality legislation of the EC is relatively progressive, and some feminist scholars have concluded that the EC in certain limited areas has proved to be more open to women than has the national state (Petersen, 1989). One could also argue that the equal opportunity level of the Community constitutes a small and relatively insignificant niche, isolated from the 'big power game' that determines the overall economic and political setting. Women's interests have certainly not been given continuous and systematic high priority by EC bodies (Schunter-Kleemann, 1990). Some scholars interpret EC legislation in this area as a consequence of the attempts of the Commission and the Parliament to enlarge the sphere of manoeuvre for the EC at the expense of the member states (Schwencke, 1992). If this is true, it does not necessarily imply that representation of women's interests will obtain a high priority in the longer run.

Whether European integration is in the interests of women is a very difficult question to answer, because the process is ongoing and affected by many different factors. It is also somewhat unpredictable. The effects may turn out to be different in different regimes, countries and regions. My suggestion is that the EC regulations will magnify differences between women, supporting those who can compete directly with men. This is especially true for women with higher education; more marginalized women will not benefit from the free mobility of labour and the prohibition on sex discrimination. These women might also carry a heavier burden of unpaid work in the family, and they cannot afford to pay others to perform it. Finally, the consequences for women's interests cannot be answered solely on the basis of an evaluation of the effects of the equality legislation. The overall effects of the integration process on the balance of market, state and family will probably affect gender relations and women's control of their options (Schunter-Kleemann, 1990). Although EC regulations have not aimed at strengthening the role of the family, they have certainly strengthened the market.

Recent discussions on unemployment confirm the highly monetarist character of the political and economic union. The principles embedded in the social dimension and the recommendations on convergence of social security systems from 1992 also suggest that basic principles of the conservative regime, in the form of insurance schemes directed towards employees, will be stressed. This reinforces a dualism between workers with secure full-time jobs and workers outside or partly attached to the labour market. This dualism is heavily structured along gender lines.

At this level, too, it will be of importance to what extent women are represented in the major political bodies. This brings the form aspect of women's interests into focus.

The form aspect of women's interests

Although the form aspect – control over choices – is closely linked to the content aspect, I will look at it separately and quite generally as women's representation and influence in a part of the formal political system, specifically the lower chambers of national legislatures. This is clearly a very narrow indicator of the form aspect, but it is a good gauge of women's influence on the conditions of choice. To Esping-Andersen's 18 nations are added some Mediterranean countries and Iceland (see Table 3.1).

Table 3.1 shows that universal suffrage was introduced at different times in these countries. There is no unambiguous connection between the time when women's suffrage was enacted and the size of women's current representation in parliaments of the different countries, with the exception of the five Nordic countries. Here women got the vote early, and these countries have for some time had the highest representation of women among the OECD countries.

Table 3.1 *Women's parliamentary representation (lower houses)*

	Universal suffrage for women	Election year	Percentage of women in Parliament
Finland	1906	1991	39
Norway	1913	1993	38
Sweden	1921	1991	34
Denmark	1915	1990	33
Iceland	1915	1991	24
Netherlands	1919	1989	23
Austria	1919	1990	22
New Zealand	1893	1993	21
Germany	1919	1990	21
Canada	1920	1993	18
Switzerland	1971	1991	18
Spain	1931	1993	16
Luxembourg	1918	1992	13
Ireland	1922	1993	12
USA	1920	1992	11
United Kingdom	1928	1992	9
Australia	1901	1993	9
Portugal	1975	1991	9
Belgium	1948	1991	9
Italy	1945	1992	8
France	1944	1993	6
Greece	1952	1993	6
Japan	1945	1993	3
European Parliament		1994	25

Note: Information on the years when women obtained the vote varies and contains an element of estimation on when the vote was extended to all groups of the population.
Source: Mackie and Rose (1991)

On this basis one could actually talk about a Scandinavian or rather Nordic model, and the political representation of women in these countries seems to reflect their integration into society more generally.

At the supranational level in terms of the EC, women's influence in the most important institutions is less than in the Nordic countries, but larger than in the liberal and conservative regimes. In the *Council of Ministers*, which has the decisive influence, women's representation is dependent on the number of women ministers in government in the member countries, and on the issues being debated. On the whole, women's share of the Council is, however, at a minimum. In the *Secretariat of the Council*, women constitute a little more than

10 per cent of the civil servants. In the *Commission*, which has the exclusive right to introduce policy proposals, there is currently one woman out of 17 commissioners, and women make up only 12 per cent of the senior civil servants. The EC *Court of Justice*, which is the final court of appeal, has no women among its 13 judges and 6 advocates-general. The highest representation of women is found in the *Parliament* where they constitute 25 per cent of the members. The parliament's power is limited, and was only insignificantly enlarged by the Maastricht Treaty.

Women's influence and representation is thus much lower than that of men in the EC system and substantially worse than in Denmark (and the other Nordic countries). It is at the same level or higher than in the other member countries. Hence, EC membership implies a worsening for women in the social democratic regime with regard to the form aspect, and to a certain extent an improvement for women in the conservative regime. However, this is on condition that the shift from the national to the EC level does not in itself reduce women's influence.

It is hardly likely that a working democracy can be established for more than 340 million people who speak different languages, and where the areas of language have very different importance. In addition the most important decisions are made in bodies which are not publicly elected. The decision-making processes are very closed in the EC system and information about possible choices is limited. Interest groups can gain influence by means of lobbying, but this requires money, power, and knowledge of the language and channels of influence in the EC bureaucracy. In order to obtain systematic influence one should probably establish a permanent office in Brussels, as the Catholic church has done. In general far fewer women than men have access to lobbying techniques, and this is also true of weak and marginalized groups compared to strong and highly organized interests. Women's problems in gaining influence are also affected by the political culture of the EC system, which is very male dominated. In conclusion there is a *democratic deficit* to the benefit of a bureaucratic male elite. Some interest representation has been institutionalized, and organized class interests have obtained a central role, which has strengthened male dominance.

In the Scandinavian countries, women seem to be more sceptical and also far more uncertain about the European integration process than men. The majority of women voted no in the first Danish referendum on the Maastricht Treaty in June 1992; in the second referendum in May 1993 more women voted yes than in the first. The gender gap was modest, but it widened from the first to the second referendum, if we look at the 'no' votes. Voting behaviour of course only reveals the subjective interests of women, and we cannot determine to what extent gender actually affects political attitudes. The scepticism of Scandinavian women might also relate to the fact that women are more supportive of welfare benefits than men are. They are also more prone than men to vote for left political parties, which are more in favour of extensive public care.

Concluding remarks

This chapter has offered evidence that gender is a factor which structures welfare states fundamentally, and variations are not fully comprehended if it is neglected. My criticism of Esping-Andersen as a central representative of the mainstream paradigm has demonstrated that the neglect of gender has serious empirical as well as theoretical implications. Regardless of how interesting it might be to study income transfers, the prominence given to these benefits limits our understanding of welfare state variations, and services must be added to the research agenda. When services such as public care and their effects on women's labour market participation are taken into consideration, one may indeed conclude that women have been commodified in Sweden and Denmark and de-commodified in the conservative regime, contrary to the conclusions of Esping-Andersen. My analysis also substantiates the view that the family constitutes a central institution which should be included systematically, and welfare states vary substantially in their mix between family, market and state. Finally, I argue that variations in the influence of the church and religion merits attention in terms of its influence on gender relations, and its role as a political actor in itself also requires investigation.

Notwithstanding these weaknesses, Esping-Andersen's typology constitutes a useful point of departure for an analysis of variations in gender structures in Western Europe. I have also applied the concept of interest, because I find it valuable to conceptualize the effects of welfare states for women and explain variations between regimes. Hence the question is whether policies improve women's control of their options.

My historical and cross-national analysis indicates that the Scandinavian welfare states, despite their preservation of a distinct gender hierarchy, have enhanced women's control of their options. Women have become more independent of men and marriage and they have gained more control at the level of the formal political system. In the conservative regime the social doctrine has been influential and it has supported a hierarchical division of labour, according to which women are mainly responsible for human care, and their options are more restricted than men's. At present one can find indications that the influence of the doctrine is limited, and the conservative regime at the point of women's labour market participation appears to converge with the social democratic. However, familism is still prevalent, and in some countries policies are still largely based on women's responsibility for human care within the family.

The regulations of the European Community are not in accordance with the social doctrine of the Catholic church on central questions like the family wage and support of a housewife–breadwinner family model. At this point in the integration process it is, however, difficult to predict how the regulations will affect the mix between the state, the market and the family. The interpretations of the effects of European integration on the interests of women so far are also ambiguous. I expect that the overall effects will differentiate women. When it comes to the form aspect, women certainly have much less power than men within EC institutions, and it is hardly likely that this will change in the immediate future.

Note

This chapter is a somewhat revised version of an article in Danish published in *Kvinder, køn & forskning*, 1, 1992: 40–62.

4

Childcare and Types of Welfare States

Siv Gustafsson

A central facet of Gøsta Esping-Andersen's regime typology is the assumption that welfare states can be understood only through their historical ideology, and that the ideological legacy shapes the present-day actions of policy-makers. Based on this reasoning he distinguishes between three different types or clusters of capitalist welfare states: the liberal or residualist, the conservative or corporatist, and the social democratic or institutional. In this chapter Esping-Andersen's typology is applied to explain differences in childcare provision and subsidization and the possible effects on labour supply of mothers with young children, comparing Sweden, the Netherlands and the United States. Whereas Esping-Andersen worked out his typology mainly for pensions, sickness benefits and the creation of jobs in the public sector, this chapter demonstrates that it can be fruitfully applied to the domain of childcare as well. The three types of welfare states are not to be seen as pure cases but as approximations, where a particular country has more defining characteristics of one of the three types of welfare states than of the other two types.

The liberal welfare state is characterized by a belief that the unfettered market brings welfare to the maximum number of citizens. Only if the market fails does the state intervene with welfare benefits which are typically means tested and often carry a social stigma. This type of welfare state can therefore also be labelled the residual welfare state. The United States is the prototype of the liberal or residual welfare state but Canada and Australia are also included in this category by Esping-Andersen (1990: 27).

The second cluster of welfare states is shaped by a corporatist statist legacy with a strong influence by the church. Welfare provisions are typically organized along occupational lines, often with preferential treatment of civil servants. The family breadwinner is the welfare recipient and married women are often excluded from any right to their own pensions or unemployment benefits. Esping-Andersen (1990: 27) mentions Austria, France, Germany and Italy as belonging to this group, and his prototype country which he analyses in more detail is Germany.

The third category is the social democratic or institutional welfare state. The most typical social democratic state is Sweden but other Nordic countries – Denmark, Norway and Finland – are also included. 'Perhaps the most salient characteristic of the social democratic regime is its fusion of welfare and work. It is at once genuinely committed to a full-employment guarantee, and entirely dependent on its attainment' (Esping-Andersen, 1990: 28). In the social democratic welfare state welfare provisions are institutional, seldom means tested and usually apply to all citizens alike.

Sweden and the United States are the prototypes used by Esping-Andersen but the Netherlands, although included in his list of conservative, corporatist welfare states, is not considered very typical. Therefore there is reason to clarify whether the Netherlands is a corporatist welfare state in Esping-Andersen's sense. An essential feature of this type of welfare state, besides its corporatist statist legacy, is the influence of the church. In analysing the historical origins of the welfare state in the Netherlands, Dutch social scientists have emphasized the importance of 'pillarization' (*verzuiling*) (Stuurman, 1993). By this expression is meant that society is organized along confessional lines where Roman Catholics and Calvinists made up the two most important pillars or columns, and socialists later formed a separate column of their own. The pillars created their own playschools, primary schools, secondary schools, universities, radio stations, newspapers, labour unions, political parties and so on. Because of pillarization a Roman Catholic seldom made friends with a fundamentalist Calvinist, and only at the very top level was there negotiation between groups. Rival churches have therefore shaped Dutch society and are primarily responsible for the breadwinner ideology which still characterizes Dutch society and which has a negative attitude to female labour force participation. Göran Therborn (1989) contrasts the backgrounds of the Swedish and the Dutch welfare states by pointing to popular movements (*folkrörelser*) in Sweden and the pillarization in the Netherlands. He also emphasizes the Roman Catholic influence in particular (1989: 210–11) and explains how a weak state was 'subsidiary' to the pillars, which were led by a strong clergy organizing welfare for members of their own pillar.

For the purpose of analysing and contrasting childcare, this chapter examines the experiences of these three types of welfare states. The main questions addressed are: how much childcare is provided by whom? How is childcare financed? Are there any subsidies for childcare, and if so under what conditions? And do childcare subsidies increase the female labour supply? In addition special attention is devoted to the historical background of family policies leading to different patterns of employment of mothers with young children.

Employment patterns of mothers

The hours of labour market work for mothers of preschool children show distinctly different patterns between the three countries. In Table 4.1 data for the years 1984 for Sweden and 1988 for the Netherlands and the United States are presented in order to enable the same definitions for the three countries. In the Netherlands the normal pattern is that mothers care for their preschool children themselves at home. Around three-quarters of all mothers do not work at all and if they do work it is only for a few hours in the week, less than half time. In the United States it is more common than in Sweden not to participate in the paid labour force. Almost half of the US mothers are full-time homemakers compared to less than a third of the Swedish preschool mothers. From the second year of the child's life the proportion of mothers who are full-time homemakers is only 20–25 per cent in Sweden as compared to twice as many, around 40–45 per cent, in the United States.

However, the proportion of full-time workers is by far the largest in the United States, where from the child's second year as many as one-third of the mothers already work 35 hours or more per week. In Sweden the proportion of mothers who are full-time workers never exceeds 26.7 per cent during the child's first five years, whereas in the United States it increases to 41.2 per cent when the child is 4–5 years old. Full-time working mothers are virtually non-existent in the Netherlands, increasing only to 6.8 per cent by the time the youngest child reaches 4–5 years.

A peculiarity of Swedish mothers is that they work 20–34 hours per week, long part-time, rather than not working at all or working full time. Working long part-time is very uncommon in the Netherlands, and it is also rather uncommon in the United States. The particular work pattern of Swedish mothers is facilitated by public policies including 15 months of paid parental leave, subsidized community-run daycare centres covering more than half of the children aged 2–6, and the right to work a six-hour workday until the child is 8 years old. Paid parental leave in 1988 (Statistics Sweden, 1989) allowed around 90 per cent of parents, father or mother, to care for their child until the child was 1 year old. This contrasts to the situation in the United States where almost one-third of (first-time) mothers were at work three months after their first child was born (Leibowitz *et al.*, 1992).

The situation regarding childcare for working mothers can be

Table 4.1 *Employment of mothers with preschool children (%)*

Age of youngest child	USA				Netherlands				Sweden			
	Hours of paid work per week											
	None	1–19	20–34	35 +	None	1–19	20–34	35 +	None	1–19	20–34	35 +
under 1	57.6	8.5	8.5	25.4	74.4	18.2	4.0	3.5	58.8	1.5	17.7	22.1
1	45.1	10.6	10.9	33.3	78.0	16.1	4.3	2.6	20.4	26.5	42.9	10.2
2–3	44.5	5.8	11.2	38.6	73.2	21.2	1.4	4.2	23.9	19.5	39.9	16.8
4–5	36.9	9.7	12.1	41.2	62.1	28.1	2.9	6.8	25.0	13.3	35.0	26.7
0–5	48.4	8.3	10.2	32.9	72.6	20.3	3.2	5.8	31.7	15.4	34.2	18.7

Source: Gustafsson and Stafford (1994). The data are based on our own analysis of National Longitudinal Surveys Young Women aged 23–30 as of 1988 n = 2650 for the USA; OSA Survey Women Aged 18–65 as of 1988 n = 1079 for the Netherlands; HUS Survey Women Aged 18–64 as of 1984 n = 379 for Sweden.

summarized as follows in the three countries. In Sweden there is subsidized good-quality public childcare which is virtually universally available, and mothers have jobs. In the United States there is a market for childcare, and mothers to a large extent have jobs. In the Netherlands until recently there has been neither a market nor subsidized childcare, and mothers have rarely had jobs. However the number of mothers with small children who work in the labour market is increasing. In 1992 almost 43 per cent of mothers of preschool children were labour force participants, according to a more recent source (Maassen van den Brink, 1994). In order to understand these different patterns, we turn to a consideration of the historical background of family policy.

Sweden: working women's rights and pronatalism

Although the public daycare system in Sweden expanded only in the 1970s and 1980s (Gustafsson and Stafford, 1992) as working mothers began to demand childcare, the ideology behind the childcare system can be traced back to discussions in the 1930s and to the acceptance of the working woman's right to have a family. Several authors have analysed the historical background of Swedish family policies (Hatje, 1974; McIntosh, 1983; Kälvemark, 1980; Popenoe, 1988; Hirdman, 1989; Carlsson, 1990). All agree that important steps were taken in the 1930s and the 1940s, and that those steps to a large extent were inspired by Alva and Gunnar Myrdal's famous book, *Crisis in the Population Question*, published in 1934. Ann-Sofie Kälvemark (1980) summarizes the arguments of the Myrdals as 'More children of better quality.' The Myrdals' objective was twofold: to increase the fertility rate of Sweden and to improve the situation of the working class. Yvonne Hirdman (1989) in her discussion of the Swedish welfare model emphasizes the influence of socialist utopians on the thinking of the Myrdals. Specifically Alva Myrdal, according to Hirdman, clearly thought that institutions, and the specialists that could be employed by institutions such as childcare centres, would do a better job in bringing up children than would ordinary mothers with no education for the job.

The 1935 population commission, which was a direct result of the Myrdals' book, argued for state institutions for childcare (Hatje, 1974). Childcare institutions at this time were generally looked upon as an unfortunate alternative, to be used only as a last resort, and they were part of poverty relief. The population commission wanted to remove the poverty connotations and advocated that part-day childcare should be made available to all children (Hatje, 1974: 77). This was motivated by the 'quality of population' argument, namely that experts in childcare institutions would improve the education of young children. Although state subsidies for childcare were discussed in parliament during 1943, they were not accepted, because of strong sentiments among Social Democrats that the problem of the working-class mother was to be able to afford to be with her children rather than to be able to leave them in care.

The fight for married women's employment developed quite differently in Sweden compared to the Netherlands and the US (Hobson, 1993). In 1939 Sweden passed an Act making it unlawful to dismiss a woman because of marriage, pregnancy or childbirth. This legislation was exceptional in an international context.

The Great Depression hit Sweden with a high unemployment rate, and mounting hostility towards married women holding jobs that were needed for male breadwinners. A government commission of 1935 (SOU, 1935: 6) recommended that women who married should be dismissed. However, Alva Myrdal and other feminists managed to change the question of married women's right to work into the question of working women's right to have a family. A special government commission on women's right to work, with Alva Myrdal as secretary, argued along the lines set out in *Crisis of the Population Question* (Hatje, 1974: 39–41). If women were dismissed, it was argued, the effects would be that working women would not be able to afford to marry and have children. The illegitimacy rate would rise, illegal abortions would increase, and those couples particularly among the working class who were dependent on two incomes would refrain from having children.

How could these arguments succeed in becoming government policy? An important fact was that Sweden in the 1930s had the lowest fertility rate in the world. The main theme of the Myrdals' book was that the remedy for Sweden's population crisis was government support of families with children. There was a strong political pronatalist sentiment, particularly among conservatives, because of the low fertility rate. Ann-Katrin Hatje (1974) describes how the working class was very influenced by neo-Malthusian ideas, which implied that the only way they could improve their standard of living was by limiting the size of their family. Consequently they were very suspicious of the pronatalist intent of the Myrdals' book and the government commission on population. However, Social Democratic intellectuals saw the book as a breakthrough in achieving broad political support. The book framed pronatalist policies as social welfare policies, and social welfare policies were made acceptable to conservative politicians because of their intended pronatalist effects.

In Sweden, the 1950s was the decade of the housewife. More women than ever married and had children but they did not combine work and family, because joint taxation of incomes made it unprofitable. Nor was there daycare for children and paid parental leave did not exist. Labour force participation of married women was lower in Sweden than in Germany and France (Schultz, 1981: 204). From the 1960s onwards Swedish economic policies have been organized around the idea of stimulating the labour supply of married women. Confronted by a labour shortage, government economic forecasts identified married women, particularly mothers of young children, as the only important reserve of labour.

One reason for the increasing acceptance of married women in the labour force was that Sweden, as opposed to Germany, did not accept the idea that foreign immigrants were guest workers. Earlier than elsewhere they were given the right to bring their families, and Swedish language instruction was to be available during paid work hours. Thus the social and business costs of immigrant workers were substantial, especially compared to the cost of bringing married women into the labour force.

The Swedish childcare system fits Esping-Andersen's defining properties of the social democratic welfare state. Childcare is universal, it is used by both the middle class and the working class. It is an example of a high-quality provision, which is supported by the middle class in the same way as Esping-Andersen characterizes the development of old age pension insurance. Access is not means tested but parental fees are usually progressive with family income. The Swedish daycare system is organized to accommodate the needs of the working mother. In order to get a place at the childcare centre both parents (or the single parent) must be working or studying at least 20 hours per week. This is important in the discussion of whether childcare subsidies increase labour supply or not. The municipalities with central state subsidies organize and run the daycare system and they have had a virtual monopoly on receiving state subsidies. In addition the municipalities have their own right of income taxation.

Table 4.2 shows the development of the childcare system in Sweden. In 1975, 15 per cent of all children had a place in the childcare system either at a childcare centre or with a daycare mother employed by the community. The corresponding figure had increased to 47 per cent in 1987, covering almost half of the whole population of children 0–6 years of age. This also includes children under the age of 1 who are cared for by parents themselves using paid parental leave, which in 1993 gave one of the parents the right to care for the child with income compensation for 15 months.

The Swedish daycare system and the working mother are typical results of the social democratic welfare state. It has alleviated the

Table 4.2 *Characteristics of public childcare in Sweden, 1975–87*

Ratio of places to children	Cost per place (1986 Skr)	Per cent of cost paid by			Labour force participation of women with children, aged 0–6
		family	community	state	
1975 0.15	20.675 (54.566)	12	50	38	58.8
1976 0.18	23.540 (56.289)	10	56	34	61.2
1977 0.20	26.960 (57.902)	10	38	52	64.4
1978 0.23	31.460 (61.373)	10	40	50	67.2
1979 0.27	34.505 (62.812)	10	38	52	70.3
1980 0.31	39.590 (63.436)	9	40	51	73.7
1981 0.34	42.700 (61.026)	8	42	50	79.6
1982 0.37	44.200 (58.196)	9	41	50	79.6
1983 0.40	47.800 (57.770)	10	40	50	81.3
1984 0.42	54.100 (60.539)	10	38	52	82.2
1985 0.45	58.100 (60.557)	10	41	49	84.2
1986 0.45	62.050 (62.050)	10	44	46	84.6
1987 0.47	62.400	10	43	47	

Source: Gustafsson and Stafford, 1992

problem of single motherhood which haunts the United States (Garfinkel and McLanahan, 1986; Hobson, Chapter 11 this volume), since a mother already has a job when she gets divorced and she already has daycare for her child. In this way, as Esping-Andersen argues, the Swedish system fuses welfare and work.

In 1991 a non-social-democratic government entered office and during 1992–93 Sweden was hit by the most severe depression since the 1930s. Unemployment increased to the average of the European Community. The municipal monopoly in receiving state subsidies has been abolished, and private organizations can now arrange daycare and receive a state subsidy. The government also has plans to use some of the childcare subsidies for a 'care subsidy allowance', which would be paid to working and non-working mothers alike. These developments may change the situation of the working mother in Sweden. If full employment is not achieved again, and available forecasts are gloomy about this, the Swedish welfare state and the provision of daycare for all children is further threatened since, as Esping-Andersen notes, 'The Swedish welfare state is at once genuinely committed to a full-employment guarantee, and entirely dependent on its attainment' (1990: 28).

The Netherlands: pillarization and subsidiarity

At most 2 per cent of Dutch preschool children under 4 and 3.7 per cent of preschool children of mothers who work in the labour market have a place in a childcare centre (Tijdens and Lieon, 1993: 24–5). To understand this contrast to Swedish policies it is important to emphasize the role of the church and its battle against state institutions:

> But the corporatist regimes are also typically shaped by the Church, and hence strongly committed to the preservation of traditional familyhood. Social insurance typically excludes nonworking wives, and family benefits encourage motherhood. Daycare and similar family services are conspicuously underdeveloped; the principle of 'subsidiarity' serves to emphasize that the state will only interfere when the family's capacity to service its members is exhausted. (Esping-Andersen, 1990: 27)

Therborn (1989) explains that the subsidiarity principle means that the state should be subsidiary not only to the family but also to the confessional pillars. This is typically visible in primary education, which is organized along confessional lines. Parochial and public schools have received equal state funding since the confessionals won 'a complete triumph' (Therborn, 1989: 204) in the great school battle of 1917. In the pillarized society there was no room for childcare except as poverty relief, and then organized along confessional lines (Rijswijk-Clerkx, 1981).

Until 1965 childcare was regulated by the Poor Laws (Pott-Buter, 1993: Chapter 9). From the 1960s until the oil crisis of 1973 was a period of tight labour markets. Firms, competing for the scarce labour force, installed daycare for their employees. Public opinion was against the working mother and against daycare, so firms never openly advertised their daycare centres. In 1973 these were estimated to comprise 10 per cent of all child places at daycare centres. As the labour shortage disappeared, firms lost interest in providing childcare and closed their daycare centres. The percentage of childcare places fell to 1 per cent in 1977. Mothers who wanted to continue to work turned to confessional centres. In response to the increased demand for their services the centres modified their rules, accepting only women who had to work out of economic necessity (Tijdens and Lieon, 1993: 13 citing Rijswijk-Clerkx).

Mothers in the Dutch society had 'a duty of presence' 24 hours a day (*aanwezigheidsplicht*) if they were to be considered good mothers. Women demanding some freedom for themselves began to question this 'duty of presence'. Part of this demand was met by shops supplying hourly-based daycare for children while mothers were shopping (Tijdens and Lieon, 1993: 13), but the most important form of daycare has become the part-day playschools (*peuterspeelzalen*).

One of the reasons for the failure to obtain jobs and full-time daycare lies in the logic of the types of welfare states. As extensively discussed by Esping-Andersen (1990: 153) the conservative, cor-poratist welfare states reacted to the rise in unemployment resulting from the oil crisis by trying to decrease labour supply (see also Hartog and Theeuwes, 1993), whereas the social democratic welfare state attempted to increase labour demand. The means of reducing labour supply have been early retirement, repatriating foreign workers, and encouraging women to remain at home. Such policies have been extensively used in the Netherlands.

In countries like Germany, Holland, France and Belgium the welfare state is strongly biased against the expansion of social services and against welfare state employment as an alternative to employment promotion. In Sweden, on the other hand, the welfare state is an important employer. Health, education and welfare services (HEW) account for around 25 per cent of total employment and over 90 per cent of HEW employment occurs in the public sector. The corresponding figures for Holland are not available, but for Germany they are 11 per cent and 58 per cent and for the United States 17 per cent and 45 per cent (Esping-Andersen, 1990: 158). Further, in 1988 almost 60 per cent of Swedish women were employed in the public sector as against 25 per cent of Swedish men (Löfström and Gustafsson, 1991: 314).

Policies of encouraging women to remain at home or even more actively to forbid them to be employed have been vigorous and have continued until recently in the Netherlands. The history of women's work in the Netherlands is a lasting story of outright legal discrimi-nation against women. Of course the discriminatory legislation was justified as protecting women from the evils of the labour market; for example forbidding women to work at night or under ground.

The Depression of the 1930s in the Netherlands strengthened earlier breadwinner arguments for excluding women from the labour market. In 1924 married women were forbidden to hold civil servants' jobs, which was most important for teachers (Kessel *et al.*, 1986; Pott-Buter, 1993; Blok, 1978). Female teachers were dismissed on their wedding day because it was unlawful for the employer to keep them, no matter how good they were. Only in 1973 did Dutch women gain the same protection as Swedish women secured in 1939, namely legislation making it unlawful for employers to dismiss a woman because of pregnancy, childbirth or marriage (Pott-Buter, 1993).

To have a job is far less important in the Netherlands than in Sweden. Therborn (1989: 234) cites a debate between the Catholic premier van Agt and the Labour leader den Uyl in 1980, where Van Agt did not agree with the social democratic idea that 'you can only completely, humanely and socially function in society when you have a paid job'. In Swedish political rhetoric no one questions that a job is an essential right, and Swedish active labour market policies since 1968 also officially include women (Gustafsson, 1984).

But things are rapidly changing in the Netherlands, and legislation to stimulate the growth of childcare institutions has become effective as of 1990 (Tijdens and Lieon, 1993: Chapter 3). In the 1980s increasingly and in the 1990s the Dutch welfare state has had to tackle the problem of financing a growing number of beneficiaries by a relatively smaller number of taxpayers. This has led to policies of trying to increase labour supply rather than decrease it. The report of the Scientific Council of the Dutch government *A Working Perspective* (WRR, 1991) has been an important contribution to this change. The new rules promoting childcare are part of these policies to stimulate greater labour force participation.

The Childcare Stimulation Act of 1990 is the first government action which explicitly caters to the needs of the working mother rather than assigning priority to educational considerations. Previously the debate pitted the needs of the child against the needs of the mother. The 1990 Act subsidizes childcare centres, daycare host parents and care for young schoolchildren but excludes (the part-day) playschools from subsidies because they are not meant for the working mother. However, the Childcare Stimulation Act of 1990 only provided subsidies during the years 1990–93, thereby increasing the proportion of children who are in subsidized childcare from 2 per cent to 4 per cent. The Act was later extended to 1997 (Tijdens and Lieon, 1993: 32).

In some respects the organization of the childcare subsidies is similar to that of Sweden in that the municipalities are given the subsidies and the responsibility to supply childcare. The financing of Swedish and Dutch subsidized childcare differs. In Sweden the municipalities have a right of taxation, and a large share of the Swedish population pays only the municipal proportional income tax (see e.g. Gustafsson and Klevmarken, 1993). Revenues from the municipal tax finance between 40 and 50 per cent of the total cost of daycare (see Table 4.2 above). Dutch municipalities on the other hand receive 95 per cent of their income from the national state. The ideal of the Dutch Childcare Stimulation Act is that daycare should be financed about one-third each by the state, parents and employers. The Dutch government intends to stimulate employers to supply childcare by having municipalities give companies subsidies out of state subsidies. Furthermore, company costs of childcare are deductible before company taxation. This is different from Sweden, where the social democratic policy has been to supply daycare in the vicinity of the child's home. In this way the children can also see their friends at weekends and parents are not tied to a particular employer who provides childcare.

In summary, the late arrival of childcare to accommodate the working mother in the Netherlands is an illustration of the functioning of the corporatist, Christian democratic pillarized welfare state. The lack of childcare is historically explained by the subsidiarity principle, previous governments' attempts to discourage labour supply, the reluctance of governments to expand budgets and engage in public production, the strong influence of church and family values, the relatively low value attached to having a job or, as Esping-Andersen (1990: 27) puts it, 'In these conservative and strongly corporatist welfare states the liberal obsession with market efficiency and commodification was never preeminent.'

The United States: the market plus poverty relief[1]

In the liberal or residual welfare state the state is involved only when the family or market fails, and this is presumed to apply to a small share or residual of the population. In the United States programmes such as Head Start and the Family Support Act of 1988 are centred on the idea that intervention is needed to encourage 'positive effects of preschool on disadvantaged children' and that the 'needs of employed mothers [be met] while providing developmentally appropriate experience for children' (Hofferth *et al.*, 1991: 8). While there is some public support for childcare extending beyond lower-middle income groups, this support is in the form of tax credits. Tax credits as a policy allows minimum government involvement, and facilitates a wide range of choice in the market. Statutory unpaid leave has been opposed on the grounds that the firm and its employees can form private agreements on an individualized market basis.

Public childcare programmes in the United States are very rare and are operated at the local level. The main policy supporting childcare is tax deductibility of childcare expenses on federal tax schedules and some modest state supplements (Michalopoulos *et al.*, 1992). It is only recently that very limited legislation allowing women to take unpaid leave from an employer has been enacted. Until the 1950s marriage and maternity bars on women's employment were common (Goldin, 1990).

From the perspective of most US economists, even those in the field of human resources, the rationale for public provision of childcare services is considered very weak. The usual justifications for government intervention are to correct market failures arising from public goods or externalities. Perhaps the closest justification for public childcare would be as a merit good or to correct an externality arising from insufficient resources devoted to childcare through choices made by individual parents or families.

This contemporary US perspective on childcare is consistent with the view of Nassau Senior, who was responsible for reforming the Poor Laws, and later Manchester liberals who emphasized individual choice and argued that social protection be offered in terms of cash payments (Esping-Andersen, 1990: 10). In terms of the residualist approach discussed by Titmuss (1958, cited by Esping-Andersen, 1990: 49), the market and family are regarded as the main and preponderant source of such services; only those who cannot use the market or have family problems are seen as needing public services.

Given a lack of consensus about the appropriate form and level of resources for preschool children, public childcare in the US is often discussed solely as an anti-poverty programme for lower-income groups to ensure child development and/or to enable welfare women to become self-sufficient via labour market skills. Virtually all programmes based on this concept have small benefit levels, are applicable only to a narrowly defined eligible population, and are often proposed to be converted to a cash basis (Rainwater, *et al.*, 1986).

Contributory social insurance programmes in the US provide a sharp contrast to such programmes for the poor. Social security is close to universally applicable. The level of revenues from social security and other payroll taxes to fund social insurance (including unemployment insurance and disability insurance) are almost as large as those from personal income taxes. Yet calls and efforts to scale back these social insurance programmes have largely been unsuccessful. The reason appears to be that benefits are based on contributions, and though some receive actuarial present values of benefits in excess of contributions, there is a sufficient element of insurance for the system not to be regarded as an income transfer programme. The potential relevance of the social security experience is that public childcare is unlikely to get much support as a policy in the US unless it is relatively universal. Without design elements emphasizing private choice and a contributory connection to benefits received, it is unlikely that public childcare or parental leave will gain popular backing.

While the US is historically a leader in developing free public education, the family and market orientation seems to have been a continuing factor shaping policy on very young children. Care of preschool children was regarded as a public obligation only in cases of poverty, widowhood or family abandonment of children. The main dialogue was over the question of whether aid should be outside the home (in orphanages or the poorhouse) or within the home. A major change was to shift toward an in-home approach during the Progressive era (1900–17) (Garfinkel and McLanahan, 1986: 97) with mother-only families receiving cash benefits on condition that the child was living in a 'suitable home', defined variously to include religious training, school performance of the child, and absence of male boarders. Very seldom did black families receive benefits, and there were usually restrictions on benefits to never-married women. Only a small share of the population received benefits, which is consistent with the residualist hypothesis about the nature of American welfare programmes. Market work of the mother was not a major objective of these early programmes of aid to dependent children.

Contemporary US policy discussion has focused on market-based expansion of childcare, with emphasis on family need. The Childcare and Development Block Grant passed by Congress in October 1990 authorized new grants to states to fund childcare assistance to low- and moderate-income families, expansion of existing tax credits for low-income parents, and added funding for Head Start (Golonka and Ooms, 1991, cited by Hofferth and Wissoker, 1992). This set of new initiatives can be classified as price reductions, income increases, and subsidies for quality of childcare. Consistent with longstanding traditions, these initiatives are targeted to only the segment of the population with limited income, and the actual services are purchased through the market and not from government providers.

For most parents the current US childcare system is a market and family based system and one which is very diverse in terms of the methods used for childcare. Of preschool-age children of employed women, 30 per cent are cared for primarily by a parent, 26 per cent in a centre, 19 per cent in family daycare and 18 per cent by relatives other than parents (Hofferth *et al.*, 1991).

The organization of childcare in the United States neatly fits Esping-Andersen's (1990: 26) characterization of the liberal welfare state:

> means-tested assistance, modest universal transfers or modest social-insurance plans predominate. Benefits cater mainly to a clientele of low-income usually working-class, state dependents. In this model, the progress of social reform has been severely circumscribed by traditional, liberal work-ethic norms: it is one where the limits of welfare equal the marginal propensity to opt for welfare instead of work. Entitlement rules are therefore strict and often associated with stigma; benefits are typically modest. In turn, the state encourages the market, either passively – by guaranteeing only a minimum – or actively – by subsidizing, private welfare schemes.

In the United States there is a market for childcare. You get the childcare you pay for, and the types and costs of childcare as well as its quality differ between families according to their incomes.

Childcare subsidies and female labour supply

A question which has interested politicians and has been analysed by economists in all three countries is whether childcare subsidies increase labour supply. If women are unable to work in the labour market even if they would like to, because of the lack of suitable daycare, there is an economic rationale for subsidizing childcare. Based on the human capital theory one can argue that the opportunity cost of not working includes not only the current forgone earnings of the mother but also her lost opportunity for on-the-job investment in market-related human capital. This theory of the interrupted labour force career originates in an article by Jacob Mincer and Solomon Polachek (1974). The human capital theory has been used by Siv Gustafsson (i.e. 1990) to argue for subsidized childcare in Sweden. In the United States childcare subsidies have been seen as an option for increasing the market potential of single mothers in order to decrease their dependence on welfare payments and their income vulnerability. In the Netherlands the recent Childcare Stimulation Act assumes that childcare subsidies will increase female labour supply.

It is not easy to estimate whether childcare subsidies do increase labour supply or if those using childcare would have worked anyway, paying the market rate for childcare. Comparing prices faced by parents with subsidies with those faced by parents without subsidies may result in comparing childcare services of vastly different quality. This is particularly true in the US but on the other hand researchers have been able to make use of the local programme character of childcare subsidies, finding a control town where there are no subsidies to compare with a town where there are subsidies.

A number of articles are collected in a special issue of the *Journal of Human Resources* (1992). Siv Gustafsson and Frank Stafford (1992) find that childcare subsidies increase labour supply in Sweden. They argue that Sweden has a uniform-quality daycare where the price paid by parents varies because communities supply different subsidy rates. The Swedish setting is therefore one of a standardized service with differing prices, which is a rare experimental situation for estimating the price elasticity of childcare on labour supply of mothers with preschool children. Wim Groot and Henriëtte Maassen van den Brink (1992) estimate the effect of the price of childcare on childcare use and female labour supply in the Netherlands. They conclude that the wage elasticity of labour supply is much higher than the elasticity of labour supply with respect to the price of childcare. A possible conclusion from this finding is that if the government wants to stimulate female labour supply it should subsidize net wages by, for example, admitting tax deductions for childcare costs as in the United States rather than by subsidizing childcare. This result can be interpreted as endangering the continuation of the Childcare Stimulation Act of 1990.

The results of American studies are mixed. David M. Blau (1992) finds that the effects of childcare subsidies on the wages of childcare workers are negligible, which implies that more childcare workers entered the market as an effect of the subsidies; that is, labour supply of childcare workers is elastic. Sandra Hofferth and Douglas Wissoker (1992) conclude that parents are very sensitive to the costs of childcare and that policies reducing the price of childcare centres increase their use, whereas policies that increase the quality of centres do not. Arleen Leibowitz, Jacob Klerman and Linda Waite (1992) find that women with higher wages and lower levels of other family income are more likely to have returned to work already when their child is three months old. Women who face a higher subsidy for childcare are also more likely to return early. Having one's own mother nearby significantly increases early return to work. Charles Michalopoulos, Philip Robins and Irwin Garfinkel (1992) find that the primary benefit of more generous subsidies is to allow users of high-quality care to purchase slightly higher-quality market care.

Conclusion

In this chapter it has been shown how childcare policies in Sweden, the Netherlands and the United States have originated from different historical considerations and that childcare provision in each country corresponds to one of the three types of welfare states outlined in Esping-Andersen's regime typology. This is a caution to economists analysing the effect on labour supply of childcare subsidies since the logics of one type of welfare state may produce a totally different result from the logics of another, even if the size of the subsidy was the same.

Note

1. This section is adapted from Gustafsson and Stafford (1994).

5

The German and British Welfare States as Employers: Patriarchal or Emancipatory?

Traute Meyer

In Germany and Britain feminist scholars of the welfare state have made a case for social policy's negative impact on the material status of women. They argue that the core policies of the welfare state are basically patriarchal because they reaffirm the gendered division of labour in society. Their perspective on the welfare state, however, derives from a certain set of premisses which is not shared by the mainstream comparative literature. By contrast, comparative studies often assume that social policy has potentially emancipatory effects. Initially this chapter compares the theoretical approaches and empirical focus of these comparative and feminist studies. I argue that both perspectives fail to do justice to the question of how social policy contributes to the incorporation of women into the public sphere and into the labour market in particular. Subsequently the chapter addresses this issue through an examination of the role of the German and British welfare states as employers of women. The analysis focuses on the development of employment participation rates and the income situation of women employed in the social services, comprising the fields of education, health and welfare.

Comparative studies: welfare states and independence from the labour market

An influential contribution to recent comparative welfare state research has been Gøsta Esping-Andersen's book *The Three Worlds of Welfare Capitalism* (1990). According to one of his central arguments, the emancipatory potential of welfare states can be measured by asking whether they enable their citizens to lead a socially acceptable life independent of the labour market. With the development of industrialization in the Western world, the majority of the population became dependent upon an income through the market. This process has 'commodified' people. In reaction to this process the welfare state provided social rights of citizenship in order to weaken dependence on the market, resulting in 'de-commodification' (1990: 21). This concept can be used to identify the differences between national welfare state regimes. In order to measure empirically the potential for de-commodification of different systems Esping-Andersen utilizes major social insurance programmes: the pension system, unemployment insurance and health insurance.

His study fits into a tradition of mainstream research characterized by the assumption that welfare states safeguard individuals against the risks caused by industrialization, the expansion of markets and the weakening of traditional community networks (e.g. Flora and Heidenheimer, 1981: 8). Empirically these studies concentrate on the question of how and under what political and economic circumstances social security systems develop. They analyse primarily levels and types of public spending as well as social insurance schemes designed to protect citizens from unemployment, sickness and poverty (e.g. Flora *et al.*, 1977; Flora and Heidenheimer, 1981; Hicks and Swank, 1992; Ritter, 1989: 23; Wilensky *et al.*, 1987). The choice of these empirical fields implies that the main function of social policy is to integrate citizens into the labour market and to shield them against the consequences of exiting from the market. In other words the focus is on the relationship between social policy and the market.

Feminist analyses: welfare states and personal dependence

The work of feminist scholars on the British and German welfare state has posed the research question in a very different way compared to mainstream studies. To put it bluntly, their main concern is not social policy's impact on independence from the market but its impact on independence from men. This is based on the assumption that the advent of capitalism not only made wage labour the dominant means of subsistence, but that in the process care work was assigned to the 'private sphere', rendering it the prime duty of women. This social organization of care work prevents women from entering the labour market on an equal footing with men. Consequently marriage and personal economic dependence became essential for women's livelihood. Referring to these processes feminist research has focused on the way in which social policy affects women's personal economic dependence on men, thus also pointing out that the social basis for 'de-commodification' is fundamentally different for men and women. The main results shed a highly unfavourable light on the welfare state's impact on the economic situation of women. Social policy is seen as reinforcing female responsibility for domestic labour and economic dependence on men. In order to maintain women's traditional role it is in the state's interest to preserve the breadwinner family (e.g. Dale and Foster, 1986; Gerhard *et al.*, 1988; Land, 1978, 1985; Neusüss, 1985; Siim, 1990; Wilson, 1977).

This main argument has been developed partly by concentrating on the question of what constitutes the public interest in this system, partly by analysing how social policy reinforces women's dependence. The earliest contributions concerning the state's interest were heavily influenced by the Marxist critique of the welfare state (McIntosh, 1978; Wilson, 1977). The state is portrayed as a mere agent of the capitalist economy. In order to create conditions for maximum profits, the smooth production and reproduction of labour need to be secured, and both are the tasks of women in the family. The social security system guarantees their proper functioning by not providing independent benefits for a married woman, which leads to economic dependence on her spouse (Wilson, 1977: 9, 40).

Later writings argue that the main public interest in women's unpaid work in the home stems from their services being a form of savings for government budgets. The more women do in the household the less the state is under pressure to finance public services (Rose, 1984). In addition families can only make use of the diverse public services through the flexible coordinating work of women who make sure that services like childcare and medical care are chosen according to the family's needs. They make ends meet, and through their flexibility can compensate for cuts in public spending and changing incomes of private households (Balbo, 1982, 1987). Another argument put forward in this context is that the state uses the fact that women's work in the home is unpaid, and therefore lacks the attributes of 'real' work, to justify low wages paid to women workers in public social services (Kickbusch, 1984: 172).

Feminist contributions focusing on the question of how the welfare state reinforces female dependency on men analyse social insurance systems, tax regulations and the level and structure of social services. Historically oriented works on the German welfare state come to the conclusion that since the founding of the social insurance system women have *de facto* been entitled to fewer benefits than men, because they were dependent on their husbands' income. For them this has proven to be an inbuilt poverty trap (Gerhard, 1988a, 1988b; Köppen, 1985; Neusüss, 1985; Riedmüller, 1988). Analyses of the German and British systems after 1945 continue in the same vein. Their main criticism is that the social security of an individual citizen depends on the labour market, leaving those whose ties to the market are weak, or who do unpaid work in the family, insufficiently protected (Riedmüller, 1984). They show that public income maintenance policies in the UK and the FRG are designed for the 'breadwinner' family, and that it is very hard for women to claim income support independent of their spouse (Land, 1978, 1985; Pascall, 1986).

They also discuss how other welfare state programmes besides social insurance constitute obstacles to the economic independence of women. For example labour market measures discriminate against mothers (Gerhard, 1988a), tax laws create incentives for wives in Germany to stay at home (Mennel, 1988), and child benefits are added to husbands' income (Slupik, 1988). A further argument is that the low level of social services for children and the elderly forces women to take on the caring responsibility in the home (Pascall, 1986: 102; Ostner, 1989). A comparison of both countries shows how mixes of different social policies coalesce into different regimes which regulate the relationships of the sexes, and how the British and German systems uphold female economic dependency on the family (Langan and Ostner, 1991). In effect these systems systematically create personal dependence and economic vulnerability for women, as manifested in widespread female poverty in old age and the situation of single mothers living on assistance (Kulawik, 1989; Koeppinghoff, 1984; Kohleiss, 1988; Schallhöfer, 1988).

The welfare state and female independence through the market?

The two strands of welfare state research presented above approach their object of analysis from different premises. While studies like Esping-Andersen's look for the emancipatory potential of social policy *vis-à-vis* the market, feminist scholars in Britain and Germany conceptualize the welfare state mainly as perpetuating the patriarchal family.

Feminist scholarship reveals the necessity of considering that not all groups of the population have the same access to benefits in assessing the quality of social security in a society. Comparative welfare state research has not given enough attention to this fact. Feminist research also presents strong arguments for taking the stratification effects of social policy into account. The significance of stratification is also emphasized by Esping-Andersen. However, he applies this concept only to different occupational groups (Esping-Andersen, 1990: 55). Last but not least, feminist contributions demonstrate that gender is also a relevant analytic category in the field of social policy. Gender determines citizens' access to resources, and different policies have different consequences for men and women.

These studies emphasize the effects of social policy in maintaining the traditional division of labour between the sexes and they generally depict the welfare state as a rather clear-cut patriarchal institution. Here Esping-Andersen's more 'positive' attitude towards the state and the idea of the emancipatory potential can serve as a basis for further explorations of the relationship between women and the welfare state. One can ask whether the welfare state may also be an agent of change for the traditional division of labour and whether it may actually weaken female economic dependence on men.

Feminist scholars have established that women's care work in the British and German welfare state does not entitle them to independent benefits, sufficient for a decent living. However, considering that they place such emphasis on the concept of an independent income, it is surprising that they have not systematically examined the fact that substantial numbers of women do get independent incomes through the welfare state – as employer. Some authors mention the employment aspect of social policy – with reference to low wages and part-time work but without detailed empirical analyses. They present this aspect merely as another argument for the discriminatory effect of social policy (e.g. Kickbusch, 1984: 172).

In this context it can be useful to concentrate on the citizens' ties to the market and social policy's impact on them, as Esping-Andersen has done, but to adapt this approach with reference to the feminist debate. Instead the empirical focus here will not be on female independence from the market through the state, but on independence from the family through the social welfare market, or on commodification through the state (cf. Orloff, 1992: 26).

Esping-Andersen recognizes the significance of the social service sector for female employment (Esping-Andersen, 1990: 157, 201). However, in his analysis he does not use it as an indicator of the state's capacity to modify poverty caused by not having access to paid work, which is a major risk for women in capitalist societies. In other words the reference to welfare employment does not change the fact that his theoretical concept is built around the notion of de-commodification as a central function of the welfare state.

Although it is uncommon to include the status of women as employees in welfare state analyses in Britain and Germany, Scandinavian welfare studies indicate the usefulness of this inclusion because it leads to different conclusions about the effects of social policy. Scandinavian feminists share the assumption with British and German researchers that female responsibility for unpaid care work is the main reason for women's economic insecurity and an obstacle to egalitarian participation of the sexes in the public sphere (e.g. Sørensen, 1984: 92). However, Scandinavian researchers maintain that in modern welfare states female independence from the family and their integration into the labour market has increased through the intervention of the state. With the expansion of the welfare states women received transfer benefits, used public social services and became employees in the public sector (Hernes, 1987a: 53; Dahlerup, 1987: 120; Borchorst and Siim, 1987: 134; Siim, 1990: 88).

The theoretical relevance of these contributions lies in the fact that they employ a broader definition of social policy, including not only the social insurance systems and services, but also the welfare state as employer. In doing so they direct attention to a neglected area as far as Britain and Germany are concerned. This neglect cannot be explained by the empirical insignificance of this area in the British and German cases. It is true that in international comparison Sweden and Denmark have the largest social welfare service sectors, whereas the German welfare state is transfer oriented and Britain occupies a position between the two (e.g. Scharpf, 1986). Nevertheless, comparative studies of the development of services in industrial societies, and the social welfare services in particular, show that the expansion of the health, education and social services sector has had a major influence on the dynamics of female employment in Britain and Germany (Cusack and Rein, 1987; Rein, 1985). Accordingly an examination of the welfare state's impact on female economic (in)dependence needs to pay attention to the welfare state as employer.

In a society where goods and commodities are almost only accessible in exchange for money the individual's autonomy depends to a large extent on an independent income. As an informal system of financial distribution, marriage is obviously inadequate. Empirical research shows that many women find it difficult to be economically dependent on their partners and that the distribution of resources inside the household is often far from equal (Dalley, 1988: 22; Graham, 1987: 221; Hobson, 1990: 236). In addition to gaining an independent income, women value the social contacts connected with employment and the opportunity to leave the closed world of the household (Becker-Schmidt *et al.*, 1985: 82). Participation in the labour market is a way of entry into the public sphere. Along with the advantages of increased personal contacts and the fact that the value of one's work is expressed in money, a workplace can provide access to the political system through involvement in a trade union. Thus compared with the status of housewife any form of employment can be considered as increasing women's personal and economic independence.

An appropriate indicator for measuring the welfare state's contribution to this form of independence is the development of the female employment rates in the two countries, especially in the public sector. The importance of the welfare state's role can be assessed by examining a longer period of time and comparing sectors of the economy with regard to women's employment. Therefore the development of the employment participation rate in the field of social welfare will be compared with other main sectors over a time span of three decades. The starting point is the early 1960s, a period during which the European welfare states began to expand.[1]

Female employment rates

United Kingdom
During the last 30 years female labour force participation rose significantly, from 47 per cent in 1962 to 61 per cent in 1990. This growth occurred unevenly. In the 1960s it was rather slow, followed by a period of rapid growth at the beginning of the 1970s; it then slowed down, leading to a period of declining participation at the beginning of the 1980s. Between 1985 and 1990 there was, however, a major upturn (Figure 5.1).

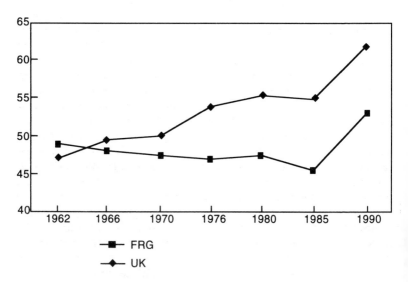

Figure 5.1   *Female employment activity rates (%) in the FRG and the UK, 1962–90*

Source: OECD *Labour Force Statistics* 1962–82 and 1971–91 (Paris 1984 and 1993b)

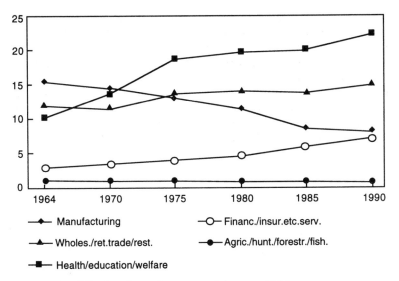

Figure 5.2   *UK – female employment activity rates (%) by sector, 1964–90*

Sources: OECD *Labour Force Statistics* 1962–82 and 1971–91 (Paris 1984 and 1993b); *Employment Gazette*, 97(11), Hist. Supplement 2 (Nov. 1989); *Employment Gazette*, 79(2) 1971, 98(11) 1990

Looking at different sectors of the economy, we find that between 1964 and 1970 manufacturing was the main sector of employment for women, followed first by the wholesale and retail trade, restaurants and hotels and secondly by the social services. During that period there was already an indication of the trend which gathered momentum in the first half of the 1970s and subsequently remained permanent. Social services moved to the top and 18 per cent of all women were employed in this sector in 1975. The trade sector expanded slightly as well. In 1975 it absorbed 13.3 per cent of all women of employable age, about as much as manufacturing. The significance of manufacturing for the female employment rate decreased continuously from then on. Even though the finance, insurance, real estate and business services did not expand much during these years, they are noteworthy because they constituted the only continuously expanding sector, with the exception of the social services.

Between 1975 and 1980 these trends continued at a slower pace, while the period between 1980 and 1985 was characterized by stagnation and decline. Labour force participation in the social services and the trade sector did not increase. At the same time manufacturing increasingly lost its significance. In 1985 only 8.5 per cent of all women were employed in this area. The financial services developed in a contrary fashion: the participation rate in this sector increased slightly, to 4.5 per cent.

In the second half of the 1980s participation increased again, mainly in the social service sector. Between 1985 and 1990 the female labour force participation rate rose from 19 to 21 per cent in this area. Meanwhile trading and manufacturing remained constant. Again a significant rise, from 6 to 8 per cent, can be observed in the financial sector (Figure 5.2).

Germany

In 1962 nearly half of all women of employable age were in the labour force. This level was similar to that in Britain, but the German female labour force participation rate increased only modestly during the next 28 years, by 4 percentage points. While the British rate rose continuously, except for the first half of the 1980s, in the FRG it fell by 3.3 percentage points until 1985. Only in the second half of the 1970s was there slight growth. In Germany the beginning of the 1980s was also characterized by the strongest decline during the whole period. Altogether there would have even been a negative trend if it had not been for the enormous leap forward between 1985 and 1990; an additional 7 per cent of all women of employable age entered the labour force during that time, producing an overall rate of 53 per cent.

Between 1962 and 1966 the three main areas accountable for women's integration into the labour force were (1) manufacturing, wholesale and retail trades; (2) restaurants and hotels; and (3) agriculture, hunting, forestry and fishing. Fourth place was occupied by the social services. Until 1970 the most important developments were the decrease of agriculture and a slight expansion of the social services; and both sectors had the same significance for female labour force participation, employing 7.5 per cent of all women.

The period between 1970 and 1976 was characterized by a decline in women's employment in manufacturing and agriculture. The growth of the social services and – to a much smaller extent – of the financial services prevented a sharper decrease. In 1976 social services were of secondary importance for female labour force participation, while trade moved down to third position.

In the second half of the 1970s the negative developments within the agricultural and manufacturing sectors continued at a slower pace. Nevertheless, the labour force participation rate increased slightly again as a result of trends within the social services, the market-oriented personal services and the financial services.

In the FRG the 1980s began with a reduction of female employment in almost all areas. Even though the main cuts within manufacturing and agriculture had taken place between 1970 and

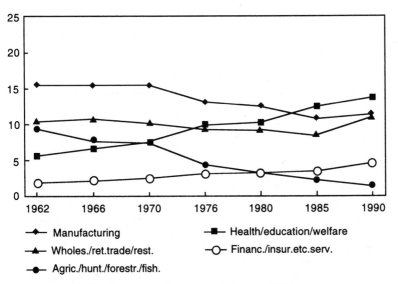

Figure 5.3 *FRG – female employment activity rates (%) by sector, 1962–90*

Sources: OECD, *Labour Force Statistics* 1962–82 and 1971–91 (Paris 1984 and 1993b); Institut Arbeitsmarkt und Berufsforschung (IAB) (ed.) Beitr AB 3.1 1981 + 1984, Nürnberg; unpublished IAB-data. 1985 health/education/welfare figures from 1986; 1966 health/education/ welfare: estimations

1976, the strongest setback of the employment rate occurred between 1980 and 1985. Contrary to the 1970s this decline was not cushioned by an expansion of the social and financial services. These growth sectors did not expand much during that time. Nevertheless from the mid-1980s social services were the most significant sector for the female employment participation rate.

Between 1985 and 1990 the trends in agriculture, the social and financial services continued. Participation in the first sector diminished further, but in the latter expanded with a pace similar to that of the first half of the 1970s. The fact that the total employment participation rate expanded was caused by reversals of downward trends in other sectors. Trading increased by 2 percentage points and small gains can also be detected in the manufacturing sector. Both sectors thus had roughly equal significance for female labour force participation, occupying second place behind the social services (see Figure 5.3).

Differences between Britain and Germany
While in Britain the employment rate increased continuously, the growth pattern in Germany was beset by reverses which were only

compensated for by a consistent increase after 1985. In both countries the social services were by far the main growth sector and they became the main employment sector as well, replacing manufacturing; in the UK the social services assumed this position from the beginning of the 1970s, in the FRG from the mid-1980s. However, during the period as a whole, these services were responsible for integrating a larger proportion of British than of German women into the labour market. In addition the growth of the financial services was stronger in the UK than in the FRG. Because the expansion of services integrated more women than men into the labour market, their stronger growth in the UK demonstrates a comparative advantage for British women. Moreover, the German employment rate is lower because of the drastic decrease within agriculture. The reduction in the manufacturing sector, however, was not as sharp for German as for British women.

Let us return to the initial question – what do these results tell us about the contribution of the welfare state as employer to the female economic independence from men? In the last three decades the changing structure of the labour market has improved the conditions for a modified division of labour between the sexes. In both countries the social services played the decisive role in this process. However, these conditions seem to have been more favourable for the United Kingdom than for Germany.

First, at the beginning of the 1990s 8 per cent more British than German women were in the labour force. As a consequence women had better opportunities to enter the public sphere and to obtain an income of their own through employment, however small. This was the result of a period of expansion, starting at the beginning of the 1960s and largely attributable to the growth of social services employment. At that time the German employment participation rate had been slightly higher than the British. Second, the two largest growth sectors – social services and financial services – were quantitatively more important for female employment in the UK. Their level was both higher in the 1960s and subsequently grew more quickly. Third, the British agricultural sector played a minor role for employment in the 1960s, while a significant proportion of German women (9 per cent) still worked in this sector. In this respect labour market structures were more 'modern' in the UK.

Employment in small family-run agricultural businesses is at best ill suited to the criteria for economic independence discussed above. There is no clear division between the household, the family and the workplace. Job and income are based on the continuity of family relationships, especially marriage, and so economic independence is limited by personal bonds. Similarly, social independence is restricted because work takes place wholly within the private sphere.

In the FRG the changing structures within the labour market did not lead to as marked an increase in the female employment participation rate as in Britain, but nevertheless the changes coincided with a modernization process in female employment. The strongest decreases took place in the agricultural sector – and the strongest increases in the social services. Accordingly a family workplace environment has been replaced by more 'modern' employment conditions, which facilitate greater economic and social independence.

All in all, the material presented here indicates that from the 1960s onwards the welfare state played a crucial role for female employment. For the women concerned this has meant an income of one's own, a de-personification of the labour conditions, and the possibility of participating in the public sphere. In other words, it has entailed progress in the sense of a reduction of personal dependence. But before any final conclusions can be drawn, an analysis of women's pay is required.

Obviously not all jobs supply their holders with an income high enough to run their own households. Not all forms of employment open up the same career opportunities or leave enough time to have children or to engage in other meaningful activities beyond the workplace. An analysis of participation rates does not allow for conclusions about the quality of the economic independence gained through public employment. It is to that aspect that we now turn.

Of all relevant criteria for evaluating the quality of a workplace the level of income seems to be the most important. The next section will deal with the question of whether women in the social services earn enough to live independently of other persons. To determine this, the main female occupations in the social welfare sector are identified, and the incomes of four comparable occupations analysed.

Occupations and incomes

In the FRG and the UK female employment in the social services consists of similar main occupations. Women are employed as nurses, teachers, medical assistants, social workers and social work assistants, administrative staff, and cleaning and kitchen staff.[2] In the course of the 1980s the share of those activities which require little formal qualification was reduced as a result of privatization or relative stagnation. Since in the British public sector employment in this area has been far more pronounced than in Germany, for example because of features such as school meals, the reductions were more noticeable in the UK. The development of employment in the main occupations dealing directly with people, however, was similar in both countries. The number of nurses, teachers and social workers, including home care for the elderly, grew. In addition, administrative employment expanded. In the next section we will look at the income of nurses, teachers, care workers, cleaners and administrative staff in the 1980s. These occupations are located in the areas of health, education and welfare and represent personal and ancillary services. They belong to expanding as well as stagnating areas of employment, and require different occupational qualifications. The income of these groups, with tax and social insurance contributions for a single person with a child between the age of 10 and 15 deducted, will be compared with the amount of social assistance to which such a person is entitled. This procedure is based on two assumptions. The first is that an income allowing for financial independence should be high enough to support at least one child. Second, the amount of social assistance a person can claim is assumed to be a rough measure of the poverty line. Even though it is arguable that being on welfare is itself a sign of poverty, an income below this level would definitely not be enough to cover daily essentials.

Female wages in the German social service sector
In the FRG in the first half of the 1980s income for all occupations was above the social assistance level. This applied not only to full-time but also to part-time workers. In the second half of the 1980s the gap between this level and earnings narrowed, due to a steep rise in benefits between 1984 and 1986. As a consequence, the wages of cleaners working part time fell slightly below the poverty line. Part-time nurses in the lowest income group and part-time administrative assistants from 1986 on did not fare much better than a single mother living on assistance. So in financial terms, for employees belonging to the lowest echelons of the pay hierarchy and working part time, dependence on state benefits could be seen as an alternative to employment.

The story is different for full-time workers. Even cleaners, at the low end of the pay scale, took home between 70 per cent (1988) and 100 per cent (1982) more than someone on social assistance would have been able to. At the other end of the spectrum, teachers' wages were sufficient to lead a life free of basic economic worries (Table 5.1). Most occupational groups in the public services fared better in the 1980s than employees in the private sector. A cleaner earned more than the average blue-collar worker in manufacturing. The wages of administrative staff were above those of clerks in the private economy. Teachers' wages exceeded female wages in all other areas.

Table 5.1 *Monthly income of full-time and part-time employees as a percentage of social assistance in the FRG, 1980–90*

	1980		1982		1984		1986		1988		1990	
	full-time	part-time	full-time	part-time	full-time	part-time	full-time	part-time	full-time	part-time	full-time	part-time
Qualified nurse												
First two years	210	116	218	121	210	117	186	102	183	101	191	106
First promotion stage	219	121	227	126	219	122	194	106	192	105	198	110
6 years' work experience	228	126	237	131	229	127	201	111	200	109	206	115
Nurse administrators	292	164	306	170	295	165	257	145	257	143	265	148
Senior nurse administrator	315	179	331	186	319	180	278	159	279	157	290	162
Primary teachers	342	191	354	196	349	194	307	172	308	171	318	177
Secondary teachers	371	210	385	215	379	213	333	189	336	189	348	195
Clerks	248	137	258	142	250	138	218	120	217	119	223	124
Office assistants	219	121	227	126	219	122	194	106	192	105	198	110
Cleaners	192	107	200	111	193	107	173	95	171	94	177	98
Monthly social assistance benefit rate	100	100	100	100	100	100	100	100	100	100	100	100

Note: Monthly income calculated as wages of the employee who is a single parent with one child, and includes residential allowance and tax deductions.
Sources: Bundesangestelltentarifvertrag (BAT); Gesamtabzugstabellen 1980–90; Statistisches Bundesamt, Fachserie 13, Reihe 2, 1980–91; 1980 social assistance benefit is from 1981

Only the nurses and carers for the elderly earned less in the public sector than someone with equivalent qualifications in the private sector, with the exception of nurses and carers in management positions.

In the course of the 1980s the earning gap between private sector and social service occupations narrowed. In 1990 private sector wages were between 46 per cent and 51 per cent higher than in 1980, whereas in the social services the rise amounted to between 30 per cent and 34 per cent. However, since the lead of the public sector nevertheless remained, employment in the public services for the majority of female employees at the end of the 1980s was still more favourable than employment in the private sector. Only the nurses, whose relative position deteriorated, would have been able to earn considerably more in the private sector (Statistisches Bundesamt, 1980–91).

Female wages in the British social service sector

On the other side of the Channel we see a completely different picture. Even among full-time employees a considerable group earned less than the social assistance benefit rate. At the bottom, kitchen workers took home about 20 per cent less than they would have done had they been dependent upon assistance in the early 1980s. Hardly better off were cleaners, whose pay was 10 per cent below this poverty threshold. Until 1990 among the manual workers only home helps had risen minimally above this level.

Nursing auxiliaries and assistants, secretaries and typists were in a somewhat better situation. Their wages rose from below the poverty level at the beginning of the 1980s to 15 per cent (nurse auxiliaries) and 42 per cent (secretaries) above it in 1990.

The highest wages of the groups examined were those of teachers in establishments for further education, closely followed by all other teachers, nurse administrators and executives. However, before 1988 even these groups did not earn more than double the amount of social assistance, and only teachers in establishments for further education and nurse administrators exceeded this level in the subsequent years. The analysis reveals the poor financial conditions experienced by part-time employees. In fact part-timers' wages, with the exception of teachers'[3] and since 1990 nurses' were well below the poverty threshold. During the 1980s the wages of teachers and nurses did rise further above this threshold, while those of unqualified workers stagnated or deteriorated, as in the case of cleaners and school helpers (Table 5.2).

Considering these results, it comes as a surprise that during the 1980s for an average female employee it was an advantage to be

Table 5.2 Weekly income of full-time and part-time employees as a percentage of social assistance in the UK, 1980–90

	1980 full-time	1980 part-time	1982 full-time	1982 part-time	1984 full-time	1984 part-time	1986 full-time	1986 part-time	1988 full-time	1988 part-time	1990 full-time	1990 part-time
Teachers in establishments for further education	155	–	173	–	184	–	190	–	201	–	207	–
Secondary teachers	137	–	149	–	157	–	170	–	187	–	198	–
Primary teachers	133	–	148	–	155	–	168	–	181	–	189	–
Other teachers	133	–	148	–	152	–	157	–	174	–	185	–
Nurse administrators and executives	148	–	147	–	149	–	166	–	179	–	203	–
Registered and enrolled nurses, midwives	108	79	109	81	117	87	129	93	133	94	158	105
Nursing auxiliaries and assistants	92	69	94	70	100	76	106	78	104	76	115	80
General clerks	98	63	99	62	107	66	113	69	117	68	124	71
Secretaries, shorthand typists	107	67	110	65	119	72	128	75	134	74	142	78
Other typists	95	65	97	63	105	70	110	72	115	71	122	75
Catering, cleaning, hairdr., other personal services	90	55	87	52	94	56	99	59	99	56	103	57
Kitchen hands	81	55	80	52	88	55	92	60	94	56	96	57
Home and domestic helpers, maids	90	60	87	57	92	61	98	64	98	63	103	66
Other cleaners	87	53	86	50	93	54	97	56	97	53	97	52
School helpers and school supervisory assistants	–	44	–	41	–	46	–	47	–	42	–	43
Weekly social assistance benefit rate	100	100	100	100	100	100	100	100	100	100	100	100

Note: Weekly income calculated as wages of the employee who is a single parent with one child and includes child benefit and tax deductions. Pay not affected by absence.

Sources: *New Earnings Survey* 1980–91, Parts F and D; CSO (1991): *Annual Abstract of Statistics*, London

employed by the state. Her income was generally higher than it would have been in the private sector. The advantage was especially evident for non-manual workers, such as nurses and teachers. At the beginning of the 1980s they earned 26 per cent more than their counterparts in the private sector. This lead was reduced to 19 per cent in the course of the decade (Brown and Rowthorn 1990: 4; *Labour Research*, January 1993: 15).

Comparing countries

The wage differences between the United Kingdom and the FRG are enormous. Female employment in the British social service sector is characterized by earnings close to the poverty threshold. This is particularly true for ancillary workers, but until the mid-1980s it applied also to qualified nurses. For a single woman with a child no economic incentives exist to be employed in occupations dominated by part-time work because the salary would be below the social assistance level and would need to be topped up by public income supplement. If the woman was solely relying on social assistance instead, she would not be worse off in economic terms. So for single mothers with low occupational qualifications economic dependence on men seems to be replaced more easily by becoming economically dependent on public transfers than by becoming an employee in the public sector. The numerous part-time positions in this area only make sense for those women who share a household with working men and who for that reason would not be entitled to state benefits anyway. Their income and the contacts they make through the job can enlarge their independence *vis-à-vis* their partners. However, because these jobs require the existence of personal economic bonds, they weaken women's socioeconomic dependence on men without making real independence possible. Since the private sector offers no better alternative, the best option for these women, if they want to achieve a modest living standard, is to live with a male wage-earner. The situation is different for women with higher occupational qualifications. A British teacher has a salary high enough to lead an independent life – even if she cannot afford the same living standard as her German colleague. Nurses' wages have improved continuously. While at the beginning of the 1980s they were so close to the social assistance level that financial independence was only possible for those without any substantial material ambitions, this wage level had increased considerably by 1990.

In the FRG on the one hand there are not as many jobs in the social services as in Britain. On the other hand, those jobs that do exist guarantee sufficiently high incomes to allow employed women to be economically independent. In comparison with the UK the gap between the social assistance level and earnings is much wider. In 1990 the British secondary teacher and the German administrative assistant both earned 98 per cent more than the amount they would have got through state benefits – a clear indication that German working women are wealthier than British.

The differences are aggravated by the different extent of part-time work prevailing in both countries. Looking at the female labour force in Britain, the share of part-timers is much higher than in Germany and this is particularly true of personal and social service employment. In 1987 for instance 33 per cent of all German but 54 per cent of all British women employed in this area worked part time (Maier, 1992: 92).

Conclusions: is less more?

The analysis of the first indicator of an improvement in women's socioeconomic status, employment participation rates, established that the welfare state has made a major contribution. As far as country differences are concerned the conditions for women's integration into the labour market were allegedly more favourable in the United Kingdom than in Germany. The analysis of the second indicator, social service wages, underlines the importance of the welfare state because it shows that the public sector is the best place to be for working women in terms of income.

With respect to Britain's comparative lead some qualifications need to be made. In the UK many women are integrated into the labour market at low wage levels and on a part-time basis. Economic independence is possible only for the better qualified workers, the majority of whom have to work full time for this autonomy. Other female workers must rely on additional sources of income in order to secure minimal material needs. The first option, reliance on a man's income, implies a personal relationship unfavourably tainted by economic dependence. The second option, state assistance, substitutes a personal dependency relationship for a formal one, regulated through legal entitlements. Nevertheless legal entitlements are an unlikely incentive to claim state benefits, considering that such reliance leads to an income only barely sufficient for a life at the poverty line and that claimants are liable to be socially stigmatized. Under such circumstances relying on a man's income in addition is the materially and socially less problematic solution: it enhances individual autonomy without threatening social status. The British state as employer has therefore created opportunities for women to improve their social and economic position – albeit on the basis of marriage or, more specifically, on the basis of a dual income partnership. This is a contribution to a more balanced relationship between the sexes which no other single institution on the market has been able to make. At the same time it does not fundamentally affect the intertwining of love and material needs in male–female relationships, a combination which for women has proven to be too prone to disastrous outcomes.

The relationship between quality and quantity of support in Germany is of a different kind. Female social service sector workers have relatively high incomes and a much lower rate of part-time work. For the highest qualified amongst them this brings higher wages; for the non-qualified it means a low living standard, which can be maintained, however, without public or male assistance. Considering its role as employer, the German state has been the most important institution in the labour market which has enabled women to live independently of men. For those employed in the public sector it means that emotional and economic bonds do not need to be entangled. Compared to Britain, being an employee of the German public sector does seem to be an advantage.

At the same time many German women do not find themselves in such an advantageous position because they remain outside the labour force altogether. Because the German social service sector as main growth area for female employment has integrated a comparatively smaller number of women into the labour force, more German than British women have had to rely on their husbands' earnings for maintenance. One reason why this sector has remained smaller in Germany is that children do not attend school in the afternoon. The negative effect of this tradition on women's employment opportunities is twofold. Children do not need to be fed and looked after by people employed for that purpose. Second, where supervisory facilities for them are lacking it is difficult for parents to have both a child and a job; in effect, mothers are driven out of the labour market. So on the whole the German state as employer facilitates the economic independence of its female employees while creating obstacles to the integration of women into the labour market. The idea of one country having done 'better' than the other seems therefore to be inappropriate. Fewer jobs with higher income do not lead to more equality than more jobs with lower income. Instead we are confronted with two different forms of women's incorporation into the public sphere. However, there is no doubt that in both countries this incorporation has taken place – and has changed the economic dimensions of the relationship between the sexes.

The preceding analysis casts a different light on the German and British feminist welfare state discussion. The thesis that social policy reinforces female economic dependence on men requires modification. The emancipatory potential of the welfare state has been underestimated in the feminist debate. Even though the state is by no means a radical promoter of sexual equality, and even though in many aspects it supports the insecure economic position of women, from the perspective of society as a whole there is no institution which has had a comparable positive impact on their economic status. The thesis that the potential of social policy can best be measured by looking at an individual's degree of independence from the labour market, as Esping-Andersen maintains, can also be questioned on this account. It is based on the assumption that attachment to the labour market is the norm for all citizens and ignores the material and social reality of women, for whom a weakening of personal dependence through employment is an emancipatory step.

Notes

1 The data for female employment mainly consist of OECD labour force statistics on civilian employment. These are supplemented by British and German national statistics. The figures cover civilian employees only, i.e. the unemployed are excluded.

OECD data are used as a central source because here the different national classifications are integrated into a homogeneous structure, making comparability possible. An additional advantage of these statistics is that the social, health and welfare services are summarized in one category. A disadvantage is that this category contains some other services as well. For the following presentation the attempt was made to subtract those from this category, using national data. Although this results in no exact figures, the statistics are a solid enough base to enable conclusions to be drawn.

2 The section on occupations in the social service sector is based on data from different official national sources which I evaluated in an unpublished manuscript.

3 Data about the situation of part-time teachers is not available. Nevertheless, since they earn more than nurses they are obviously above the social assistance minimum.

6

Work, Welfare and Gender Equality: A New Typology

Alan Siaroff

Gender inequality is not merely something which is present in the economic, social and political realms (Norris, 1987), but more specifically is a reality embedded in social policies and welfare states. There is of course a vast literature on welfare states and welfare state regimes (Pierson, 1991; Esping-Andersen, 1990; Castles and Mitchell, 1993; Schmidt, 1988; Therborn, 1987) which tends to produce overlapping typologies. Despite the theoretical importance of such typologies, however, they have tended to be gender blind – thus missing some salient distinctions.

Moreover, such typologies often rely on simple aggregates of state intervention and spending. Yet it behoves us to ask whether welfare state spending benefits women as much as men. Later on in this chapter we will produce a more family-specific measure of the welfare state. Certainly, however, if a welfare state is targeted towards 'workers' rather than all citizens, and/or favours certain workers over others, then gender variations in labour force participation and employment patterns become crucial.

The purpose of this chapter is, first, to examine a variety of indicators of gender (in)equality in work and welfare; and secondly to use these to construct a new 'gender sensitive' typology of welfare state regimes. To this end, we shall contrast comparatively the female reality of what has been called the 'work–welfare choice' (Castles and Mitchell, 1993: 104; cf. Esping-Andersen, 1990: 54). This concept includes such issues as whether one has to work in order to draw at some point social benefits (or better social benefits), whether social benefits adequately replace one's earnings, who specifically receives these benefits, and ultimately whether partaking of the welfare state can be seen as an alternative to employment.

Obviously, a more generous, less employment-dependent welfare state provides a greater incentive to use it than a minimal, employment-based system. However, since we are speaking of a *choice* between working and utilizing the welfare state, then the nature of 'working' – in terms of wages, conditions and availability of work as well as work-related benefits – must enter into everyone's calculation. That is, what are the incentives or disincentives to work? One obvious factor is the level of (un)employment, as this clearly affects the likelihood of finding work in the first place.

Yet the nature of 'working' as we have summarized it is obviously not the same for every individual. The realities of the labour market vary according to one's age, education, social class – and certainly one's sex. The bulk of this chapter will consist of analysing data on the 23 OECD democracies to assess the relative incentives and disincentives of working *as they apply to women in comparison with men*. This variation will be compared with aspects of the welfare state as they particularly apply to families and women. These dimensions will then be combined into a new typology, the types of which are explained in terms of broader social, political and historical factors.

Gender variations in work

Female/male differences in unemployment and employment
Inasmuch as we have stressed the notion of work versus welfare (and thus the choice between them), we first need to examine the gender equality of work as an end in itself. Breaking down unemployment rates by gender is a logical place to start. As Table 6.1 shows, official unemployment rates for the 1980s range from 10 per cent or more in Spain, Ireland, Belgium and Italy down to below 1 per cent in Switzerland and Iceland. Normally, the key dichotomy involves distinguishing between those nations that have or have not maintained full employment, that is, rates of below 4 per cent.

Yet official unemployment rates for women range from as high as 22.1 per cent in Spain down to 0.7 per cent in Switzerland. However, these are also the second highest and the lowest nations, respectively, in terms of male unemployment. It is not the range of female or male unemployment performance alone which is so striking here. Rather, it is the *ratio* between the two. Across our sample of countries, female unemployment is normally more than a third higher than the male figures. The correlation between the two values is a highly significant 0.756. In only three countries – the United Kingdom, Ireland and Finland – was female unemployment lower than males' in the 1980s. Indeed, female rates were more than double those of men in Italy, Portugal, Greece and Belgium.

On the other hand, the seven nations which in terms of Table 6.1 have maintained full employment – Switzerland, Iceland, Luxembourg, Sweden, Japan, Norway and Austria – appear to have done so

Table 6.1 *Gender variations in unemployment, 1980–90* (%)

Nation	Female Unemployment	Male Unemployment	Total	Female/ Male Percentage
Spain	22.1	15.1	17.4	146
Italy	16.3	6.6	10.0	247
Belgium	15.9	7.6	10.9	209
France	12.0	6.9	9.0	174
Netherlands	11.8	8.3	9.6	142
Ireland	11.2	15.6	14.2	72
Portugal	10.6	4.6	7.1	230
Greece	10.3	4.7	6.7	219
Canada	9.5	8.9	9.2	107
Denmark	8.9	7.4	8.1	120
Australia	8.3	6.6	7.4	126
F.R. Germany	7.8	6.0	6.7	130
United States	7.1	6.9	7.0	103
United Kingdom	6.5	10.9	9.2	60
New Zealand	5.3	4.6	4.8	115
Finland	4.4	5.0	4.7	88
Austria	3.8	3.0	3.3	127
Norway	3.3	2.8	3.0	118
Sweden	2.5	2.3	2.4	109
Japan	2.5	2.4	2.5	104
Luxembourg	(1.6)	(1.1)	1.3	145
Iceland	(1.0)	(0.8)	0.9	125
Switzerland	0.7	0.5	0.6	140
mean	8.0	6.0	6.8	137
std.dev.	5.4	4.0	4.2	49

Source: Author's calculations and estimates from OECD data

for women as well as for men. This is even more the case for the borderline full employment nation of Finland.

However, by its very nature unemployment is a problematical variable. It is, of course, not an individual total but a *ratio* of those registered as unemployed compared to the national labour force. In other words, one is not in fact *either* employed *or* unemployed; rather a person is *one of*: (1) employed; (2) unemployed; or (3) not in the labour force. Cross-national variations are thus quite possible in terms of who is considered (by government statisticians) to be registered unemployed, and especially in terms of who are deemed to be actually in the labour force.

This is perhaps most problematical in terms of Japan. Koji Taira (1983) has noted that Japanese unemployment figures treat as employed people who have a job contract or even an understanding of one, but who have not actually started working yet! Equally, if one is not pursuing a search for work as diligently and as frequently as certain employment survey questions imply, one is likely to be ultimately classified as 'not in the labour force'. This latter factor is particularly noticeable for Japanese women.

Consequently, Taira attempts to recalculate Japanese unemployment levels based on the measures and assumptions used in the United States. For the years of 1977 to 1980, Taira on average increases the national Japanese unemployment figures by a factor of 1.78. However, whereas his figures for male unemployment show an increase of only 1.27 times, those for women show a correction of 2.85 times (this author's calculations from Taira, 1983: 6–8).

If we assume that this statistical discrepancy holds to exactly the same extent for the period 1980–90, then this would produce the following 'US -measurement' unemployment figures for Japan:

4.36 per cent nationally
3.10 per cent for men
7.05 per cent for women

This would give a female/male percentage of 227 (more than double). Even if one does not accept the estimated values at this level of precision, Japan does appear to be a case of *full employment for men but not for women*.

Certainly, in recessions the labour force participation rate of Japanese women does fall off noticeably. A similar pattern has been stressed for Switzerland. For example, Manfred G. Schmidt (1985: 43) notes that low unemployment has been maintained in Switzerland (especially after the first OPEC shock), not just by the repatriation of border and seasonal workers, but also by the withdrawal of Swiss women into the 'silent labour market reserve' (*'Stillen Arbeitsmarktreserve'*). Lack of obligatory unemployment insurance in Switzerland until 1977 was also a clearly related factor here. For his part, Wolfgang Blaas (1992: 375) stresses that whereas '[t]he outstanding achievement of the Swiss economy is full employment . . . it is more appropriate to talk about full employment for (male) Swiss citizens' *only*.

For these reasons at a minimum, one should be suspicious of certain low female unemployment values (or the lower figures in Ireland for women as opposed to men). However, merely looking at levels of total employment does not allow for cross-national variations in the age structure of the population. Moreover, increases in employment are ultimately higher in nations with a sharply growing population, such as the high-immigrant societies of Australia,

Table 6.2 *Employment–population ratios and gender, 1980–90*

| Nation | Employment–population ratio | | | Female/ Male Percentage |
	Female	Male	Total	
Sweden	76.0	83.5	79.8	91
Finland	69.4	77.7	73.5	89
Denmark	68.3	81.9	75.2	83
Norway	65.9	84.7	75.4	78
Iceland	(63.8)	(91.7)	77.9	70
United States	59.4	78.7	68.9	75
Canada	56.8	77.6	67.2	73
United Kingdom	56.7	78.5	67.6	72
Switzerland	56.1	93.6	75.0	60
Japan	56.0	86.1	70.9	65
Australia	51.3	80.6	66.1	64
Portugal	51.0	85.3	65.8	60
New Zealand	50.4	80.6	(65.6)	63
F.R. Germany	49.7	77.6	63.7	64
Austria	49.7	78.8	64.0	63
France	48.6	72.2	60.4	67
Luxembourg	(44.1)	(86.7)	65.1	51
Belgium	41.7	69.4	55.6	60
Netherlands	38.4	72.0	(55.4)	53
Greece	36.1	74.2	54.9	49
Italy	35.0	74.6	54.5	47
Ireland	33.2	72.2	53.0	46
Spain	27.5	67.3	47.3	41
mean	51.5	79.4	65.3	64.5
std.dev.	12.6	6.8	8.8	13.5

Source: Author's calculations and estimates from OECD data

Canada and the United States. The statistical 'solution' to this problem is to use the *employment–population* ratio, which relates the level of employment to the working-age population (those aged 15–64), regardless of whether or not (individual) people are officially considered to be in the labour force. It is a highly useful tool in comparing labour market performance (Leon, 1981), not least because its cross-national measurement is more standardized than for unemployment alone.

Since people can be employed after the age of 64 (or in some less developed nations before 15), the employment–population ratio can in theory go above 100. However, the essential point is that the ratio allows us to compare levels of employment across OECD nations. Furthermore, we can calculate this ratio for each sex. The results of these calculations are shown in Table 6.2, which ranks OECD democracies by the level of their female employment–population ratio. This ranges sharply from Sweden at 76 per cent (followed by Finland) down to Spain at 27.5 per cent. Male ratios and overall ratios are also given, as well as the female ratio as a percentage of the male value. As was the case for unemployment, the variation (standard deviation) within male values is much less than for women.

Crucially, in every nation the female ratio is less than the male ratio. However, this 'ratio of ratios' also varies sharply, again going from Sweden at 91 per cent (followed by Finland) to Spain at 41 per cent. Besides Spain, the female ratio is less than half of the male ratio in Ireland, Italy and Greece. Indeed, the variation in female rates explains virtually all of the overall variation: $r = 0.953$.

Furthermore, there is an inverse relationship between gender variations in unemployment and gender variations in the employment–population ratio; that is to say, the higher the relative female unemployment (compared to males'), the lower is the female employment ratio (compared to males'). The correlation here is -0.474, which is significant at the 0.05 level. This relationship is far from perfect, since it depends on the extent to which in a given nation non-employed women are treated as officially unemployed as opposed to not being in the labour force.

For example, the Republic of Ireland is perhaps the biggest statistical outlier in this relationship: it is one of the three nations where official female unemployment is lower than that of men, yet in contrast to the United Kingdom and Finland relative *employment* of women is low in Ireland. This difference is due to the tradition of extremely low labour force participation by Irish women. Generally, then, rising female labour force participation may lead to increased official unemployment; conversely, the lack of such an increase certainly helps explain lower official unemployment in the German-speaking nations and in Japan (Rhein-Kress, 1993: 160–5).[1]

Female/male differences in the nature of employment

Of course, merely finding some sort of employment says nothing about wages, benefits, and the general availability of 'good jobs' versus 'bad' or dead-end 'junk jobs' (Esping-Andersen, 1990: 199). Table 6.3 presents certain data in this regard – all in terms of female-to-male ratios for the mid-to late 1980s. The first column ranks the nations by wage ratios in industry, which range from 90 per cent of men's in Iceland down to 52 per cent in Japan. It should be

Table 6.3 *Female to male ratios in wages and desirable positions, 1980s*

Nation	Industrial wages	Managerial workers	Post-secondary students	'Elites'
Iceland	90	n.d.	113	(68)
Sweden	87	n.d.	89	(56)
Denmark	86	16	97	56.5
Australia	85	42	91	66.5
Norway	81	28	113	70.5
Italy	80	60	88	74
Netherlands	79	14	70	42
Austria	78	14	80	47
Finland	77	24	99	61.5
France	77	10	97	61.5
Portugal	76	17	113	65
New Zealand	75	21	89	55
Belgium	75	15	89	52
F.R. Germany	73	20	72	46
Spain	72	6	96	51
Greece	71	18	94	56
United Kingdom	68	29	81	55
Switzerland	68	6	47	26.5
Ireland	66	19	76	47.5
Canada	63	54	113	83.5
Luxembourg	63	6	52	29
United States	61	61	110	85.5
Japan	52	8	56	32
mean	74.0	23.2	88.0	55.6
std.dev.	9.3	17.1	19.3	15.4

Sources: UN 1991a, 1991b

noted that such similarity (or variation) relates closely to the overall absence or presence of wage dispersion in industry.

The remaining columns in Table 6.3 focus on the most desirable jobs, and the means of achieving them. The second column gives the ratio of total administrative and managerial workers. The third column gives the ratio of university and college students. The correlation of these two is 0.510. These last two columns are then averaged together to give a total for female 'elites'.[2] One sees that although the Nordic nations score highly in 'elites', the highest scores in fact belong to the United States and Canada – yet the two North American nations are still near the bottom in terms of wage levels in industry. Of course, the missing factor here is that whereas well-educated North American women are normally in professional or

Table 6.4 *A summary measure of female work desirability,*
1980s

Nation	Average of wage ratios and 'elites'[‡] 100	Weighted employment gender ratio*	Multiplied score
Finland	0.6925	0.942	0.652
Sweden	(0.7150)	0.912	0.652
Norway	0.7575	0.792	0.600
Denmark	0.7125	0.833	0.594
United States	0.7325	0.798	0.585
Iceland	(0.7900)	0.717	0.566
Canada	0.7325	0.773	0.566
United Kingdom	0.6150	0.913	0.561
Australia	0.7575	0.668	0.506
New Zealand	0.6500	0.674	0.438
France	0.6525	0.653	0.426
Austria	0.6250	0.663	0.414
Portugal	0.7050	0.565	0.398
F.R. Germany	0.5950	0.666	0.396
Ireland	0.5675	0.647	0.367
Belgium	0.6350	0.576	0.366
Italy	0.7700	0.456	0.351
Netherlands	0.6050	0.567	0.343
Greece	0.6350	0.481	0.305
Japan	0.4200	0.712	0.299
Switzerland	0.4725	0.622	0.294
Spain	0.6150	0.464	0.285
Luxembourg	0.4600	0.545	0.251
mean	0.6484	0.680	0.444
std.dev.	0.0999	0.141	0.128

[‡] from Table 6.3
* Ratio of female to male employment–population ratios and male to female
unemployment rates (both 1980–90), weighted 4 : 1.

administrative and managerial positions, we are still speaking of a
privileged minority here. As Pippa Norris (1987: 69) stresses:

> Middle-class women are relatively successful in getting ahead in board-
> rooms and executive offices in the United States, yet the vast majority of
> American women are entering poorly paid jobs as typists and clerks,
> cashiers, restaurant waitresses, office cleaners and factory assemblers.

On the other hand, the lowest-scoring nations in terms of 'elites' –
Switzerland, Luxembourg and Japan – are also at or near the bottom
in terms of gender ratios in industrial wages.

We are now able to arrive at a composite, if crude, measure for
female work desirability, as shown in Table 6.4. This is calculated by

first averaging the values for industrial wage ratios and 'elites', then dividing this by 100 to produce decimal scores. This figure is then multiplied by a weighted average of female to male ratios in the employment–population ratio and in official unemployment.[3] The resulting figure is our score of 'female work desirability'. Given certain estimated data, and the fact that the correlation of the two components (average of wage ratios and elites with the weighted employment gender ratio) is only 0.250, one should treat the resulting summary value as more of an ordinal than an integral measure. However, it is still highly useful in that it basically dichotomizes the OECD democracies into those where it is relatively attractive for women to work and those where women are clearly discriminated against 'more than average'.

On this measure, New Zealand falls slightly below the mean. However, like the vast majority of nations above the mean, New Zealand has a tax system that is favourable to two-income families (in that it does not extensively penalize a couple in terms of deductions and other benefits when the wife works as opposed to when the husband earns more by himself).[4] Consequently, we would tentatively want to push New Zealand 'up' into the higher group. In contrast, the tax system in France is one of those biased against two-income families.

In summary, we can see that 'female work desirability' exists in two distinct groups of nations: the Nordic group (Finland, Sweden, Norway, Denmark, Iceland); and *certain* Anglo-Saxon nations (the United States, Canada, Australia, the United Kingdom). The lack of 'female work desirability' is basically found in Central and Southern Europe, plus Ireland (often treated as a quasi-Southern European nation anyway), and of course Japan. We have earlier noted that Japan effectively – and uniquely – combines high unemployment for women with full employment for men.

Of course, work desirability says nothing about the welfare state proper, except that in those nations where there is low labour de-commodification as well as high female work desirability (again, the Anglo-Saxon group) women have a further incentive to work! That is, they cannot partake equally of the welfare state otherwise. What, however, of women benefiting from the welfare state independent of unemployment? To this we now turn.

Gender variations in welfare and family benefits

A more generous welfare state is likely to benefit women as much as men (or perhaps even more), so the comparative extent of social welfare spending is certainly a relevant factor. However, within the welfare state certain programmes are clearly targeted at women. One obvious example is maternity benefits. Another type of social spending often targeted at women consists of child or family allowances, which in most advanced nations began in the 1930s or 1940s (Bock and Thane, 1991: 5). But as we shall see, this presupposes that the benefit is paid to the mother.

More generally, the International Labour Organization provides data on overall family policy expenditures – including family allowances, daycare, parental leave and so on – as a share of public spending. Recalculating these expenditures as a share of national GDP, the levels of spending range from over 4 per cent of GDP in Sweden to next to nothing in the United States – the only OECD democracy where there are almost *no* such national programmes. Switzerland and Japan also spend practically nothing in this regard.

Furthermore, an attempt to assess more broadly how various welfare states affect women and families specifically has been made by Harold L. Wilensky (1990: especially p. 2), who rank-orders 18 OECD nations in terms of their 'innovative and expansive family policies' in three areas: (1) maternity and parental leave; (2) public daycare programmes, and (3) flexibility of retirement systems. His rankings 'measure government action to assure care of children and maximize choices in balancing work and family demands for everyone' (Wilensky, 1990: 2). In this analysis we utilize his data on childcare and maternity and parental leave.

Again, the issue here is whether welfare states do offer women a real choice in terms of working volitionally versus partaking of social programmes. As Jennifer Dale and Peggy Foster (1986: 128) stress: 'Feminists' intention is not to force women with children to look for work, but to give them the choice of staying at home to look after children without thereby becoming dependent on a male bread-winner.' Dependence on male partners is of course only one potential consequence of women staying at home with their children. The other is that by not working one forgoes aspects of the social welfare state, especially pensions, *where these are earnings related and thus 'commodified'*. A more desirable welfare state from the point of view of women as mothers would not merely aid them when their children are young (through family allowances and public daycare) but also ensure that lifetime benefits are not sacrificed or indeed that these directly reflect the time spent raising children. This latter point is reflected to some extent in Wilensky's broad measurements.

The raw scores of Wilensky's data are based on a five-point scale, which we have adjusted so that '5' reflects the most generous 'pro-family' policies, and '1' the least. Where possible, the data have been updated and expanded to assess all 23 OECD democracies.

Table 6.5 *Family welfare orientation*

	(5-point scales)				
Nation	Social security spending, 1984–86	Family policy spending, 1985–87	Wilensky rank order: Child care	Mat./par. leave*	Overall average
Sweden	5	5	4	5	4.75
France	4	5	5	4	4.50
Finland	5	5	3	5	4.50
Belgium	4	4	5	4	4.25
Norway	4	5	4	4	4.25
Denmark	5	5	4	3	4.25
Austria	4	4	2	4	3.50
Netherlands	5	4	2	2	3.25
Luxembourg	3	3	(2)	(4)	3.00
F.R. Germany	4	2	2	4	3.00
Iceland	2	5	(2)	(3)	3.00
Ireland	4	2	(2)	2	2.50
Portugal	1	2	n.d.	(4)	2.33
United Kingdom	2	3	2	2	2.25
Greece	2	2	(2)	(3)	2.25
Italy	1	1	3	3	2.00
Spain	2	1	(2)	(3)	2.00
New Zealand	3	2	1	2	2.00
Canada	2	2	1	2	1.75
Switzerland	2	1	2	2	1.75
Australia	1	2	2	1	1.50
United States	2	1	2	1	1.50
Japan	1	1	1	2	1.25
mean					2.84
std.dev.					1.12

* Maternity and parental leave.
Sources: Author's calculations from ILO (1992: Table 5); Ólafsson 1993; Nordic Statistical Secretariat (1990); Wilensky (1990) and a personal communication which graciously provided his raw data (22 March 1993); OECD (1990); Child Care Advocacy Association of Canada (1993: 4)

However, in order to compare directly the two other relevant factors noted earlier – total spending and family policy benefits – these must also be grouped into five-point scales.[5]

These four (or in some cases three) scores are then averaged to produce a summary measure of family welfare, by which the 23 OECD democracies are ranked. The results are given in Table 6.5.

The average score is highest in Sweden, France and Finland; and lowest in Japan, the United States and Australia. These summary scores of family welfare provide a clear – if somewhat crude – *family-sensitive* ranking of OECD welfare states, which basically dichotomizes these nations.

Yet 'family welfare' is not quite the same as 'female welfare' or 'maternal welfare', in that one further distinction must be noted: the actual recipient of the benefits. As Irene Wennemo (1992: 206–7, 1994) notes, OECD democracies can be basically divided into those nations where family benefits are universal and thus paid to all mothers (Nordic and Anglo-Saxon nations) and those nations (in Central and Southern Europe and Japan) where the benefits are paid to the father as a supplement to the presumed breadwinner's income.[6] It must be stressed that only where the benefits are paid to the mother can high *family* welfare be said to translate into high *female* welfare.

Moreover, the values on family welfare orientation do relate to Gøsta Esping-Andersen's (1990: 74) clustering of welfare state regimes, but with the following qualification: nations that are *either* social democratic (such as Sweden) *or* conservative (such as France) score highly on our measure, thus 'collapsing' these two clusters together. In contrast, nations that reflect liberalism in their overall welfare state (United States, Switzerland, Japan) have low scores on our measure. Indeed, for the 18 nations Esping-Andersen discusses, the correlation between his score on 'liberalism' and our summary measure of female and family welfare is a significant −0.629. One may wish to protest here that a key distinction between social democratic and conservative welfare states relates to their effects on the overall employment structure, and women's place within this (Esping-Andersen, 1990: Chapters 6–8). This is a valid point, which is best dealt with by integrating our earlier concept of 'female work desirability' with our analysis of women and the welfare state proper. Figure 6.1 does this by providing a scatterplot of the scores on family welfare with the scores on female work desirability. The main beneficiary – father or mother – of family allowances payments is also noted. A third category here includes nations without comparative information on this factor, nations (Belgium and France) where certain benefits go to the father and others to the mother, and the Republic of Ireland, which in 1974 switched from making payments to the father to making payments to the mother.

A new typology

These three factors – family welfare orientation, which parent is the recipient of benefits, and female work desirability – provide us with a

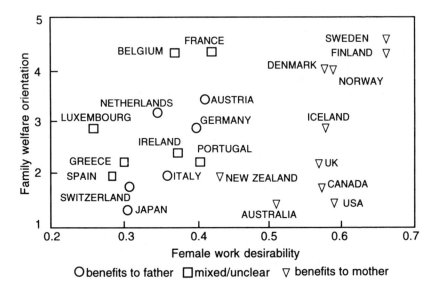

Figure 6.1   *Work and welfare incentives for women*

Note: family welfare orientation represents the overall average as shown
in Table 6.5. Female work desirability represents the multiplied score as
shown in Table 6.4

tentative new typology. We can first note that family welfare orientation is statistically independent of the other factors. That is, the correlation between family welfare and female work desirability is an insignificant 0.387; likewise the correlation between family welfare and mother as chief recipient is an insignificant 0.177.[7] Again, family welfare reflects 'non-liberalism' in welfare state principles. In contrast, the correlation between female work desirability and family benefits going to the female is a highly significant 0.784.

However, the variations on female work desirability presented in both Table 6.4 and Figure 6.1 do not appear to relate clearly to any of Esping-Andersen's welfare state types.[8] One might speculate, based on theories of modernization and industrialization (Pierson, 1991: 13–24), that female work desirability would be greater in the most advanced nations; however, the correlation between said measure and wealth is only 0.335.[9]

Yet female work desirability does relate clearly to one causal factor, and this is *Protestantism* – here the correlation is a robust 0.815.[10] This result confirms Schmidt's (1993b: 208) stress on the statistical and causal relationship between Protestantism and increasing female labour force participation. This causality relates both to Protestantism's greater stress on individual rights, [11] and to the fact that Catholicism (and other traditional religions) have had stricter views that the place of women should be in the home (Schmidt, 1993b: 208). Of course, although there would be a negative correlation with Catholicism in our data, this correlation would be less, as Greece and Japan – low scorers, both – are neither Protestant nor Catholic. There is a further significant correlation between Protestantism and payment of family benefits to mothers (rather than to fathers or mixed): $r = 0.715$.

Secondly and consequently, Figure 6.1 – bearing in mind the mean score of 2.84 on family welfare – does seem to provide a clustering of almost all OECD nations into four groupings, which thus define our new typology. In the upper right cluster are Denmark, Finland, Norway and Sweden. These are the only nations to provide (comparatively) a true 'work–welfare choice' for women, in that female work as an end in itself is relatively desirable. Moreover, family benefits are high, and are always paid to the mother. The overall nature of welfare states in these nations (Finland with qualifications) combined with their religion would lead us to call these cases of *Protestant social democratic welfare states*.

More specifically, there is a virtuous circle relating social democratic welfare states and relative female equality in these nations. As Schmidt (1993a: 278–9) notes, female employment tends to increase where the service sector (as opposed to industry) is relatively dominant, and where there is high government employment. Both of these patterns are now true in Scandinavia. Indeed, there large welfare states tend to involve *female* labour-intensive provision of services, such as childcare, rather than merely cash transfers.

The lower right cluster comprises those nations with minimal family welfare yet a relatively egalitarian gender situation in the labour market. Family benefits are paid to the mother, but these are rather inadequate and tend not to include supplemental child support or housing allowances (Kamerman and Kahn, 1988: 356, Table 14.2). Women in these countries thus have both a direct incentive to work (in terms of the nature of employment) and a broader incentive in terms of commodified welfare benefits. However, in such nations the large female labour force faces the clear burden of inadequate (public) daycare. This cluster of nations contains most – but not all – of the Anglo-Saxon or English-speaking world: Australia, Canada, New Zealand (effectively), the United Kingdom and the United States. 'Englishness' has in fact been related to public policy 'awfulness' by Castles and Merrill (1989); in our context, these nations are 'awful' in terms of family welfare but *not* in terms of the recipient of family benefits or especially female work desirability. Moreover, this cluster does not contain Ireland, which is highly

Catholic. So in terms of gender effects, welfare systems and payments, and religion the most appropriate terms for these cases would be *Protestant liberal welfare states*.

In between these two Protestant groupings we find Iceland. Iceland is a fully Protestant nation; but it is also unique in that it is a Nordic country wherein social democracy has been much weaker than the other Nordic countries (Ólafsson, 1993: 62–3). Consequently Iceland never developed a comprehensive, social democratic welfare state. However, certain benefits that affect families do compare favourably with the other Nordic nations. It follows that Iceland has a unique pattern: one that approaches but still remains distinct from the four Protestant social democratic welfare states.

The complete opposite to the Protestant liberal welfare state is provided by the nations in the upper left cluster: Austria, Belgium, France, (West) Germany, Luxembourg and the Netherlands. The first four of these are classified by Esping-Andersen (1990: 74) as having strongly 'conservative' welfare states. In any case, in all six nations in this cluster there are no great incentives for women to work, but (or rather) strong incentives not to work and to stay at home. Being the direct recipient of all family benefits is normally *not* one of these incentives. Yet there are others; for example, in the 1980s the Christian Democratic led government of the Federal Republic of Germany changed the pension system to grant claims specifically to mothers, graduated by the number of children (Offe 1992a: 145; Schmidt 1988: 90). This Claus Offe (1992a: 145) calls 'conservative state feminism'.

Such patterns relate to general *Catholic* notions of encouraging families *and* discouraging women from working (Wilensky, 1990). However, the *poorer* Catholic nations of Europe (Ireland, Portugal, Spain and, historically, Italy) are not in this cluster – although perhaps they would 'like to be'. In any case, two terms are possible for this cluster: the first would be 'advanced Catholic welfare states'. Yet the Netherlands, what was West Germany, and especially reunified Germany are in fact more Protestant than Catholic. Consequently, a better term might be *advanced Christian Democratic welfare states*. This is logical even if there is no specific Christian Democratic party in the French Fifth Republic, since the Catholic MRP (*Mouvement républicain populaire*) was a central player in the Fourth Republic – and this party staunchly worked for the maintenance and expansion of French family policy (Lenoir, 1991: 145).

The final grouping is the lower left cluster of nations in Figure 6.1: a seemingly eclectic mixture of Greece, Ireland, Italy, Japan, Portugal, Spain, and Switzerland. Indeed, Esping-Andersen (1990: 74) classifies Japan and Switzerland as 'liberal' in terms of their overall welfare state regime, Italy as 'conservative', Ireland as moderately 'conservative', and does not discuss Greece, Portugal or Spain! Moreover, whereas Greece, Portugal, Ireland and Spain are in that order the poorest of the OECD democracies, Switzerland and Japan are among the very wealthiest. (Italy falls nowadays in the middle.) Consequently, this is not merely a grouping of less advanced countries, even if wealth does improve women's relative situation.[12] The main factor uniting most of these nations seems to be the *absence* of Protestantism, although Switzerland is again an exception here. Indeed, one might have expected Switzerland to be in the bottom right cluster, given the latter's term of 'Protestant liberal welfare states'. Yet unlike all dominantly Protestant nations, in Switzerland family benefits are paid to the father. (This is also true of the mixed Protestant–Catholic Netherlands and West Germany; whereas Canada pays the benefits to the mother.)

Moreover, Switzerland also differs from all other Protestant or mixed Protestant–Catholic nations of the OECD in one perhaps obvious but certainly crucial way: the granting of the suffrage to women. Whereas in most of the Protestant or mixed OECD nations women had the vote by the end of the First World War (or even before, in the Antipodes), women in Switzerland did not gain the right to vote nationally until 1971 – the last OECD democracy to provide female suffrage, where males had already had this. Table 6.6 shows the year in which universal female suffrage was granted, as well as the basic extent of Protestantism in a nation. In Iceland, it should be noted, female suffrage occurred while the country was ruled by Denmark.

Of course, the suffrage can be removed as well as granted. For example, although women received the vote in Spain in 1933, *nobody* voted in Spain during the decades of the Franco regime. Table 6.6 thus calculates the number of years in which women have been voting in democratic periods since they received the suffrage. Here we can see greater coherence with regard to the lower left cluster of Figure 6.1. Portugal, Switzerland, Spain and Greece rank at the very bottom of female voting duration, whilst Japan and Italy are also near the bottom. In these nations women have simply been late entrants into the political process. Even now they are weakly represented in parliament and cabinet.

Ireland is of course exceptional, in that universal female suffrage was granted there in 1923 – the first Catholic country to give women the vote. However, women over 30 had already received the vote in 1918 when Ireland was a part of the United Kingdom. The first Irish electoral law merely equalized the situation for men and women (as occurred in the United Kingdom in 1928). In any case, Irish women

Table 6.6 *Female voting and Protestantism in OECD democracies*

Nation	Years to 1994 of female voting	Universal female suffrage*	Dominantly Protestant or mixed
New Zealand	102	1893	yes
Australia	94	1901	yes
Finland	89	1906	yes
Iceland	80	1915	yes
Norway	77	1913 *[1940–45]*	yes
Canada	77	1918	mixed
Denmark	75	1915 *[1940–45]*	yes
United States	75	1920	yes
Sweden	74	1921	yes
Ireland	72	1923	no
Netherlands	71	1919 *[1940–45]*	mixed
Luxembourg	71	1919 *[1940–45]*	no
United Kingdom	67	1928	yes
Austria	66	1918 *[1934–45]*	no
F.R. Germany	64	1919 *[1933–45]*	mixed
France	51	1944	no
Italy	50	1945	no
Japan	50	1945	no
Belgium	47	1948**	no
Greece	36	1952 *[1967–74]*	no
Spain	24	1933 *[1939–77]*	no
Switzerland	24	1971	mixed
Portugal	19	1976	no

* Periods of *non*-democratic interludes within national periods of female suffrage are italicized in brackets.
** However, Belgian women could stand for parliament in 1921.
Source (first two columns): UN (1991a: Table 3)

were to remain very marginal politically. As Chubb (1992: 34) notes, between 1922 and 1977 only 4 per cent of those elected to the Dáil Éireann (Irish parliament) were women.

The key contrast in this regard is with nations in the upper left cluster such as Austria, Germany, the Netherlands and Luxembourg, where women have been voting for much longer *and* where they have generally been mobilized by Christian democratic parties. In short, then, we would tentatively want to call the bottom left cluster that of *late female mobilization welfare states*, rounding out our new typology.

Conclusions

If we compare our findings with Esping-Andersen's *Three Worlds*, there is obviously a close match between his socialist cluster and our list of Protestant social democratic welfare states; likewise, there is a clear overlap between his conservative cluster and our grouping of advanced Christian democratic welfare states. Only on the placement of the Netherlands is there a major difference. However, Esping-Andersen's (1990: 74) third and final cluster is a liberal one comprising Australia, Canada, Japan, Switzerland and the United States. In the second part of his work, on welfare states and employment structures, Esping-Andersen goes on to use the United States, Sweden and West Germany as representative nations of each of his three clusters. Our analysis would support such a procedure for Sweden and Germany. However, the nature of the 'post-industrial employment trajectory' (Esping-Andersen, 1990: Chapter 8) in the United States, and in particular its strong sexual desegregation (Esping-Andersen, 1990: 208–10) seems a relatively unique evolution. Specifically, whereas Canada and Australia may approximate the United States in this regard, the situation in Japan and Switzerland is quite different.

The analyses we have made of gender variations suggests that the combination of Protestantism and liberalism found in most Anglo-Saxon nations does produce its own cluster. However, neither Japan nor Switzerland belongs to this category. Instead, these two nations (which are often paired in comparative political economy) fall clearly into the category of late female mobilization welfare states. It is the notion and definition of this final welfare state cluster which is perhaps the most novel result of our analysis.

In conclusion, although previous typologies have advanced our comparative understanding and conceptualization of welfare states, they tend to gloss over certain aspects of the 'work–welfare trade-off', especially as this applies to women. In this chapter we have examined various gender differences in the natures of work and welfare states (and benefit orientation). Putting these dimensions together has produced a new typology of welfare state regimes. This typology not only provides a 'gender sensitive view' of work and welfare, but it also hopefully suggests new ways of analysing welfare states in general.

Notes

1 Specifically, in analysing the period 1973–83 Gaby von Rhein-Kress (1993: 164) has calculated that if the labour force participation of women in Austria, the Federal Republic of Germany and Switzerland had grown at the OECD average (instead of

remaining stagnant), and assuming this increase would have translated directly into open unemployment, then by 1983 the unemployment rates in these three nations would have been respectively 4.5, 4.6 and 5.0 per cent higher than they were.

2   There are no data or no comparable data for Iceland and Sweden in terms of administrative and managerial workers (in the latter case because of a blurring with the category of clerical, sales and service workers). Consequently the average of the remaining nations is used as an estimate in order to arrive at values for 'elites' – an admittedly crude correction.

3   Since unemployment is a negative effect, we use the male rate divided by the female ratio. The weighting of combination of employment–population ratios and unemployment is 4:1, reflecting the far greater honesty in the former measure.

4   For a fuller discussion of the extent to which national tax structures encourage married women to work, or discourage them from doing so, see OECD 1990: 163–9. This factor has been found to be significantly related to increasing female labour force participation – see Schmidt (1993b: 202).

5   This is done by calculating the quintiles of a normal distribution based on the mean and standard deviation of the raw data.

6   The United States has no national programme of family allowances; the few meagre benefits which are given are paid to the mother. In Belgium, the father receives the benefits if he is self-employed; otherwise these go to the mother.

7   This calculation is based on a trichotomy of OECD democracies into: benefits going to the mother [=3]; recipient of benefits varying or unclear [=2]; and benefits going to the father [=1].

8   For example, the correlation between female work desirability and Esping-Andersen's score on 'liberalism' is a non-significant −0.249.

9   For this calculation, 'wealth' is defined as GDP per capita at purchasing power parities for 1984 to 1986; the data are from OECD (1993a).

10   This calculation is based on a simple trichotomy of OECD democracies into: dominantly Protestant [=3]; half Protestant (and half Catholic) [=2]; and non-Protestant [=1].

11   For example, Schmidt (1993b: 208, footnote 10) finds a clear relationship between Protestantism and favourable tax treatment of married women's work.

12   In this regard, one can note that the four Protestant social democratic nations are all wealthy. See also Schmidt (1993b: 192).

7

Comparing Welfare States: Towards a Gender Friendly Approach

Mary Daly

The welfare state has fed a large volume of academic investigation but the core of its scholarship has been on the relationship between class forces and different systems of welfare. This has led it to prioritize the experience of men. Feminist research, in attempting to redress this bias, has investigated the relationship between women, family, work and welfare states. It is now time to bring these two sets of literature closer together. I propose to do so by focusing on the market–family–state triangle and by suggesting ways to make gender part of a theoretical and empirical framework for studying welfare state variation. To these ends, the two sets of literature – 'mainstream' and feminist[1] – are first briefly examined for what they reveal about welfare state variations and effects. I then move on to look at one of the most influential recent typologies of welfare states, that of Gøsta Esping-Andersen (1990). Key shortcomings are identified when the criteria underlying this typology are examined from a gender perspective. In effect, it will be seen that the family–state nexus has not been rigorously integrated into the analysis and that the utility of the de-commodification concept for differentiating welfare states is thrown into question. The remainder of the chapter elucidates how family considerations and the male/female relations shaped by these can be integrated into a framework for comparative analysis of welfare states.

It is appropriate at the outset to define gender and from that to consider what is required of a framework for investigating it in relation to the welfare state. Gender can be defined as the structural, relational and symbolic differentiations between women and men (Acker, 1989: 238). As such it prioritizes the study of social relations between the sexes and in particular sees these relations as socially constructed. A gender framework as applied to the welfare state must, therefore, account for the treatment and experience of both women and men and the role of the state in constructing female and male access to its resources and those located elsewhere in the social system. This refocuses the analysis in two ways in the present context: at a micro-level resource-based relationships between women and men as they are constructed or influenced by welfare state structure and practice become central; at the macro-level, we search for how the welfare state interacts with other institutional domains to determine female and male life chances and role constructions.

The welfare state in scholarship

For most of its history welfare state theory has privileged the relationship between state and class, class being configured largely in terms of men's experience (Shaver, 1991: 145). As a consequence, the experience of women has been either ignored or downgraded. With the advent of woman-centred scholarship women's relationship to the state and state policy began to be studied in its own right. Most but not all of this work has been feminist in orientation.[2] Looked at from this viewpoint, one can say that two sets of literature on the welfare state exist. As will become clear, they are not easily reconciled and both, especially the former, are adrift of a gender perspective. Terming the first 'mainstream' and the second 'feminist', I will briefly review their main insights from the point of view of what they reveal about how welfare states are to be defined and understood.

Mainstream work on the welfare state

As a core structural component of contemporary Western society, the welfare state has fed a broad-ranging debate about changing modes of societal organization and the formative role of welfare institutions therein. Investigation of the welfare state has tended to concentrate on a delimited number of directions. One of the most longstanding and fertile fields of study has sought the seeds of welfare state gestation and subsequent growth and development. Around this has sprung a vast literature on the influences shaping and the political dynamics surrounding welfare states.[3] The quest for the shaping influences has in fact dominated theoretical scholarship in the field – debate bouncing back and forth between structural factors (often identified as general background conditions or stages of economic development) and political agency which treats of a wide gamut of social actors from organized labour to state bureaucracy to political parties.

Along with its focus on identifying and explaining the historical landmarks of welfare states, three further characteristics distinguish mainstream scholarship. First, the roots of welfare state history and

subsequent development have been located in either the modernization or industrialization process, the logic or inherent contradictions
of capitalism, the independent action of state resources, the political
agency of social democratic parties or class alliances more generally.
Partly as a consequence, and second, the (labour) market has been
privileged among contingent institutions. The form of the welfare
state and its own shaping influences are located first and foremost,
and often exclusively, in the (labour) market. Third, the welfare state
has been conceptualized largely as a quantitative entity, most
commonly operationally clad in aggregate levels of welfare expenditures. Such foci of scholarship have resulted in a representation of the
welfare state in the mainstream literature as a product of political
(read: class) forces whose main significance lies in its capacity to
either uphold or modify class and economic status differences.

A key commonality in the *explanans* of the theories is their heavy
reliance on class dynamics as the mainspring for social provision.
Different theories weigh differently the causal role of capital, labour
and the state in bringing political form to social welfare. But they
commonly assume that class politics provided the template for social
policy innovation, just as they regularly conclude that the resulting
redistribution is significant only or mainly for class politics (Mink,
1990: 92). While the agency of interest group politics is allowed for in
some cases, this too is ultimately reduced to class politics. The
possibility of gender politics did not seriously exercise the minds of
mainstream welfare state analysts or, if it did, it never saw the light of
day in their work. This has had two consequences: the possibility of a
male/female dynamic as a shaping influence in contests over redistribution has been ignored or downgraded; and political engagement on
the part of women is sidelined by the existing mainstream theories. I
take serious issue with the theoretical marginalization of gender and
women. It is not my intention to dispute the critical importance of
class in understanding the welfare state: there is no doubt that
welfare provisions are 'classed'. But I do claim that bringing gender
into the analysis forces us to rethink whether a class framework is by
itself capable of accounting for how women as well as men experience
the welfare state.

Feminist insights

Feminist research has devoted some attention to redressing the
imbalances of existing scholarship in excluding women, although it is
with neo-Marxist theory of the welfare state that it has mainly
engaged. As things stand now, I think it fair to say that no feminist
theory of the welfare state dominates. A likely explanation for this
may be that theoretical energies have been focused elsewhere: in

searching for a general theory to explain 'women's oppression'. In some cases the welfare state has been lost in this demanding endeavour. What has feminist scholarship contributed to the study of the welfare state?

First, the family has been placed centre stage and the role of the state in sustaining certain forms of family and certain types of family relationships has been explored (Barrett, 1980; McIntosh, 1978). Feminist work has demonstrated that to better understand the more public systems of state welfare, their connections to welfare within the household/family system and to women and men inside and outside that system must be explicated. A second contribution has rested on the examination of the ideologies that underlie welfare, especially as they relate to women (Fraser, 1989b; Lewis, 1983, 1992a). Analysis has emerged to demonstrate how welfare state policies and practice have reinforced and distinctively shaped women's secondary status to and dependence on men. Rooted in a 'familialist' ideology inherent in welfare policies, many examples of such practices have been identified – lower-level payments for women, income and earnings restrictions on partners or spouses, differential conditions of access to welfare for women and men. A third contribution of feminist work has been to show how the welfare state is heavily dependent on arrangements outside the formal economy and/or public provision through which women provide unwaged/low-waged welfare services (Siim, 1987b). A key focus of interest here has been the relationship between paid and unpaid work and the state's role in sustaining this division. One of the main contributions has rested on an exploration of care work, social reproduction if you wish, illustrating that the boundaries between what is accepted as a public responsibility and that which is consigned to the private sphere vary across states but are closely shaped by welfare state policies within countries. A fourth focus of feminist work has been the citizenship paradigm. The degree to which gender is a source of inequality in citizenship rights, and the nature of social citizenship in particular, implicates the welfare state as a carrier of gender differentiation and of a poorer-quality, female citizenship (Leira, 1992; Pateman, 1988). Different forms of citizenship have been associated with different bases of political organization, leading to work positing dual citizenship (Hernes, 1987b) and a 'two-track' welfare state (applied especially to the United States) (Fraser, 1989b; Nelson, 1990).

Notwithstanding the fact that it has helped to fill a hole in mainstream work – the exclusion of women – feminist scholarship has some delimitations for studying gender differences in a comparative welfare state context. Because the welfare state has been studied mainly as a site of female oppression, whether patriarchal, capitalist or both, the work has not developed much in the way of a framework for gender analysis. That is, since its focus has been largely, if not exclusively, on women, the role of welfare states in constructing systematic differences between women and men has been under-played. In addition, feminist studies have tended to produce a generic model of welfare states, thus failing to probe differences within and among welfare systems.

So, neither set of scholarship provides a blueprint for the analysis of the gendered character of welfare states, although from each certain insights can be retained while others need to be developed. For the present purpose, the historical development of Western welfare states is less important than their current forms. My interest inheres more in the shape and outcomes or consequences of modern welfare systems. What becomes most germane to this interest is which aspects of the programmatic content of welfare states are most relevant to a gender analysis and how one can best identify gendered outcomes of the organization of welfare systems. These direct attention to another type of literature on the welfare state – that which explores empirically the structure and (some) outcomes of welfare state policies.

Research comparing systems of welfare

The last years have seen the growth of a new 'school' in welfare state research: work that has begun to explore the qualitative character of welfare states from a comparative perspective (Esping-Andersen, 1990; Jones, 1985; van Kersbergen, 1991; Leibfried, 1990b). This work has spawned a different way of comparing welfare states – in terms of typologies derived on the basis of variations in structural characteristics.

Welfare state typologies
Esping-Andersen (1990) arguably develops one of the most sophisti-cated sets of indicators, to some extent replacing the welfare state concept with that of social policy regime. His historically sensitive analysis selects the following as the key criteria differentiating modern welfare states: their logic of organization (especially their capacity to de-commodify individuals), their social stratification effects, and their employment regimes. Evaluated on these charac-teristics, 18 advanced capitalist welfare states are judged by Esping-Andersen to cluster into three distinct types of regime: the now familiar social democratic, conservative and liberal welfare regimes.

Apart from the fact that it represents a considerable advance in our understanding of welfare state–society relations, Esping-Andersen's work is useful to the present purpose for a number of reasons. First, at a macro-level it helps to identify key features of welfare state structure and content. For the purpose of trying to discern general patterning, it is useful to be able to group welfare states and the criteria used by the 'new typologists' for doing so are undoubtedly more discriminating than the aggregate social expenditures so favoured in the past. Clarifying their distributive mechanisms and empirically tracing the features of welfare states on the basis of whether rights hinge on citizenship, performance or need is a welcome advance. Second, a focus on the more qualitative characteristics, generally translated by Esping-Andersen into quantitative indicators, is helpful. Although utilized by Esping-Andersen as a heuristic device to isolate the principles organizing social policy regimes and to set up explanatory circuits, they can also help in providing a bridge between the welfare state as a macro-institution and welfare practice as affecting women and men in real life. To the extent that this genre of work captures both the material resources provided by the state to individuals or families and the conditions under which they are conferred, it should be fruitful for an analysis of outcomes, those that are gendered included. However, in the latter lies the rub.

Problems from a gender perspective
When considered through a gender lens, important inherent limitations of this type of work are spotlighted. For a start, Esping-Andersen's typologies rely almost exclusively on an analysis of the state–market nexus. Although his theoretical framework incorporates the triangle of market, family and state, in practice the key analytical relationship is between the state and the market. This is evident, for instance, in his view of stratification which largely confines it to class inequalities. It also underlies the construction of private provision as market provision. In effect, the theoretical status of the family in the schema is unclear. In the empirical analysis, it is most integrated for the 'conservative' regimes (although not in a disaggregated way – in the sense of the gendered division of labour that characterizes most families and especially those in the 'conservative' welfare states of Germany, Italy, the Netherlands and France) but hardly appears at all for the social democratic or liberal welfare states.

To help unravel the issues involved, it might be useful to consider why the family needs to be included at all? I think an answer to this question lies in a recognition of the welfare functions performed by the family and the close interrelationship which has always existed between the state organization of welfare in society and the family (not to mention other 'welfare' institutions like the semi-public and voluntary sectors, the wider kinship system and neighbour networks). In any case to say that welfare states relate to the family in different ways begs the questions of why and how. While the first question is beyond our scope here, to answer the second we need to integrate the family centrally into the analysis and consider the interplay of family and state in welfare provision and the effects of welfare state policies on different types of families and relations within families.

In point of fact, the family remains the most significant provider of welfare and care in all welfare states, even in those which are classified as social democratic.[4] This is not to claim that the boundaries between the family and welfare states have not shifted but rather that (a) this varies empirically, and (b) that the relationship between the welfare state and the family needs to be theorized in its own right. Apart from its caring functions, the family may also be important as a basis of claims on the welfare state. If we take the situation of married women who are not in the labour market, for instance, it appears that the basis of their claim to benefits in many welfare states derives from their marital and other family relationships. For men too, family status is likely to be an important factor shaping the benefits they receive from the state and, indeed, their treatment in the market. This basis of claim cannot be readily accommodated within the threefold citizenship, need or work framework.

A second issue raised by gender considerations refers to the discriminating properties of the concept of de-commodification – one of the key analytic hinges of Esping-Andersen's typology. For Esping-Andersen the extent to which the state confers on individuals the capacity to live outside the market, its de-commodification potential, is a fundamental differentiator of welfare states. To the extent that they de-commodify, Esping-Andersen regards welfare states as conferring independence (a stark contrast to one of the main currents in feminist work which has emphasized the welfare state as a locus of dependence for women). In his hands the concept embraces not just the levels of income replacement provided but the surrounding fabric of eligibility and benefit rules. Moreover, de-commodification is a matter of degree – in its pure form a condition that is probably unrealizable in capitalist societies. Operationalized as it is, the implicit evaluation in Esping-Andersen's work implies a positive correlation between the level of welfare state advancement and the degree of de-commodification.

The de-commodification concept is gender blind and obscures

gender variations in social rights. First, it is constructed with male lifestyles in mind: men spend most of their life in the market and when they cannot are paid a wage substitute by the state. To the extent that welfare state programmes are constructed only around male life-cycle patterns, de-commodification is an adequate indicator of one of their component characteristics. However, welfare states also relate to other spheres apart from the market, to other units apart from the individual and to other individuals apart from men. In effect, significant welfare programme inputs are directed to people outside the market, most of whom are women, and to families or households as collectivities and, via that, to adult and child 'dependants'. Applying the concept of de-commodification to typical female lifestyles raises three issues.

The first relates to the scope of the concept. Based on formal, waged labour, the de-commodification concept takes no account of the fact that many women live now and have always lived outside the market. This is not because they have been de-commodified but, rather, because they are not commodified. The extent, therefore, to which a dual conception of commodification–de-commodification can embrace the relationship of the welfare state to the citizenship of women in general is limited. The core issue centres on the notion of independence that underpins the concept. While it may be true to claim that welfare systems confer independence of the market on men, female independence is of a different calibre. This is for two reasons. First, in effect most women derive the lion's share of their income from sources other than the market or the state. Sweden apart, the majority of married women are economically dependent on their husbands (see Hobson, Chapter 11 in this volume). Second, there is the fact that large numbers of employed women are not conferred with financial independence by the market anyway (because of their average lower wages relative to men, higher propensity towards part-time work and more frequent interruptions of employment). In the heel of the hunt, the most important 'source' of income for women as a group is the men with whom they are having intimate relations. So, Esping-Andersen's twofold classification of dependence is too simplistic when women are brought into the picture. Women's independence is conditioned by their relationships and status within the family as much as by welfare state policies or labour market participation.[5] A key empirical question arising from this is how welfare states affect the volume and sources of resources available to men and women, and in particular how they affect women's reliance on male incomes.

A second complication is revealed when women's labour relations and the role of the welfare state in this regard are considered. The fact is that, in contrast to men, women are as likely to be commodified by the state as to be de-commodified by it. This can occur in two ways. First, through the welfare state as employer: witness the large numbers of women in the social welfare labour market and their predominance over men in this arena across countries (Rein, 1985; Meyer, Chapter 5 in this volume). So, the implicit market/state relationship, whereby the former is the commodifier and the latter the de-commodifier, is not as neat as Esping-Andersen presents it. Furthermore, the dynamics surrounding women's labour relations, and their distinctiveness from those of men, should be emphasized. Women's decisions to enter into and exit from the labour market are not determined by social security provisions in the same way as those of men. Family situation, in the guise of both labour responsibilities and socio-emotional factors, influences women's capacity for paid labour to a much greater extent than is true for men. A further question then, and one left unanswered by Esping-Andersen's framework, is how and if the welfare state has a role in moulding the pattern of differential male/female construction of and access to paid/unpaid labour.

There is a further problem with de-commodification from a gender perspective. This is the possibility that de-commodification is itself a gendered phenomenon. While they share some states of de-commodification, women and men are generally de-commodified for different purposes and usually under different conditions. As an indicator of this, consider the sex differentiation that has been found amongst recipients of different programmes. Diane Sainsbury (1993a), for instance, demonstrates that American, British and Dutch income maintenance programmes, although not the Swedish, are dominated by one sex or the other. Women are predominant amongst programmes specifically targeted at them (for example maternity and special 'caring' measures) and as recipients of social assistance, while men are more likely to be claimants of insurance, that is, rights-based, benefits.[6] Significant differences characterize the two sets of programmes, especially in relation to the nature of the right involved and the conditions attaching to receipt (Fraser, 1989b). The extent to which men and women relate to different parts of benefit systems is an important question for empirical exploration.

The forgoing discussion raises three key issues requiring clarification in the context of a gender-sensitive framework for comparing welfare states: the scope of welfare state intervention; the ideologies underlying welfare policy and practice; concrete outcomes for women and men in terms of their interrelationships, access to resources and respective roles and responsibilities.

The scope of welfare state intervention

Even the most cursory glance across countries shows that different 'welfare mixes' exist, that is, that different roles are played by the state, the family and the market in the provision of caring services. Two empirical indicators can serve to disentangle welfare states' approaches to caring work (by which I refer to the tasks involved in caring for others, especially the young, the ill and the elderly). The first is the extent of state involvement in service provision related to caring and the second is the extent of financial support given by states to those who do the caring work within the family.

As regards state service provision, huge variation can be seen empirically: across states, caring work is organized on the basis of a continuum from private to public. While it is not by any means the only determinant, the welfare state is a key actor in constructing the boundaries between what is considered as a public responsibility, a market option or a private obligation. In this regard, welfare states have a number of alternatives. They can undertake to provide caring services directly (Sweden being the most advanced in this regard), to subsidize this work through income replacement (either in the market or in the home) or to leave it completely private (allowing it to find its own 'price' in the market or in the home). In reality most welfare states choose some mixture of all three options.

Appraised from the viewpoint of the organization of care work, Esping-Andersen's regime clusters are not watertight. While it is true that the Scandinavian states have moved furthest towards the socialization of care work, they are not undifferentiated in regard to the extent of state involvement in caring or the primacy of the state in raising female labour force participation. Arnlaug Leira's work (1992) highlights important differences within the social democratic cluster. Norway is especially divergent: its childcare policies, being oriented to the socialization of the child, emphasize private, family care for young children, unlike Sweden and Denmark where reproduction policies are closely coordinated with labour market policies. So the Norwegian welfare state has played a very modest role in facilitating the economic activity of mothers.

Within the conservative regime cluster, comparison of France and Germany reveals very wide differences in how these two welfare states have institutionalized care for children. In the former, state involvement in caring is high for children of all ages, whereas the German welfare state constructs childcare as a largely private matter, placing quite strict limits on public childcare provision (especially for children up to the age of three) and offering payments to stay-at-home parents. Of Esping-Andersen's three regimes, only the liberal cluster seems to cohere when the spotlight is turned on state service provision for caring. However, if the second empirical indicator I suggested above is taken – the extent of state support for carers within the family – it will be seen that regime clusters vary widely and in a fashion that is not consistent with accepted logics of welfare state variation. Sheila Shaver and Jonathan Bradshaw's (1993) examination of the extent of state support for a stay-at-home spouse/partner in 15 countries indicates no obvious association between the degree of variation empirically and the regime types proposed by Esping-Andersen. They conclude: 'apparently welfare states do not, through the levels of support they provide, favour one pattern of wifely support over another in any clear and consistent fashion' (1993: 22). I suggest, therefore, that the utility of the indicators of state involvement in caring services and its support for private caring in predicting welfare state variation should be explored empirically.

The ideologies underlying welfare

This has been a more favoured theme, especially in feminist research. Its importance in the present context lies in clarifying further the relationship between the state and the family and the nature of the woman/state relation.

Taken together, feminist work proffers substantial evidence to support the thesis that welfare states have operated with and helped to sustain a particular model of the family. Investigation of the history of debate surrounding the construction of welfare policy in many countries has identified an ideology of the family wage as a formative influence on the programmatic content of welfare states (Land, 1978; Sapiro, 1986; Zaretsky, 1986). Variously conceptualized, this argument posits the maintenance of the traditional family form of breadwinner husband/dependent wife as one of the long-term organizing principles of welfare. As an attempt to theorize the relationship between welfare and domestic labour, it poses a challenge to the view that the work ethic is the main organizing logic of welfare. However, there is a large (theoretical) gap between identifying a family wage ideology as a common organizing principle of welfare and claiming that the welfare state maintains a specific form of family or household for capitalist purposes. In particular, variations and changes in the relationship between the state and the family must be accounted for. Different states support the family to different degrees (Gauthier, 1991). To take account of such variations, a more nuanced approach is needed.

Significant steps towards a more refined approach have been taken by Jane Lewis and Ilona Ostner (1991; Lewis, 1992a). These analyses have centred on the assumptions regarding the role of women which are embedded in welfare policies. In particular, a number of European welfare states are compared on the basis of whether they recognize and cater for women solely as wives and mothers and/or also as workers. From this analysis, Lewis and Ostner derive a threefold categorization of several contemporary European welfare states: those with strong, moderate and weak breadwinner models.

Britain, Germany and the Netherlands are categorized as strong male-breadwinner countries. All have tended to treat adult women as dependent wives for the purpose of social entitlements, although they have differed in the extent to which they have developed policies, transfers or services to promote marriage and family life (Lewis and Ostner, 1991: 30). France is categorized as a 'moderate male breadwinner' state because women there have gained entitlements as both citizen mothers and citizen workers. Female labour market participation is encouraged but, at the same time, the policy framework is strongly supportive of families. Motherhood is treated as a social function rather than a private matter by family-centred, pronatalist-inspired social policies. Post-1970 Sweden and Denmark constitute the third variant in the framework, being 'weak male-breadwinner' states. Supporting a 'two-breadwinner family', the basis of women's social entitlements has been transformed: they have been treated as workers and have been compensated for their unpaid work as mothers at rates they could command as members of the labour force (1991: 42).

The Lewis and Ostner framework is useful, not least because it offers a more differentiated approach to the state/family/woman relationship. In this regard it identifies and draws upon an apparently widespread theme in diverse European welfare systems (in the process arriving at a somewhat different clustering of welfare states to that of Esping-Andersen). In practice, Lewis and Ostner transcend the rather simplistic application of the family wage concept and demonstrate that, while common, it is by no means uniform. To some extent, this type of framework liberates us from the use of the breadwinner model as the *bête noire* of welfare systems for women. However, theirs is clearly a model in the making rather than a finished product. It might benefit from a wider empirical application since one gets the impression that the national systems selected are the ones that best fit the model. Also at times, Lewis and Ostner fail to be systematic about the exact policy package involved in each prototype and the specific outcomes for women.

While the model requires greater empirical development, an important point about this work is that it introduces a new set of criteria for clustering welfare regimes: on the basis of indicators of women's roles. The framework has special promise because it begins to unravel women's treatment in different welfare state forms, while at the same time recognizing diversity. I suggest that the framework's utility could be increased by two modifications. First, it should be made more flexible so as to be able to incorporate role combinations better. In the case of women, Lewis and Ostner speak of a two-dimensional relationship to the state: mothers and workers. But, to my mind, modern welfare states are more likely to encourage combinations of activities on the part of women, and, indeed, to pursue contradictory and even ambivalent policies rather than to operate to a singular role construction. Second, the conceptualization should be reviewed for its capacity to incorporate the male/state relationship. Men tend to be represented in welfare state research in a very uniform manner – as workers/breadwinners. But men's claims as citizens are also related to their family status, through, for example, the generally more favourable tax treatment of married as against single men, in some countries the payment of additional allowances to married men for their adult and child 'dependants'.

Gendered outcomes of welfare

One of the key themes underlying this chapter is a question not always made explicit: how do welfare states affect relations between women and men? Programmatic content and the conditions surrounding welfare receipt (as well as the degree and form of state service provision considered above) are at the empirical coalface here, as independent variables, as it were. Three elements of welfare systems are relevant in this regard: the 'risks' covered; the bases of entitlement and the treatment of family members. Of most interest are their effects in leading to particular role constructions for women and men and specific material outcomes in terms of levels of benefit payments.

At their core, welfare systems, and social insurance in particular, attempt to cover income losses. However, states are selective about the risks they collectivize. A glance at history suggests that, in part at least, this selection process has been underlied by gender. Across welfare states contingencies typical of male lifestyles (such as retirement, industrial accidents, unemployment) were more readily incorporated into social programmes than those of women (widowhood, family caring and pregnancy) (Daly, 1994). The bias, then, was towards de-commodifying male risks. To the extent that this was or is the case, welfare systems tend to construct men as workers and women as unpaid carers; in a very concrete sense, then, reinforcing a traditional division of labour and dependencies between women and men. However, welfare provision is by no means static. A discernible trend in recent years has been towards incorporating caring as a social risk. Relevant developments here include the widespread introduction of parental leave, in Britain and Ireland the institutionalization of special non-contributory payments for carers and, more widely, the establishment of 'benefit credits' which allow carers to retain existing or build up new contributions for the period of their caring activity. It is probably not far-fetched to claim that provision for caring and carers constitutes one of the few new developments in the social security systems of industrialized countries. Such provision is innovative because it has been introduced in a manner that modifies existing principles. These benefits transgress and blur the traditional structures, introducing elements of means-testing into insurance systems and principles of universalism into both social assistance and insurance-based provisions (Bieback, 1992: 239). An empirical question remaining to be determined is whether and how these innovations alter the distribution of income, roles and responsibilities between women and men and their ramifications for the organizing logics of welfare systems.

The basis of entitlement constructs the framework in which individuals and/or collective units are granted access to income support. It is usually taken for granted that social rights are individual-based. However, in national contexts the basis of entitlement varies, some benefits being granted to a collective unit.

To the extent that benefits are granted to a collective unit, welfare state constructions and treatment of 'dependants' are important empirically. The constructions involved derive not only from the basis and calculation of payment but from the surrounding rules of entitlement. For instance, receipt of social security often carries with it conditions about both partners' labour market involvement. Often these rules make it a rational decision for only one partner to be employed. Since the man is usually the higher earner, effectively it is the woman who is discouraged from employment. In addition, the existence of earnings thresholds for qualification to social insurance debars many women, as low-income earners, from personal rights. At the most concrete level, this means that they have no personal right to a welfare payment and that the circuit of distribution that is established/reinforced is from man to woman.

In a sense all of the discussion here turns on the thorny issue of how to evaluate outcomes of welfare. Quite a lot of feminist literature has considered this for women. And while there is no consensus, there is a tendency to compare positive and negative outcomes and then evaluate welfare states as being good or bad for women. But it is more complex than this. In particular, on what scale is the state's effect to be judged and which criteria are to be used to evaluate the outcomes as good or bad? I would suggest two parameters: the degree of financial support offered to women and men in the context of the income inequalities that exist between them; and the consequences of state support for male/female power relations.

Conclusion: suggestions for a gender framework

If I have done my job properly in this chapter, I should have convinced even the more sceptical reader that there exist gendered elements in the welfare state which largely remain to be explored. One point brooks no ambiguity: the position of one sex in relation to the welfare state cannot be read off from that of the other. There is no shortage of indicators to suggest that the nature of female and male interactions with the welfare state differ substantially.

For the purpose of constructing a framework for exploring these gender dimensions, it may be helpful to differentiate between *explanandum*, and *explanans*. With regard to the former, I suggest that the most appropriate way of evaluating welfare states' gender outcomes is through their effects on: (a) resource-based relationships between women and men; and (b) female and male role constructions. Such indicators are sufficiently broad to facilitate cross-national comparison while at the same time liberating us from normative constructions such as dependence.

As *explanans*, I suggest that the welfare state should be conceived of in a threefold way: as a sphere of intervention, as a set of ideological practices and as a framework for redistribution. Adding considerations about relationships between and the resource capacities of women and men brings into the limelight hitherto overlooked elements in each case.

Let us first think of the welfare state as a two-dimensional form of intervention. There are two important angles here, roughly corresponding to the questions: intervention where? and with what? In terms of the former, I maintain that the family is an important site of welfare state intervention/interdependency and should, therefore, be inserted alongside the more familiar market/state nexus. In empirical terms, this means that public service provision deserves to rank alongside income maintenance programmes. Turning to the content of the welfare state, it seems to me that three functional areas are important: service provision, employment and the system of income maintenance. Their interactions are likely to be quite complex because all three are connected in a dynamic fashion.

In specific national contexts, an interesting comparative task would be to consider where the boundaries are drawn between the public, private and market spheres in relation to caring activities. Points of comparison here include to what extent and how state policies intervene to support different types of family activities, in the process affecting the commodification of male and female labour. Analytically, it is useful to differentiate welfare states on both the extent (how much) and nature (which kind of services are provided, whose caring labour is substituted) of their service involvement.

A second element of the welfare state which I emphasize is its ideological structure. Welfare embodies norms and values about appropriate activities and behaviour. This brings into focus welfare states' institutional structures and the specific imprints of policies. In this regard welfare states may be compared on the following indicators:

1 the range of risks covered and the extent to which income risks of women as well as those of men are covered;
2 the location of 'male' and 'female' risks; that is, whether in social insurance or means-tested assistance;
3 the conditions of entitlement to welfare and the rights attaching to caring as compared with those from earning;
4 the unit of entitlement and of calculation for different programmes;
5 the constructions of and proscriptions on female and male labour.

Utilizing such indicators enables us to explore the bases of both women's and men's claims to welfare, the ideological constructions underlying welfare, the extent of gender differentiation in access that is built into income maintenance programmes and the prevailing concept(s) of family or collective unit. Key empirical questions relate to the variations in the principles underpinning welfare in different states, the assumptions with regard to gender that are built into welfare and the type of family form and activity that is favoured.

Third, the welfare state can be regarded as a mechanism of redistribution – it redistributes both resources across different risk categories or groups and life chances in terms of the opportunities made available to members of society to effect a change in their circumstances. As we have seen, the circuits of redistribution to women may well be different from those to men. Women are involved in a triangle of income sources – the state, the market and men – whereas the state – market nexus defines men's income configuration.

In trying to elucidate the welfare state's role in this regard, the following are some important empirical indicators:

1 the range of cash supports provided for families and the type of family caring activities which they target;
2 wage or income replacement levels for all payments;

3 the construction of family payments and the level of payment for adult and child 'dependants' and to whom they are directed;
4 the fabric of conditions attaching to receipt of benefits, especially as they relate to labour market involvement of both partners.

What is of greatest importance here is how welfare states set up circuits of redistribution for men and women individually and as members of families.

This initial sketch of the possibilities inherent in the relationship between the welfare state and gender indicates, I suggest, a veritable Pandora's box of treasures for those who will but lift the lid.

Notes

1 In the realm of theory, Ann Orloff's 1993 paper on gender and the social rights of citizenship within a comparative perspective is one of the foremost attempts to integrate gender into one of the 'mainstream' perspectives on the welfare state. The paper suggests how the central concepts of the power resources approach to the welfare state can be broadened and new dimensions added to produce a gendered version of the model.

2 Feminist work, as well as placing women at the centre of the analysis, operated with the convictions that significant differences of interest exist between women and men and that women have been systematically disempowered by existing and past institutional arrangements. Moreover, men are regarded as prime beneficiaries of these arrangements. Work that focuses on women's position is not exclusively feminist. In the present discussion other relevant works include Jon Kolberg's (1991) analysis of the gender dimension of the Scandinavian welfare states, Christopher Pierson's (1991) consideration of the future of the welfare state and Norman Ginsburg's (1992) analysis of welfare divisions in Sweden, the Federal Republic of Germany, the United States and Britain.

3 Jill Quadagno (1987), Kees van Kersbergen (1991) and Christopher Pierson (1991) provide useful overviews of this literature.

4 In Norway, for instance, public authorities deliver less than one-fifth of the total volume of non-residential care (Kolberg, 1991: 132). Having estimated the total volume of non-paid caring work in Norway, Kolberg comments that the Scandinavian model is more than a welfare state; it remains a mixed economy at the empirical level (1991: 134–6).

5 So much so that Julia O'Connor (1993) suggests that the concept of personal autonomy (freedom from personal and/or public economic, social and personal dependency) should be used along with de-commodification in classifying regimes.

6 In light of this, Esping-Andersen's analysis, which was limited to employment, sickness and pension programmes, may also have been biased against a gender effect in this respect as well.

8

Men's Welfare State, Women's Welfare State: Tendencies to Convergence in Practice and Theory?

Lois Bryson, Michael Bittman and Sue Donath

In 1977, in a ground-breaking book, Elizabeth Wilson pointed to the inadequacy of any analysis of the welfare state which is not based on a satisfactory 'understanding of the position of women in modern society' (1977: 59). More than 15 years, and a substantial body of feminist literature later, we have a far better understanding of women's position in society, though as a number of the chapters in this book demonstrate, insights provided by feminist scholarship are not always heeded in mainstream (or as some feminists would term it 'malestream') theory and research on the welfare state.

Feminist writers have demonstrated the need to understand the welfare state as produced by a mix of state, market and family mechanisms. This is not something with which mainstream theory would disagree. The difference lies in the weight given to the three elements. Mainstream theorists have emphasized the relationship between the market and the state, while feminist theorists have emphasized the family. Because the family is recognized as funda-mental, feminist theory has been particularly concerned with the unpaid as well as the paid work of women, something which mainstream theory has virtually ignored (e.g. Brannen and Moss, 1988; Dalley, 1988; Finch and Groves, 1983; Hernes, 1987a; Leira, 1992; Waring, 1988). Current estimates put the value of this labour, consisting of unpaid domestic labour and non-market economic activity in the informal economy, at between 40 and 60 per cent of gross domestic product in Western countries (ABS, 1990), and confirm that most is done by women (Bittman, 1991; Waring, 1988). Given the sheer volume of unpaid labour it is surprising that we still lack a body of comparative research investigating the links between this non-market work, market work and different forms of social policy.

Any analysis of welfare states which is to be based on a satisfactory 'understanding of the position of women in modern society' must cover both forms of labour because while paid labour provides a key window on to the public sphere, unpaid labour allows us simultaneously to consider that traditionally undervalued work within the family or private sphere. Here we focus on the sites of market and family and investigate the extent to which gender equality is promoted in practice by state policies. This addresses the question of the degree of convergence of men's and women's welfare states in practice. We are also concerned with convergence in theory and the degree to which mainstream theory provides an adequate framework for addressing the issue of gender relations. That is, is there convergence of mainstream and feminist approaches?

Mainstream theory has largely treated the welfare state as a unitary concept, primarily focusing on welfare state provisions that support people outside the labour market, or to use the term popularized by Esping-Andersen (1990), provisions that de-commodify labour. Yet historically it is largely men who have been socially constructed as workers in the labour market. Women have historically been constructed as unpaid workers in families and approached by the welfare state on the basis of their family status. As a consequence, feminist analysis has identified a highly gendered dual system, in effect two welfare states: one which applies to men and one to women (Fraser, 1987; Bryson, 1992; Pateman, 1989b).

We approach mainstream theory via the typologies of welfare states which have been evolved over a number of decades through much research and theorizing (e.g. Marshall, 1950; Titmuss, 1963; Wilensky and Lebeaux, 1965; Mishra, 1990). As with a number of other contributors to this book, we draw particularly on the most recent work within this lineage, that of Esping-Andersen (1990). In his much-quoted analysis of capitalist welfare state regimes, Esping-Andersen recognizes the welfare state as having at its core the promotion of social citizenship, with rights granted 'on the basis of citizenship rather than performance'. He sees this as involving two major elements. First, the 'de-commodification of labour', that is providing a financial buffer for citizens when they are unable to support themselves on the labour market (that is they are unable to sell their labour as a commodity). Second, the promotion of equality through modifying the effects of social stratification. As he remarks, the aim of welfare policies is to ensure that 'one's status as a citizen will compete with, or even replace, one's class position' (Esping-Andersen, 1990: 21). Esping-Andersen does not explicitly raise the issue of whether citizenship status might replace gender as well as class position, though this is implied by his approach to social citizenship, and it is a point we consider here.

In this chapter we empirically and theoretically assess this form of mainstream welfare state theory and a feminist dual welfare states approach, through a study of time use in two countries which in mainstream theory are identified as having different types of social policy regimes. Our data are drawn from time use surveys, which have a long international history as a standardized research tool. The data are typically collected on the basis of a 24-hour diary, and because the diary covers all activities the data simultaneously provide a picture of respondents' involvement in paid and unpaid work.

Studying men's and women's welfare states

The data on paid and unpaid work on which the empirical analysis rests come from national time use surveys undertaken in 1987 in Australia and Finland. These countries have relatively similar levels of economic development, as well as a number of contrasting characteristics which render them valuable sites for the comparative study of the links between gender and welfare state regimes.

When assessed in terms of gross domestic product, Australia is ranked ninth and Finland thirteenth on the United Nation's Human Development Index (UN, 1991b: 119). There is similarity too, in the position of women and men in their respective labour markets, each of which displays marked horizontal and vertical segregation. For example, at the time of the surveys, 71 per cent of the female labour force in both Australia and Finland were employed in the private sector, while 57 per cent of Australian and 56 per cent of Finnish women were employed in three industry classifications: wholesale/ retail, restaurant and hotels; financing, insurance, real estate and business services; community, social and personal services (Affirmative Action Agency, 1987; Central Statistical Office of Finland, 1991).

Although Australia has a slight edge in economic development, Finland is ahead in social development. Finland made a relatively late move from a highly agricultural economy but is now regularly classified in mainstream analysis as a social democratic welfare state, along with other Scandinavian countries. Australia, on the other hand, is regularly classified with other English-speaking nations as having an underdeveloped welfare state of the liberal variety (Esping-Andersen, 1990), though Castles and Mitchell (1992) suggest it has been more 'radical' than most because of the historic strength of its labour movement.

The two countries display quite different female labour force participation rates, however, as is revealed by Jallinoja's classification of prevailing family systems in 14 nations. When female labour force participation is over 70 per cent, Jallinoja classifies a nation as having a pattern of 'egalitarian families'. Finland alone among non-communist countries corresponds to this 'egalitarian' pattern, and has had such a pattern since 1970. Those countries in which the majority of younger married women are housewives she refers to as having a 'traditional' family system and in 1980 identified only Italy and the Netherlands as exhibiting this pattern. In the third, and largest, group of 'moderate' countries, women are frequently employed part time, and because family norms require a full-time mother, rather than a full-time housewife, women have 'some sort of career'. On this basis Australia had a 'traditional' family pattern in 1960 but shifted to 'moderate' in 1970, where it has remained (Jallinoja, 1989: 107–9).

Given a degree of similarity in economic development and a degree of difference in social development, Australia and Finland provide a convenient location within which to initially consider the links between market, state and family mechanisms and the implications of these links for our understanding of men's and women's position within welfare states, both on the ground and in theory. Clearly, however, comparing only two countries has limitations. In particular, the addition of an example of Esping-Andersen's third type of corporatist welfare state regime to our examples of social democratic and liberal welfare states would strengthen the analysis. Nonetheless, this initial comparison does allow us to come to grips with key issues and to assess the value of focusing on unpaid as well as paid labour for both empirical and theoretical purposes.

Convergence in practice? Women's and men's time use in Australia and Finland

The market – time spent in paid labour

Not surprisingly, when we consider time spent in paid work in the two nations (Table 8.1) we find a very gendered pattern. Excluding breaks at work and travel, Australian men work the longest hours, 1.63 hours per week more than their Finnish counterparts. Given that the figures are averaged over the population, it can reasonably be claimed that these shorter hours for men represent an index of a more advanced Finnish welfare state. In Esping-Andersen's terms, Finnish men's labour is more effectively de-commodified. However, of greater import for our task is the comparison of men's and women's patterns. Men's hours of paid work actually provide the point at which the two nations most closely resemble each other. The contrast between the sexes is much more dramatic. The cross-national difference in the hours Finnish and Australian women spend in paid

Table 8.1 *Time spent in paid and unpaid work*
(weighted population means – hours per week)

	Women	Men	Gender gap
	PAID WORK		
Australia	13.65	28.93	−15.28
Finland	18.55	27.30	−8.75
National gap	−4.90	1.63	6.53
	UNPAID WORK		
Australia	33.02	15.40	17.62
Finland	25.78	15.17	10.61
National gap	7.24	0.23	7.01
	PAID AND UNPAID WORK		
Australia	46.67	44.33	2.34
Finland	44.33	42.47	1.86
National gap	2.34	1.86	0.48

Source: The table (and all the data on time use drawn on in this chapter) is based on a secondary analysis of data from Time Use Surveys undertaken by the Bureaus of Statistics of Australia and Finland in 1987

employment is three times larger and the trend is in the opposite direction. Finnish women work considerably longer hours (just under five hours more) than do Australian women. Hence while the mainstream focus on the de-commodification effects of state policies does offer an explanation of the quite small national difference for men, it is silent on the much greater difference between men and women.

The difference between women across the two nations is overshadowed by the gap between the sexes within both countries. The most profound difference is between time spent in paid work by Australian women and men, this being almost double the gap for Finland. The dramatic differences between women's and men's patterns support an analytic approach which does place these differences at centre stage. The fact that such differences are largely ignored in mainstream theory can only be interpreted as a result of their being naturalized and thus taken for granted, hardly an adequate theoretical response.

Figure 8.1 plots the time devoted to paid work by women and men in both countries in hours per week according to age, when other major factors (marital status, day of week, education, age of youngest child) are held constant.[1] This graphically shows that, while marked differences remain, there is far greater convergence of gender patterns in Finland. The graph lines for Australia are likely to have moved somewhat closer together since 1987, as Australian

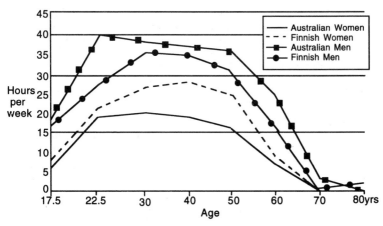

Figure 8.1   *Time spent in paid work by age, hours per week, 1987*

Source: adjusted Multiple Classification Analysis (MCA) figures

women increasingly participate in paid work while men's workforce participation has been slowly decreasing. Nonetheless, the change is far from sufficient to alter the general picture.

A dramatic and highly gendered effect is exerted on paid work time by age of youngest child. This is significantly[2] related to both Australian and Finnish women's labour force participation, but not to men's in either country. Not surprisingly, age of youngest child has its largest influence when the youngest is less than 5 years of age (see Figure 8.2). This reduces Australian women's paid work participation to 17 per cent, and Finnish women's to 44 per cent, of its average value. Men remain relatively unaffected by both the presence and age of children. These divergent effects reinforce the appropriateness of distinguishing between men's and women's welfare states.

Marriage is associated with significantly reduced labour force participation for Australian, but not for Finnish women, while it is associated with a significant increase in paid work for Finnish men. While gendered patterns remain overall, and Finnish women's careers are disrupted by motherhood, they are far less affected than their Australian counterparts and there is no evidence that their careers are diminished by marriage *per se*. This reduced effect of ascribed roles and greater gender convergence in Finland suggests that more generalized social citizenship has been achieved and confirms Finland as a more developed welfare state. But the Finnish situation is still a far cry from gender equality, and from the point of view of mainstream analysis, the convergence is brought about by the greater commodification of women's labour, rather than its de-commodification, as Esping-Andersen's analysis would imply.

There are clearly more barriers to women's absorption into the full-time labour force in Australia. These barriers can be traced back to the strength of traditional patterns, or what Esping-Andersen would call pre-commodified family values. They are also due to the lingering effects of historic processes through which the labour movement achieved a family wage which effectively aimed to remove married women from the workforce. This history adds weight to the proposition that welfare states need to be approached as dual-gendered systems.

Australia's underdeveloped liberal welfare state has proved less successful than the social democratic Finnish welfare state in overcoming barriers to women's workforce participation. In social democratic regimes, according to Esping-Andersen, 'the ideal is not to maximize dependence on the family but capacities for individual independence' (1990: 28). Certainly Finland is closer to this ideal than is Australia. Where women are in the full-time workforce in Australia, however, their pay rates are closer to men's than in Finland, an effect attributable to the flow on effects from a strong centralized industrial regulation system, achieved largely by a strong male labour movement. Around the time of the surveys, full-time Finnish women workers earned on average 71 per cent of men's earnings, while the figure for Australian women was 79 per cent. This rate was diminished to 66 per cent, however, when all Australian women workers were included, because of a rate of 40 per cent in part-time work (Affirmative Action Agency, 1987: 1). In Finland only 10 per cent of women workers were employed part time (Niemi and Paakkonen, 1990: 22).

What accounts for the greater convergence of gender patterns in Finland? A quick and late transition from a highly agricultural economy, in which women were traditionally centrally involved, has been an important factor, but that history is beyond the scope of this chapter. What we will focus on are the current effects of the more highly developed welfare state. As is discussed more fully later, Finland has well developed maternity/family policies and extensive provision of childcare and, unlike other Scandinavian social democratic welfare states, Finnish social policy does not encourage women into part-time employment. These well developed childcare provisions not only underpin far higher levels of paid labour than in Australia, but also effectively reduce the burden of unpaid work.

The family – time spent in unpaid work

If we consider the average total time devoted to producing non-market goods and services at home – cooking, cleaning, laundry, childcare, shopping and garden/house/car maintenance we find, not unexpectedly, that for both countries the distribution is the obverse of that for paid work, with women doing far more than men (see Table 8.1). The mean weekly unpaid work time of Australian women, at 33 hours, is by far the highest. Finnish women spend 22 per cent less (just under 26 hours). Australian women's unpaid labour time is also higher than the highest average amount of paid work time, which is 29 hours for Australian men (see Table 8.1). The gap between women's and men's hours within the nations is substantially larger than the same gender gaps across the national boundaries, and is even larger than for paid work, suggesting that unpaid work is a particularly fruitful area for study. There is virtually no difference between the countries in men's unpaid work times. The striking difference between the sexes again highlights the inadequacy of a unitary approach.

When unpaid and paid work are added together, the differences between women and men and between the nations are reduced markedly. Nonetheless, in both countries women remain worse off in terms of total average time expended in work per week. However merely to respond to total time expended would be to ignore the social context of the activities. It is clear that in both countries market labour activity provides far greater economic, power and status rewards than does domestic labour. There is also evidence that such labour is broadly preferred over many of the tasks involved in domestic labour (Berk and Berk, 1979: 230). Our time use analysis is also focused only on primary activities. This is likely to underestimate women's contribution more than men's because multiple activities are more often recorded in the home than the workplace and women's leisure activities more often overlap with domestic labour. In addition it has been suggested that women take their home role to work with them because they cannot readily escape their domestic managerial role. It has been suggested that women perform their family and market labour roles simultaneously, while men do this sequentially (Wolcott, 1986), which means that women's work time has a greater intensity.

As with paid work, unpaid work provides a clear index of the greater convergence of women's and men's time use patterns in Finland. This is certainly not accounted for by Finnish men doing more unpaid work than their Australian counterparts. Progress towards gender equality in Finland seems to have come from a reduction of time spent in unpaid labour by women. A similar effect

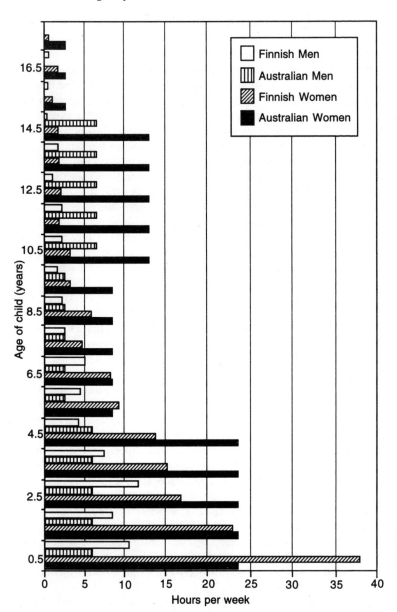

Figure 8.2   *Hours per week spent in face-to-face childcare, by age of youngest child, 1987*

is found in Australia among women in full-time employment who reduce their unpaid labour time even though their partners do not do appreciably more.

When major time-consuming tasks are separately examined, for example cooking, laundry and childcare, each reflects the overall pattern. Full-time employment reduces the amount of time devoted to each task and it is striking that part-time employment has relatively little effect. Laundry proves something of a test of the segregation of domestic labour, since on average the time women in both countries spend on this task is nine times that of men. Australian women between the ages of 35 and 44 spend over 15 times longer on laundry, ironing and clothes care than Australian men, and Finnish men manage to do even less laundry than their Australian counterparts. For both cooking and laundry, the time commitment of women increases significantly upon marriage and diminishes when they are separated, widowed or divorced. The opposite is the case for men: their time reduces on marriage and increases when they are separated, widowed or divorced. Clearly these are tasks that are assigned on a traditional ascribed gender basis. Harking back to Esping-Andersen's second core element of welfare states and substituting gender for class, we must conclude that 'status as citizen' does not 'compete with or even displace' gender position in responsibility for unpaid work.

The pattern for childcare also conforms to the broad picture for other unpaid work, with Australian women expending most time, followed by Finnish women. Having a child below 5 years of age greatly increases the time spent in childcare, especially by Finnish women. Men have a pattern of three to four times lower involvement in childcare, with Finnish men being involved least overall. Finnish men remain on a plateau of about 10 hours per week until the child reaches the age of 3, when direct face-to-face care gradually diminishes, so that by the time children reach 10 years, it is less than two hours a week (see Figure 8.2), though by this stage Finnish women's contribution is much the same. For both Finnish and Australian men, working life is barely interrupted by the appearance of a new child. Unlike their Australian counterparts, however, and thanks to the Finnish state, when Finnish men become parents it does not mean that their spouses will be as burdened by the responsibilities of care as are Australian mothers. This is due largely to the provisions of the Finnish welfare state. Finnish women's rights as citizens do modify the effects of their gender position.

Policy differences and their effects

Differences between the amount of unpaid work that Australian and Finnish women do must largely be seen against the greater rate of participation of Finnish women in full-time employment and the childcare policies which facilitate this. The importance of this explanation is underscored by the fact that women in full-time paid work in Australia also reduce the time they spend on domestic labour. Yet there remain some differences that cannot be explained in this way. Take for instance the extra time Australian women, even those in full-time employment, spend doing laundry. The explanation for at least part of this difference (and other differences) lies in cultural and lifestyle patterns. Australian families mostly live in detached houses and use outdoor clothes-lines for the drying of clothes, something which increases laundry time.

Different social policy settings with respect to childcare are, however, fundamental and account for a major part of the observed differences (see Figure 8.2). Such policies are effective beyond just reducing direct childcare time because cooking and cleaning time, for example, are also reduced if chidren are cared for away from home for a significant part of the day. From a theoretical perspective, such explanations of the effect of welfare state provisions run counter to the emphasis of mainstream theorizing. Rather than being aimed at de-commodifying labour, such policies, in allowing women to join the labour market, are aimed at its commodification and simultaneously affect patterns of domestic labour.

Provisions for childcare confirm mainstream assessments of the Finnish welfare state as the more developed. In 1987 childcare facilities in Australia far from met demand, with only 37 per cent of children catered for, compared with 78 per cent of Finnish children (Huttunen and Tamminen, 1989; ABS 1992). And even this figure of 37 per cent can mislead, because some care is only partial, for example one day per week. Over the past decade provisions have greatly improved, a clear move to facilitate the commodification of women's labour. Even so, in 1990, 29 per cent of the parents of preschoolers claimed that their demands for formal childcare were unmet (Australian Bureau of Statistics, 1992: 58).

Nor are most Australian women compensated when they care for their child themselves. Unpaid maternity leave, usually of one year, has been a right for all women workers for about a decade. Effectively this means merely that a job must be kept available for a mother's return to the workforce. From 1991 unpaid leave became available to fathers under similar conditions to those for mothers. Relatively few women are entitled to paid maternity leave. Most who are, are employed in the public service. After the period of unpaid leave there is no entitlement to shorter working hours, though acceptance of this practice is growing. Even so, such shorter hours are not recompensed and, like most maternity and all paternity leave, this does not represent a de-commodified right in the sense used by Esping-Andersen. In the absence of a replacement of earnings, a mother's (or father's) dependence rather than independence is assumed.

In contrast to Australia (particularly in 1987), Finland has a well developed network of services and provision which met the needs of about four-fifths of the parents who were employed in 1988, with the bulk of places as long daycare of 8–10 hours a day (Huttunen and Tamminen, 1989: 7). Expectant mothers in Finland are eligible for a government grant of three months' maternity leave at full replacement of their previous pay. All parents are granted a further seven and a half months' parental leave at 80 per cent of previous earnings. Parents can divide this leave so that the father's share is up to but not exceeding six and a half months. In practice only 5 per cent of fathers take up this opportunity but, as occurs in other countries with similar provisions, most take the available 12 days off work after the birth of their child (Huttunen and Tamminen, 1989: 10).

After the expiry of maternity/paternity leave, parents are entitled to care leave until their child reaches the age of 3. Employers whose employees choose to take this leave must guarantee the employee her/his job for the duration of the leave, but they forfeit their salary. They are then eligible for a homecare allowance – a cash benefit equivalent to the costs incurred by the state in the provision of municipal daycare. Parents can decide whether to pay for private daycare or to claim the benefit in respect of their own caring activity. Parents of children under 4 years of age and children just beginning school also qualify for state-compensated reduced working hours. Parents can choose to reduce their working day by two hours, either from the beginning or the end of the day, and are eligible for compensation for this time (up to 325 Fmk – US$75 – per month in 1989). The quality of childcare services is regulated and private day centres, which are subsidized by the state, must conform to the state standards (Huttunen and Tamminen, 1989).

The generous maternity/paternity leave available during the child's first year, universal coverage, and reluctant fathers, combine to ensure that most Finnish children are cared for by their mothers for the first year of their life (see Figure 8.2). Childcare as a primary activity halves for Finnish women at the end of this period as a large proportion return to work, despite the availability of a substantial benefit to those who stay at home to care for their children. After the first 24 months of the child's life, Finnish mothers' time spent in direct primary childcare begins to more closely resemble that of Finnish fathers and continues to fall until children reach school age (7 years of age). Thereafter there is an even closer convergence.

The patterns of time spent in childcare show distinctive gender and national patterns (see Figure 8.2). For Finnish women these very clearly mirror the state provisions, and relatively similar time is spent on childcare regardless of whether they are employed full time or part time; this indicates that childcare is provided on a more universal basis. In Australia, demonstrated need and rationing are factors, and if a woman is not actually working away from home she almost invariably cares for her children herself.

Conclusion

It is clear that as women's labour has become increasingly commodified there has been a convergence of the patterns of men's and women's market positions. Even here, though, the process is far from complete as the higher average hours of paid work of men, highly sex-segregated workforces and lower wages for women illustrate. The importance of gender shows up very clearly in our cross-national comparison in the fact that Finnish and Australian men's patterns of time spent in paid work are far more similar than they are to the women in their own countries. When we turn to the family site, through the study of unpaid work, evidence of convergence of gender patterns is minimal. Again though, men's patterns across countries are uncannily close, far closer than they are to the patterns for the opposite sex within their own country. Nonetheless, there remain considerable national differences for women, and it is clear that welfare state regimes do have an effect. The childcare facilities provided by the social democratic Finnish welfare state do reduce women's unpaid workload in the childcare area, and this spills over to an extent to other aspects of unpaid labour, though these are less affected.

While Esping-Andersen's typology acknowledges the significance of family policy and while it does have some value for understanding the patterns of time use we found, it cannot take us far in understanding gender relations. It would be expected, on the basis of the mainstream analysis, that social democratic welfare state regimes which rely on universalistic principles would promote the greatest allocation of women's time to labour market activities and exhibit the smallest differences between men and women in the domestic sphere. Our results are consistent with this, even though very significant gender differences remain. Further analysis is obviously necessary before we could comment on the full typology of capitalist welfare states or on non-capitalist regimes, where both high female labour force participation and high domestic labour responsibilities have been the pattern.

While this initial comparison of only two nations is not adequate to make broad claims, it is clear that mainstream analysis cannot fully illuminate the relationship between the sexes. The simultaneous analysis of social policy regimes, domestic labour patterns and labour market involvement has far greater potential to cast light on gender relations and social citizenship. Despite their very different welfare state regimes and obvious historical and social policy differences, Finland and Australia both still display very gendered patterns of paid and unpaid work. The patterns for women, on average, in the two countries more closely resemble each other than they do the patterns of their male co-citizens. On top of this, the national differences between the patterns for women are very much greater than for men.

It is transparently clear that a particularly telling way of approaching the comparative study of welfare state regimes is through women's rather than men's situations. Because of the more marked differences, this offers a more promising site for the study of social citizenship than the classic site, which has been the position of the male worker/citizen. At the very least our analysis suggests that understanding the nature of welfare states and forming typologies requires greater convergence of mainstream and feminist approaches. At a minimum what is required is a gendered approach through the conjoint analysis of women's and men's welfare states.

Notes

This study was supported by a grant from the Australian Research Council.

1 Multiple Classification Analysis (MCA) was employed to control for variables with a known influence on time use. This technique is derived from regression analysis and is used throughout the world by national statistical agencies for the multivariate analysis of time use data.

2 In the discussion of MCA effects, 'significant' denotes significant at the 0.05 level or better.

9

German Pension Insurance, Gendered Times and Stratification

Kirsten Scheiwe

The analysis of stratification in mainstream comparative welfare state analysis has centred on class, occupation and status. Mainstream researchers have characterized the German pension regime as 'status maintenance' of different classes of employees according to their status as blue-collar, white-collar employees or civil servants based on occupational performance and earnings (Esping-Andersen *et al.*, 1988; Esping-Andersen, 1990). Joakim Palme (1990) has categorized German pension insurance as a typical example of the 'income maintenance' category, where the preservation of a proportion of former earnings is more important than providing a general needs-oriented minimum or 'basic security'. However, the gender system as an interacting stratifying structure is ignored in these (pension) regime typologies which focus nearly exclusively on the interaction of the market and the state. Mainstream analysis does not analyse the interdependent family system in any depth, and it fails to consider how pension regimes recognize care activities, unpaid work or family status in varying ways. No attention is paid to marriage as a traditionally important alternative social security institution to provide old age income for women; and entitlements based on marriage (or cohabitation) are not included as an element of the 'public–private pension mix'.

Although some welfare state regime typologies are in my view open to being 'gendered' (Bussemaker and van Kersbergen, Chapter 2 in this volume), this has scarcely been done for pension regimes. Women have sometimes been 'counted in',[1] as Mary Daly (Chapter 7 in this volume) characterizes the limited recognition of gender at the level of outcomes. Recently more comparative empirical work on elderly women and poverty has been published (for example Hutton and Whiteford, 1992; Sørensen, 1992). Little attention has been paid to embedded *gender structures and institutional features* that contribute to different outcomes for women and men. Research including the importance of institutions has mainly been limited to single-country analysis.[2] I propose to take up the question of how social rights to old age income are provided through the interrelated systems of the market, the state and the family and how 'work merit' is recognized not only as employment participation, but also as care work. Disadvantages stemming from involvement in care activities are not the same under all pension regimes. The disadvantages are different in pension systems based on need, on citizenship (or residence) or on employment participation. Pension systems which provide minimum pensions or flat-rate pensions are less male biased than occupational or strictly employment-related public pension systems.

In this chapter I deal with the gender dimension of the German pension system and how the 'time frame' enshrined in institutional rules affects pension differences between women and men. First, I focus on gendered outcomes by examining how social rights to old age income are provided through the interrelated systems of the market, the state and the family. Second, besides looking at gender stratification I analyse the interaction of gender and class in the German pension regime. Third, I compare pension outcomes of the former West Germany and the ex-GDR.

My analytical framework takes time seriously. The analysis of gendered time models is used to counter the market and employement bias inherent in mainstream theory. Mainstream theory has focused predominantly on money flows and cash transfers from the market and the state to employees. Money matters, but not only as a reward for market-related activities. Instead I argue that *time* is another basic resource of crucial importance, which is distributed in a highly uneven fashion (Bryson *et al.*, Chapter 8 in this volume), and financially compensated unequally and in a gendered and hierarchical way. All welfare states have implemented policies which reward certain uses of time, or what I term *time policies*: these policies and regulations affect time patterns in the market, the public sector, civil society and the family. Access to labour law protection and social insurance rights is often shaped by time requirements such as minimum working hours, duration and continuity of employment or contribution periods.

Two types of time models can be envisaged. I call these *female and male times*. Underlying them are different expectations about gender roles and the division of labour. One type assumes full availability for paid work on time schedules that inhibit simultaneous fulfilment of caring responsibilities outside employment, since continuous, life-long employment and full-time work with upward time flexibility are assumed. The other type relates to larger time investments in unpaid care activities and servicing work outside the labour market (family law is strongly involved here) and to discontinuous time patterns of employment or substandard working hours (Scheiwe, 1991, 1993).

Besides the well-researched stratification based on occupation and status, time policies and their institutionalization should be analysed as stratification systems in their own right which interact with other dimensions. I apply the concept of *institutionalized 'gendered times'* to analyse how the time factor plays a role in access to social rights and insurance benefits through minimum working hours, contribution periods, continuity of employment or other time thresholds. These are especially important in German social insurance regulation. 'Female times' are particularly disadvantaged by the strong labour market ties of benefits and by special requirements of length and continuity of employment, inadequate recognition of childcare periods and disincentives in social security provisions and tax law which put a premium on marriage but penalize full-time employment of married women. If one takes social rights as a criterion for comparative welfare state analysis, the analysis of the underlying 'time frame' can be a useful category to discover the gender dimension comparatively.

The time factor in German pension insurance

If one differentiates national pension schemes according to the criterion of whether the time factor plays no role, a minor role or an important one, the German system definitely falls within the latter group. Time is a key factor in explaining gender differences in access to retirement pensions and pension differences between women and men. This also affects retirement age: contrary to popular belief, women retire later than men.

Comparative research has shown that Germany is the extreme case where pensions are strictly contribution and earnings related without provision of minimum pensions. On the basis of the length of contribution period required for a full pension in 1985, Palme (1990: 53) distinguishes three groups. Some countries have no such conditions; in the second group the number of contribution years is relatively short and does not exceed 35 years (Ireland, Sweden); and in the third group more than 35 years are needed for a full pension (Austria, Germany, France, Italy, Switzerland, the United States). Germany is the leader of the third group, with 45 years of contributions required for a full pension. Gabriele Rolf and Gert Wagner (1992) locate national pension systems along a continuum where at one end the individual's employment record plays no role in access to pensions (such as the Dutch and Danish 'people's pension'), and at the opposite end the pension system is neatly tied to the employment career, with Germany as a forerunner of the latter group.

Time politics is enshrined in various institutional rules under pension law as

minimum working hours for compulsory insurance;
contribution periods and insurance years for entitlement to pensions;
pension age;
continuity requirements and treatment of employment interruptions;
treatment of care times; child credits;
time factor in pension benefit calculation.

The gender effects of such rules can vary according to changing behavioural patterns, but here I am concerned with effects related to special institutional features.

Time thresholds

A time threshold for access to compulsory pension insurance is imposed by a *minimum working hours* requirement. This excludes part-time employees working fewer than 15 hours per week and earning less than DM 560 (£212) a month (1994). This time threshold also bars part-time employees from access to sickness insurance; while compulsory unemployment insurance requires at least 18 working hours per week. Employers save considerably on insurance contributions, while workers in this employment category – mainly women – are excluded from benefits. This highly gendered construction has been challenged as indirect discrimination against women under EC law on equal treatment in social security; a few cases are pending before the European Court of Justice. A similar German labour law rule that excluded part-timers with under 10 hours per week from statutory sick pay by the employer has already been judged as an infringement of EC law.[3]

German pension law envisages a *typical work career of 45 years* full-time employment at an average wage level reflected in male earnings. Deviations, such as most care-related employment interruptions or part-time work, are penalized by a lower pension, or possible loss of those types of pensions which require long contributory periods. As long as retirement age for women and men was different (65 years for men, 60 years for women), women's ideal pension career was five years shorter and lasted 40 years. The Pension Reform Act 1992 equalized pension ages, set at 65 years irrespective of sex for all persons retiring after the year 2010. This typical work career is very long compared to other countries, although the average *contribution period* required to get a full pension has been extended over the last decades in all pension systems. Palme (1990: 53), who analyses data from 18 OECD countries, shows that on average 13 years in 1960 were sufficient, while in 1985 26 years were needed.

The underlying philosophy of the German 'income security' pension regime is that pensions should substitute for earnings over one's lifetime. Since 1957, pension benefits have been indexed to the average wages of the economically active population and adjusted yearly. This has contributed to a substantial reduction in old age poverty in Germany, but the gender gap in old age poverty has survived. The replacement rate of a standard pension amounted to 68.5 per cent of average net wages (1993) after 45 insurance years. Since pensions are strictly based on 'work merit' and calculated on the basis of contribution periods and former earnings, access to different pension types and the benefit structure display a high degree of inequalities. Gender stratification is a striking feature among pension recipients.

Gendered tracks into different pension types

The public pension system consists of invalidity pensions and of different old age pension categories:

    normal old age retirement at 65 years;
    flexible retirement at 63;
    early retirement at the age of 60 for the unemployed;
    old age retirement for women at the age of 60;
    old age retirement of disabled employees at 60.

Insurance and contribution periods required for access to old age pensions vary between 35 and five years (Table 9.1).

Women less frequently than men meet substantial time require-ments, and this results in gendered tracks into different pension types. An inspection of Table 9.2 reveals that nearly half of all female retirees in 1988 left the labour market with a normal old age pension at the age of 65 which requires only five years' insurance, while only 17.8 per cent of new male pensioners did. By contrast, the most important category for men was invalidity pensions; nearly 40 per cent of men – mainly blue-collar workers – fell into this category, compared to 17.7 per cent of women. Although only five years' insurance are required, the additional qualifying condition of three years' compulsory contributions paid before the event of disablement bars many women from access, especially those with children who interrupted employment.[4]

Table 9.1 *Pension types and eligibility rules*

Retirement type	Pension age	For whom?	Time requirements
Invalidity pensions		Occupational or generally disabled employees	5 years' insurance; during the last 5 years before the event of invalidity at least 3 years obligatory contributions paid
Early retirement for unemployed	60 years	Unemployed	One year unemployment during the last 1.5 years; at least 8 years' obligatory contributions paid during the last 20 years
Early retirement for women	60 years	Women	15 years' insurance; at least 10 years' obligatory contributions paid during the last 20 years
Flexible old age pension for disabled employees	60 years	Disabled employees	35 years' insurance
Flexible old age pension for long insured	63 years	All insured	35 years' insurance
Normal old age pension	65 years	All insured	5 years' insurance

While the majority of male pensioners in 1988 had left the labour market at the latest at the age of 60, nearly half of all female retirees had worked until the age of 65. It is certainly not the better health of women which explains this difference.

Gender differences in insurance periods

The average number of insurance years reveals large differences between women and men, and between white-collar and blue-collar employees. In 1988 male pensioners had on average 10 insurance years more than their female counterparts if they had been white-collar employees, and 14 years more in the case of manual workers (Table 9.3).

While the average male employee in the FRG had acquired 36 years of pension insurance by the age of 55, women at the same age were insured only for 28 years. The requirement of 35 insurance years

Table 9.2 *New pension beneficiaries in 1988, by pension type, age and sex*

Pension age	Pension type	Male pensioners 100%	Female pensioners 100%
60 years or older	Invalidity pension	38.5	17.8
	Early retirement pension for unemployed	13.1	1.4
60 years or older	Early retirement pension for women		30.5
60 years	Old age pensions for disabled employees	12.6	0.9
63 years	Flexible old-age pension	17.9	1.3
65 years	Normal old-age pension	17.9	48.1

Source: *Bundesarbeitsblatt* 1(1990): 7

was fulfilled in 1988 by 68.8 per cent of men, but by only 21.9 per cent of women (*Pension Report*, 1989). In all old age pension categories requiring 35 insurance years, the proportion of all male beneficiaries is at least ten times as high as the respective share of female retirees (Table 9.2). In 1991, three-quarters of all male pensioners, but only one-quarter of the female retirees had more than 30 insurance years. The average insurance period among all female pensioners in 1992 was 21.6 years for women and 38.7 years for men in the former West Germany (*Pension Report*, 1993).

Pension age: women retire later than men

Contrary to popular belief, employed women retire later than men. Table 9.4, which presents the pension ages of new retirees in the late 1980s, shows that nearly half of the women compared to less than one-fifth of the men were 65 years or older when they retired.

This outcome appears to be an effect of first, women's disadvantages in access to earlier retirement pensions as a result of shorter insurance periods and, second, of female employees' decisions to extend their employment beyond the retirement age of 60 for financial reasons; they continue to augment their low pension entitlements. Low pensions are a combined effect of shorter contribution periods and low pay. These two factors, time and earnings, are of crucial importance in the German pension calculation formula. For women, this can be a vicious circle: mothers interrupt employment more often than fathers, since their earnings losses are smaller, and

Table 9.3 *Average insurance years of retired women and men in 1988*

	Average number of insured years		Pensions based on more than 40 years' insurance as a % of all old age pensions	
	Blue-collar pension insurance	White-collar pension insurance	Blue-collar pension insurance	White-collar pension insurance
Women	22.2	27.1	8.0	19.0
Men	36.1	37.6	52.8	57.4

Source: *Pension Report 1988*, BT-Drucksache 11/3735: 61ff.

these interruptions bring about human capital losses and relatively lower wages when they re-enter the labour market, or penalties for part-time work,[5] and this leads to lower pensions.

Usually, these differences are explained by behavioural differences: women interrupt employment more often than men because of their domestic tasks, and the labour force attachment especially of married women and older cohorts is lower. At face value, this is true, but simply descriptive: it does not question the social construction of gendered institutional rules. As Jill Quadagno has pointed out in her historical analysis of US pension eligibility rules, women's failure to meet these requirements is not merely a function of their dual family and work roles:

> No automatic causal link exists between lack of benefits and discontinuous career patterns. Instead the price that women pay in the market for their domestic labour is a social construction. . . . Penalizing women in old age for family responsibilities that create irregular work histories is a *political* decision. (Quadagno, 1988: 555ff.)

A look at the different treatment of various employment interruptions and its male bias backs up this argument.

Table 9.4 *Pension age of men and women retiring in 1988*

Pension age	Male pensioners 100%	Female pensioners 100%
54 and younger	17	8
55 to 59	15	7
60	22	27
61 to 64	28	9
65	16	41
Older than 65	2	8

Source: *Bundesarbeitsblatt* 1(1990): 17

Breaks in employment: 'male times' privileged over 'female times'

Certain employment interruptions are treated more favourably under pension law than others. A systematic analysis reveals that these cases relate more frequently to male life circumstances. German pension law provides coverage for interruptions in employment, such as military service, registered unemployment, university studies and training periods after the age of 16, sickness and so on. These complex provisions formerly included various forms of direct sex discrimination.[6] But even after the abolition of discriminatory rules, 'male times' are treated more favourably than 'care times'. Periods of military service during the war, of imprisonment or of expatriation before or immediately after 1945 are recognized as insurance periods and evaluated on the basis of 90 per cent of former gross income. The same calculation formula is applied to other interruptions due to sickness, disablement or rehabilitation measures (including anti-drug or anti-alcohol treatment). Registered unemployment and disablement of persons in receipt of insurance benefits are recognized as contribution periods calculated on the basis of 80 per cent of former gross earnings. These interruptions, experienced more frequently by men, are covered by on average higher pension credits or recognized for longer periods than 'care times'.

How are breaks in employment treated when they relate to female life circumstances? There are various ways in which the welfare state can compensate women for *care periods under pension schemes*. Systems that grant minimum pensions based on citizenship or residence provide a general coverage of earnings-free periods. Flat-rate pensions in contributory schemes may have the same effect. Under 'employment merit' oriented pension systems with lower time requirements for access to a full pension where pensions are calculated on the basis of earnings in a certain number of years (for example, 20 years in France), employees can choose 'the best years', and women may eliminate those years when they reduced or interrupted employment. Another possibility is to grant child credits or care credits. The traditional solution of linking compensation for women's unpaid work to marriage under private law and to grant derived rights (survivors' pensions) to the widows of properly insured men will be discussed later.

Until 1986, *care periods* were acknowledged as contribution periods only in the case of statutory maternity leave. During this relatively short period (14 weeks) contribution payments for the employed mother continued. A longer maternity leave that existed from 1979 to 1983 continued for a further four months and was evaluated only with about 30 per cent of average earnings. In 1986 pension credits of one year per child for the caring parent were introduced, and later the child credit was extended to three years per child born after 1992. Pension contributions are granted at the level of 75 per cent of average salaries. The fact that contributions do not total 100 per cent of the average contributions has caused harsh criticism and has also been questioned by the German Federal Constitutional Court. Child credits can be granted to every mother/father independent of employment status. However, the regulations contain several disincentives for a mother to continue her employment during the first three years after the birth of a child, since her own pension contributions and the child credit cannot be added together. If she already pays contributions at the level of 75 per cent or more of average salaries, she gains nothing from childcare credits. If her own contributions are lower, only the difference up to the 75 per cent level will be covered through the credits. The 'double burden' of a working mother is not recognized by allowing her to accumulate own entitlements and child credits. Instead an implicit gendered norm – 'the mother of a child under three should stay at home' – underlies the 1986 parental leave package implemented by the Christian Democrat/Liberal government.

If one calculates how much these child credits pay, they can result in a maximum monthly increase of DM 28 (£11) per child born before 1992 and somewhat more for a child born later, but exact estimates are difficult. It depends on the personal pension biography. The effect of child credits for entitled female pensioners in 1991 was that insurance pensions increased on average by DM 64.20 (£26) per month – a small sum which might suffice to buy a monthly ticket for public transport in a big German city. Besides the criticism of the disincentives for female employment built into child credit regulations, it has been pointed out that child credits are totally insuffficient to compensate for the pension losses due to longer interruptions or to part-time work, as simulations for several model female work careers with different income chances have shown (Rolf, 1991).

Other *care times* have not been acknowledged under pension law, with two minor exceptions introduced recently. First, childcare periods can be taken into account to remedy continuity gaps which might bar mothers who interrupted employment from access to *invalidity pensions*. A close time nexus between the event of disablement and the last contribution payment is required (see Table 9.1). Mothers who interrupted employment were covered only until the age of 6 of a child born before 1992; this has now been prolonged until the age of 11 of the youngest child. It should be mentioned that no such thing as a disability pension for housewives, as in the UK or Norway, exists in Germany.[7] Childcare periods up to the age of 10 of the child can also be taken into account to bridge gaps between insurance periods in order to qualify for early pension requiring 35 insured years. A similar rule was introduced for general care of the sick or disabled: if a woman interrupts or reduces her employment to nurse a seriously disabled person, she has the option to pay voluntary pension contributions and bridge gaps in her pension record. No pension credits are granted in these cases, but gaps in the insurance contributions period can be partially bridged. Since both reforms were introduced by the 1992 Pension Reform Act, it is still too early to assess the impact of these changes. However, they are far from an adequate upgrading of 'care times' in law and are an insufficient response to the criticism of the discriminatory character of the German pension system.[8]

Differences in pension benefits: gender and occupation

There is a direct link between contribution periods and pension benefits: the more years insured, the higher pensions will be. The 'earnings points' gained each year are added up over the whole insurance period up to a maximum of 50 years' insurance. The 'earnings points' reflect the relation between personal earnings and average earnings of all insured persons in a given year. This benefit formula translates low pay into low pensions, and penalizes part-time work and employment interruptions. It also reproduces differences based on class and occupational status, as set out in Table 9.5.

The gender gap is, however, wider than the differences between white-collar and blue-collar workers. If one compares women's pension benefits and average male pension benefits in 1992, the ratio of the average woman's pension to average man is 39.3 per cent for blue-collar employees and 48 per cent for white-collar employees in the West. The personal pension entitlements of women in the old *Länder* were only half or even less than half of average male pensions. The gender difference is smaller for the ex-GDR where women's pension benefits were about one-third lower than men's. The ratio of female to male pensions in the East is 77.7 per cent of average male pensions for blue-collar pensioners and 76.8 for white-collar employees. Differences between manual and non-manual workers are negligible in the new *Länder* (for women and for men).

Looking at *stratification along occupational lines* in the West, it is evident that this cleavage also plays an important role for men.

Table 9.5 *Average monthly pensions paid to women and men in 1992 (DM)*

	Blue-collar insurance		White-collar insurance	
	Individual pension	Widow/er pension	Individual pension	Widow/er pension
Old *Länder*				
Women	572	826	955	1147
Men	1456	249	1989	398
New *Länder*				
Women	819	479	839	472
Men	1209	176	1255	197

Source: Statistisches Bundesamt (1993)

Average male pensions of blue-collar employees are about a quarter lower than those of their white-collar counterparts. Female blue-collar employees have 40 per cent lower individual insurance pensions than women in white-collar jobs. The female blue-collar employees in the old *Länder* lose out most and occupy the lowest position. Being a woman and a blue-collar employee is the worst bargain in the German pension system in terms of personal pension rights. The story becomes more complicated if one considers marriage as another important variable.

If one looks at pension entitlements of employees from the ex-GDR, the importance of men's later pension age and a long and uninterrupted pension career becomes clear: gender differences are smaller, but nonetheless significant. In 1992 men in the new *Länder* had on average 45.1 insurance years and women 30.4 (38.7 and 21.6 years in the old *Länder* respectively) (*Pension Report*, 1993). Women's lower earnings also play a role – a phenomenon that also existed in the ex-GDR. However, differences between high and low wages in the ex-GDR were relatively small, so that even after reunification pensions in the new *Länder* are clustered closer together than in the old *Länder*.

The status-maintaining effects of the German pension system are even more striking when one looks not only at average pensions, but at pension distribution according to different income strata (Figure 9.1).

More than half of all female blue-collar pensioners in the West had individual monthly pension benefits which were less than DM 500. Hardly any women received a personal pension above DM 1500, which was the norm for most male pensioners. Although female

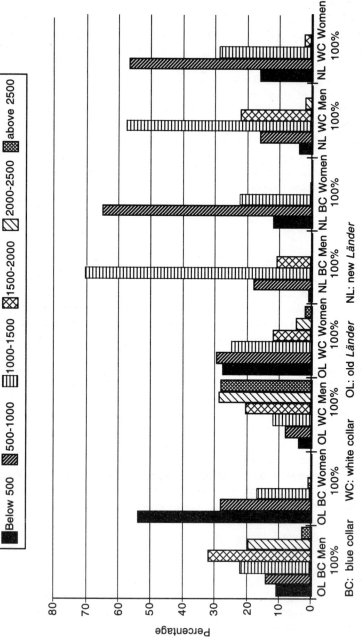

Figure 9.1 *Insurance pensions for blue-collar and white-collar workers in the old and new Länder by sex, 1992 (DM)*

BC: blue collar   WC: white collar   OL: old *Länder*   NL: new *Länder*

BC: blue collar   WC: white collar   OL: old *Länder*   NL: new *Länder*

Below 500   500-1000   1000-1500   1500-2000   2000-2500   above 2500 white-collar pensioners fared somewhat better and only 25 per cent have less than DM 500, the majority are still clustered below the DM 1000 line. Women's low insurance pensions are a notorious feature of the German pension system. This induces financial dependence either upon individual men or upon means-tested income support. In the new *Länder*, the most significant features are that occupational differences were very small, and gender differences were smaller than in the West. Women's pensions were about one-third lower than men's, and most female pensioners were clustered in the income stratum between 500 and 1000 DM monthly, while most men received DM 1000 to 1500 monthly.

This shows that pension differences along gender lines are greater than along occupational lines – but to complete the picture, one has to take into account marriage as an important institution in providing old age income for women. Family status is another important variable in explaining stratification and gender differences.

Survivor pensions: marriage and status maintenance

To explain the welfare state as a system of gender stratification one must also consider the institution of marriage and family status. Social rights are linked in various ways to family status (married, unmarried or cohabiting, or, for a child, born in or out of wedlock). A feminist approach to welfare state analysis not only addresses the question of how social rights enhance independence from the market, but also how social rights construct women's dependence or independence from individual men (Daly and Hobson, Chapters 7 and 11 in this volume; O'Connor, 1993).

Only since the 1950s have pensions provided the main source of income for the elderly, granting some degree of independence from the market (Esping-Andersen *et al.*, 1988). Formerly pensions were too low to provide an adequate living for women and men; they had to be supplemented by continuing waged work or family support. This is still the rule for many elderly women, but only for a smaller proportion of men whose pensions are below the poverty line. Market dependency for employed women ends on average later than for men, as the analysis of pension ages has shown. Whether women rely mainly on their own insurance pension, income sharing within a household (family support), derived pension rights as a widow or means-tested state benefit is highly correlated with their family status. Institutional rules reinforce a rigid 'either-or' alternative – dependency on the market or on marriage – by creating employment disincentives for married women and favouring reliance on marriage for income security in old age.

Insurance pensions do not include any 'dependency allowance' for a married or cohabiting partner or a child.[9] Pensions are individualized, which means that pension benefits are dependent on labour market performance and do not take family responsibilities into account. Pension law constructs dependency on marriage *directly* only through survivor pensions. As in most countries, marriage is a requirement for access to widows' pensions; unmarried cohabitees are excluded. Remarriage nullifies entitlement to a survivor's pension and shifts dependency from the old to the new spouse. Divorce does not necessarily cut off all rights to a survivor's pension; entitlement to a special 'divorced widow's pension' was introduced in 1957. For all women divorcing after 1977 this right was abolished and substituted by the 'pension splitting' procedure which guarantees an equal share in all pension entitlements acquired during marriage. But this introduces a time factor: only entitlements acquired during marriage are divided up. This provision under social security and divorce law to grant pension rights based on marriage even in the case of marital breakdown illustrates the importance the German pension regime attaches to this institution. A divorced woman is still cared for better than those who never married. And it is not the importance of caring for a child which is the criterion for this redistribution, but the pure fact of legal marriage.

How did these provisions linked to dependency on individual men develop? In Germany widows' pensions were introduced in 1911, with a special class feature: while white-collar widows received this pension unconditionally in case of the insured spouse's death, blue-collar widows had access only if they could prove their disability for paid work. This status differentiation among widows was abolished only in 1957 when pension reform equalized the basis entitlement for white- and blue-collar widows of appropriately insured men. Since the normative goal of this pension type was to substitute for loss of marital maintenance, until 1985 widowers were entitled only if the insured deceased wife had been the main family provider.

The principle of formal equality led to the extension of the derived right to a survivor's pension to married men. Following a ruling of the Federal Constitutional Court in 1975, widowers have been able to receive a survivor's pension independent of the proportion which the deceased wife's earnings contributed to family income since 1986. However, the personal income of the survivor is partly deducted; the 1986 reform introduced an income ceiling above which a widow(er)'s pension is reduced by 40 per cent of the amount exceeding the threshold. Despite these small changes, no general reform took place. Survivors' pensions based on the assumption of women's marital dependency have not been abolished for future generations or replaced by provision of independent old age security for carers or persons with incomplete pension careers (unlike other countries such as Sweden or Denmark). The basic construction inherited from the beginning of the century was kept intact: dependence on the market and dependence on marriage are basic normative orientations, and both institutional settings are neatly intertwined, cross-cutting the distinctions between private law and social security institutions.

Eligibility criteria for widow(er)s' pensions are fairly generous. No minimum duration of marriage is required. No contributions have to be paid for a dependent spouse. The deceased spouse must have been insured for at least five years. Widow(er)s' pensions are paid at the level of 60 per cent of pension entitlements of the deceased spouse for a widow(er) aged over 45. A younger widow(er) receives a reduced rate (25 per cent of the deceased spouse's pension entitlement), except if she cares for a child under 18 from the marriage or is unable to work. Earnings or other income could be topped up with a survivor's pension unconditionally until 1976. Nowadays, when replacement earnings of the widow(er) exceed DM 1125 (£450) monthly (1992) plus amounts for children, the survivor's pension is reduced by a rate of 40 per cent of the excess amount. Survivors' pensions in the ex-GDR were considerably lower[10] and have increased since reunification.

If a widow in the new *Länder* receives an individual plus a survivor's pension at average level, the proportion of a widow's pension out of this total old age income is 37 per cent for blue-collar widows and 36 per cent for white-collar widows.

Widows' pensions in the old *Länder* are a more important source of old age income than individual insurance pensions for women (see Table 9.5). If one adds up the average individual pension and widows' pension of women in the West, the derived pension entitlement makes up 59 per cent of this 'pension package' for blue-collar widows and 55 per cent for white-collar widows. The lack of minimum pensions, flat-rate contributory pensions or other elements redistributing towards low earners or persons with incomplete pension careers increases the importance of survivors' pensions. Whether personal pension entitlement of a widow plus a survivor's pension provide a decent living, depends also on the class and income position of the deceased husband. This stratification dimension cross-cuts the dividing lines between married and single elderly women. Best off are the widows of high earners who can combine their own earnings or pension entitlements with survivor benefits (until 1986 without income thresholds), while single female blue-collar pensioners are in a worse position. The gap widens for those without a proper work career, possibly due to care obligations, who also lack the proper relationship to an insured man. The German state steps in only via means-tested income support.

Conclusions

If one assumes that an outstanding criterion for social rights should be the degree to which they permit people to have living standards relatively independent of pure market forces and also of individual men, the question is how 'female times', especially child-rearing and care obligations, influence the possibility of making a decent living compared to 'male times'. Social rights should be evaluated on the basis of whether they also provide women individually with access to a decent income of their own through salaries or social security benefits even when bringing up children or performing other care activities. The reliance on the family as an alternative social security institution has been weakened for men and women at a different pace. How welfare states intervened through 'time politics' to tighten or loosen these links is an area of inquiry which cuts across the often separated research subjects of the market and the family sphere and integrates gender as one stratifying dimension.

The analysis of institutionalized gendered times in this chapter has shown the relevance of this institutional structure as an explanatory factor which influences stratification of male and female pension recipients. Eligibility criteria are heavily biased towards the life circumstances of men and disadvantage 'female times'. Marriage is still very important in providing old age security for women. Social rights connected directly to 'care times' are minimal and tied to a traditional family model where 'a mother with a child under three should stay at home'. 'Care times' are overwhelmingly privatized; they have to be provided and compensated for within the family or marriage. Social rights are highly bifurcated: either entitlements are market based, or they are derived through marriage. For those who fall between, there are no universal social rights; only means-tested state benefits as the last resort.

Notes

1 Hutton and Whiteford (1992) review the comparative empirical literature on the income situation of elderly people and find that only two out of nine studies reviewed specifically analysed the circumstances of women compared with men.

2 For Germany, see the contributions in Mechthild Veil *et al.* (1992) and Claudia Gather *et al.* (1991). The article by Jay Ginn and Sara Arber (1992) is exceptional since it compares institutional factors interacting with behavioural patterns for three countries and locates the analysis in the framework of welfare regime typologies.

Martin Tracy (1988) and Diether Döring *et al.* (1992) describe comparatively the institutional rules affecting the pension entitlements of women and men differently, but do not theorize the underlying gender dynamics.

3 See Scheiwe (forthcoming) on the disadvantages of 'female times' in German labour law.

4 The eligibility criterion that at least three years' obligatory contributions must have been paid during the five years preceding the event of invalidity was introduced in 1984 and reduced the number of invalidity pensions by nearly 50 per cent. Women were disproportionately affected.

5 See Heinz Galler (1988) and Hugh Davies and Heather Joshi (1990) for economic estimates of mothers' forgone earnings through employment interruptions or part-time work. Galler (1988) estimates the loss of income capacity for university graduates at 12 per cent when interrupting employment for one year, and up to 50 per cent for ten years' interruption. Davies and Joshi (1990) calculate the forgone earnings caused by child-rearing as about half of the earnings of a comparable female employee without a child after the age of motherhood, assuming that a mother of two children stays out of employment until the youngest child is 6.

6 Until 1983, the *evaluation of training periods* under pension law discriminated against women, since women's pension credits for this period were evaluated as 25 per cent lower than men's (who got contributions calculated on the basis of 100 per cent of average income). This was justified by the argument that female wages were lower. Only in 1981, after a judgment of the Federal Constitutional Court, were pension credits for training periods set equally at 90 per cent of the average income (75 per cent from 1992 on).

7 The risk of *work accidents at domestic work* with the consequence of partial or total disability to work is not covered by social insurance. This unequal treatment is discriminatory especially since various other forms of unpaid work are insured against these risks: help to construct a family home, blood donation, etc. (para. 539 I no. 8 ff. Imperial Insurance Act). See Bieback (1990) on the question of indirect discrimination against women by this regulation.

8 For a short overview on the Pension Reform Act 1992 see Winfried Schmähl (1993); for an extensive discussion of the gender dimension, including the consequences for women after German reunification see Veil *et al.* (1992) and Gather *et al.* (1991).

9 Child dependency allowances that existed under GDR law were maintained if they were acquired before July 1991.

10 Under GDR law a widow was entitled to 60 per cent of the deceased spouse's pension. If she also had an individual pension, only 25 per cent of the lower pension or a minimum amount were paid as a survivor's pension.

10

Women's and Men's Social Rights: Gendering Dimensions of Welfare States

Diane Sainsbury

Gendering welfare states – bringing gender into the comparative analysis of welfare states – has moved to the top of the research agenda. While the importance of this project is increasingly recognized, opinions differ about how to gender welfare states. The most obvious method would be to apply mainstream theories and frameworks to an analysis of welfare states that explicitly focuses on women and men. An objection to this seemingly straightforward approach has been that central concepts and assumptions of mainstream research often contain a male bias. A prerequisite then is to illuminate how these concepts and assumptions are gendered by clarifying their implications for women and men and to what extent the implications differ. An additional objection is that mainstream analysis has totally omitted gender but its centrality makes it necessary to avoid procedures that merely 'add-on' gender to existing frameworks (Lewis and Ostner, 1991). This position represents a second approach which argues that new models and typologies must be devised if gender is to be incorporated into the study of welfare states and policy regimes. A third stance is that the best course is to build gender into mainstream frameworks of analysis (Orloff, 1993).

The strategy adopted here has not been to build gender into existing mainstream typologies but rather to separate it out. On the basis of the feminist critique of mainstream theories and research, I identify a number of dimensions of variation that have been either marginalized or not included in the mainstream models and typologies. As a heuristic exercise these dimensions are presented as contrasting ideal types. The dimensions of the models are the variations that I am interested in comparing cross-nationally in an empirical analysis of women's and men's social rights. I do not assume, however, that the ideal types would be replicated in reality or that variations across countries necessarily follow the logic of the models. Quite the contrary, the analysis is exploratory. Its purposes are to determine the usefulness of the framework, to discover eventual deviations, and to improve the models on this basis.

The first part of this chapter discusses feminist criticisms of mainstream research. Drawing on the major points of this discussion, I present two models of social policy. The dimensions of variation of the models are then employed to analyse policies and women's and men's social rights in four countries – the UK, the US, the Netherlands and Sweden – in order to delineate similarities and differences and to determine to what extent the countries cluster into types. The final section comments on the implications of the analysis for gendering welfare state analysis and refining the original models and other typologies.

The feminist critique

Although mainstream research has produced many significant insights, it has not been very informative about the differing consequences of welfare states for women and men. I believe the reason for this is that the mainstream perspective is fundamentally incomplete, and that it must be complemented by a new set of dimensions of variation with respect to gender. Feminist scholarship can help us establish what is missing in the mainstream models.

As distinct from the mainstream debate on the determinants of welfare state development that has stressed economic processes – especially industrialization – and more recently class politics, feminists have emphasized the interrelationships of the family, the state and the market. They have concentrated on the dynamics and the shifting boundary between the private and public spheres, that is, both their interdependence and separation. Feminist research has pointed to a significant change in state–family relations – the extent to which tasks of reproduction and socialization, formerly activities of the family, have become functions of the public sector. As aptly put by Helga Hernes, the issue is the degree to which caring tasks and reproduction work, previously done in the home, have gone public (Hernes, 1984, 1987a).

Feminists have also highlighted how ideological constructs shape women's lives, and this emphasis has informed feminist accounts of the welfare state. Contrary to mainstream analysis, feminist writings on the welfare state have dealt extensively with the influence of familial ideology in structuring social policies and reproducing the social division of labour between the sexes. Initially discussions focused on the breadwinner ideology which holds that the husband is responsible for earning a living and providing for the family. Eventually more attention was given to ideological prescriptions concerning women and their role as caregivers. These prescriptions stress the wife's inherent domesticity and her duties in nurturing and caring for members of the family in the form of unpaid labour in exchange for the support of her husband.

In short, feminist theorizing on the welfare state makes it clear that even if mainstream models and typologies were gendered through explicitly including women and men in the analysis, such a step does not go far enough. Gendering welfare states requires specific attention to the interplay of the public and the private and a conceptualization of welfare provision in terms of a public–private mix (Hernes, 1987a; Leira, 1992). This dictates an examination of not only paid work but also unpaid work both inside and outside the home. Second, feminists have stressed the necessity of studying how the welfare state in providing employment and services affects the situation of women as workers, consumers, mothers and clients. Third, feminists have stressed the role of familial and gender ideologies in structuring welfare policies.

Gendering dimensions of variation

Implicit in the feminist critique are a number of dimensions of variation. These consist of the type of familial ideology; its influence on social policy in terms of the unit of benefits and contributions and the nature of entitlement; its influence in other policy areas reinforcing the actual division of labour within the family; the boundary between the public and private spheres; and the degree to which women's work is paid or unpaid. These dimensions of variation are summarized in Table 10.1 as contrasting ideal types: the breadwinner model and the individual model.

In the breadwinner model, the familial ideology celebrates marriage and a strict division of labour between husband and wife. The husband is the head of the household, and it is his duty to provide for the members of his family – his wife and children – through full-time employment. The duties of the wife are to make a good home and provide care for her husband and children. This division of labour shapes practice, and it is codified in family law, social and labour legislation, and the tax system. The unit of benefit is the family, and minimum benefits and pay embody the notion of the family wage. Entitlement is differentiated between husband and wife. Eligibility is based on breadwinner status and the principle of maintenance. Accordingly, most wives' rights to benefits are derived from their status as dependants within the family and their husbands' entitlements. As a result, married women may lack individual entitlement to benefits. The family or household is the unit of social insurance contributions and taxation. The family provider receives tax relief to

Table 10.1 *Dimensions of variation of the breadwinner and the individual models of social policy*

Dimension	Breadwinner model	Individual model
Familial ideology	Strict division of labour Husband = earner Wife = carer	Shared roles Husband = earner/carer Wife = earner/carer
Entitlement	Differentiated among spouses	Uniform
Basis of entitlement	Breadwinner	Other
Recipient of benefits	Head of household	Individual
Unit of benefit	Household or family	Individual
Unit of contributions	Household	Individual
Taxation	Joint taxation Deductions for dependants	Separate taxation Equal tax relief
Employment and wage policies	Priority to men	Aimed at both sexes
Sphere of care	Primarily private	Strong state involvement
Caring work	Unpaid	Paid component

compensate for the maintenance of his wife and offspring. The division of labour prescribed by familial ideology also affects wage and labour market policies – assigning priority to men's employment and earnings. The boundary between the private and public sphere is strictly enforced. Caring and reproduction tasks are located in the private sphere, primarily in the home, and this work is unpaid.

The familial ideology of the individual model prescribes that each spouse is individually responsible for his or her own maintenance, and that husband and wife share the tasks of financial support and care of their children. The unit of benefit, contributions and taxation is the individual with no deductions or allowances for dependants. Labour market policies are aimed at both sexes. The boundary between the private and public spheres is fluid. Many reproductive tasks are performed in the public sector. Care, even in the home, can be paid work and provide entitlement to social security benefits.

Admittedly this presentation is skeletal, but it seems to me that there are a number of advantages of using this sort of analytic construct at the present stage of gendering welfare state analysis. The dimensions of variation are clearly formulated. Earlier models have not always been very explicit on this point. For example, Jane Lewis and Ilona Ostner's typology seems to be based on a single underlying dimension – the strength of the male breadwinner model in terms of the traditional division of labour between the sexes and its implications for social entitlements. The resulting typology is 'strong', 'modified' and 'weak' male breadwinner states (see Daly and Hobson, Chapters 7 and 11 in this volume); and the final category – weak male breadwinner states – is especially problematic. It seems to indicate what a country's policies are not rather than what they are.

A further advantage of the models is their potential applicability. In principle the dimensions of variation presented here can be used to analyse the policies of any country over time. A family of nations approach, or typologies based on the policies of specific countries, runs the risk of limited relevance to those countries.

Finally, by isolating dimensions of variation related to gender it is possible to examine the interaction between these dimensions and the welfare state variations designated as important by mainstream analysis. This possibility is more difficult, if not impossible, when the feminist and mainstream perspectives are compounded in single ideal types or policy regimes.

Women's and men's social rights

In analysing women's and men's social rights the dimensions of variation in Table 10.1 are applied to the policies of the UK, the US, the Netherlands and Sweden during the late 1960s. This is an important period to examine for a number of reasons. First these years offer an important benchmark because it was in the 1970s that equality of the sexes moved on to the policy agenda, resulting in major reforms in all four countries.[1] Second, since few gender equality reforms had been enacted one might expect to find less variation between the four countries during this period. Third, many feminists initially argued that the breadwinner model was encoded in the social legislation of the industrial nations, and that it was part and parcel of the welfare state. Gradually the breadwinner model has come to be viewed as varying in strength across countries. Typically, however, most variations are presented as fairly recent developments, coinciding with women's exodus into the labour market. The strength of Swedish women's social rights is seen as the result of their higher rate of labour market participation. The latter years of the 1960s, combined with digressions tracing policies back in time, allow us to probe assumptions concerning the recentness in the development of variations. The analysis also casts light on newer assumptions that the male breadwinner model had decisive influence in the formative period of welfare states, and that early welfare states were basically 'paternalist' in nature (Orloff, 1993: 323; Skocpol, 1992: 2, 8–10).

Applying the dimensions in Table 10.1 results in strong divergences in the policy patterns of the four countries, and the clustering of countries is quite different from the clusters produced by mainstream typologies. Using mainstream models the Netherlands and Sweden have often been bracketed together as ambitious or comprehensive welfare states scoring high on de-commodification (eliminating dependence on the market), while the US and the UK have been categorized as both less ambitious and less de-commodifying (Castles, 1978; Sainsbury, 1991; Esping-Andersen, 1990).[2]

An analysis using the dimensions of variation in Table 10.1 yields quite a different picture. Although social rights in all four countries were influenced by a traditional familial ideology in the 1960s, the Netherlands approximated most closely the breadwinner model, while Sweden least resembled it. The UK and the US occupied middle positions, but the policies of both countries bore much stronger similarities to those of the Netherlands than to those of Sweden. In the three countries social rights were tied to the principle of maintenance and tax benefits to the family provider, while Sweden differed in that motherhood and the principle of care exerted a much stronger influence on women's social rights. A second difference that further strengthened Swedish women's social rights was the extent of entitlements based on citizenship, and in these cases there were points of convergence with the individual model. Entitlement and benefits of pensions were uniform between spouses, and the recipient of benefits was the individual.

The Netherlands: the principle of maintenance and a family minimum

In the Netherlands the Catholic principle of subsidiarity and the Protestant doctrine of sphere sovereignty have assigned a central importance to the family in its traditional form. Religious teachings have sanctioned state action to protect the family from economic hardships and to aid the family provider in meeting his obligations of support (Borchorst, Chapter 3 in this volume). The principle of maintenance is firmly entrenched in social provision; and the construction of benefits and contributions has revolved around the family as the norm – and the notion of a family minimum.

During the 1960s minimum pension benefits were linked to the minimum wage, and the standard minimum was set for a couple, while single individuals received a smaller amount. Subsequently the social minimum was upgraded and extended to a wider range of benefits. The beneficiary has been the person responsible for maintenance, and benefits have been calculated on the basis of family responsibilities. Accordingly, when fully upgraded, the social minimum was roughly equivalent to the net minimum wage for couples, 90 per cent for single parent families, with lower rates for single persons, and young adults living at home. This system contrasts with the UK and the US where the construction of benefits has been based on the individual, with supplements for dependants.

The unit of contributions to the national insurance schemes was also the household and was paid by the head of the household, based on family income. Compulsory health insurance automatically covered family members without an income with no additional contributions required (Roebroek and Berben, 1987: 689). *Because the household was the unit of benefits and contributions, married women lacked individual entitlement to 'national' insurance benefits.* The most severe discrimination against married women was their ineligibility for the basic old age pension, extended unemployment benefits, and later general disablement benefits when introduced in the mid-1970s.

The importance of family protection and the family as the norm can also be seen in the compulsory employee insurance schemes. Through relatively high replacement rates (generally 80 per cent of the daily wage) without special allowances for dependants, these schemes safeguarded the earnings of the breadwinner against the eventualities of sickness, unemployment and disability.

The principle of maintenance and the notion of the father as provider for his children influenced family allowances, which unlike in Britain and Sweden, are social insurance transfers and not a non-contributory benefit. Family allowances have been paid to the insured person responsible for maintenance of the child – usually the father. Furthermore, the responsibility of maintenance has extended to children in early adulthood (to the age of 27) with limited or no earnings or permanently ill. The amount of the allowance increased with the number of children, and older children (over 16) and children with special needs entitled the father to larger compensation, reflecting their financial burden on the family (ISSR, 1970: 48–9). In contrast to Britain and Sweden, family allowances were indexed, and they were more generous, especially compared to Britain. As a proportion of the standard wage the Dutch allowances were roughly twice as high as those in Britain in the late 1960s (Kaim-Caudle, 1973: 271–2, 283; cf. Wennemo, 1994). Finally the father received child tax exemptions. The combination of family allowances and tax exemptions meant that the Dutch father, regardless of his economic position, was aided in meeting his family responsibilities.

In conclusion, the costs of familyhood were socialized through subsidies to the family provider. The guarantee of a minimum wage, a social minimum eventually pegged at roughly the same level as the minimum wage, the high replacement rates of employee insurance schemes, and indexed family allowances tailored to large families and reflecting the varying costs of children provided the breadwinner with a substantial buffer of security in supporting the family. These policies produced a situation which seems closer to the ideal of a family wage for the vast majority of wage-earner families.

The breadwinner ideology was also reflected in labour legislation and the tax system. Legislation privileged men as earners with respect to job opportunities, wages and tax relief. Marriage bans curtailed a wife's possibilities of employment. As noted by Siv Gustafsson (Chapter 4 in this volume), legislation prohibiting employers from firing a woman because of pregnancy, childbirth or marriage was not introduced until the early 1970s. Nor have married women without breadwinner status always been entitled to the minimum wage. Married couples' incomes were jointly taxed, without the option of separate taxation; and working wives received no tax allowance as they did in the other countries.

Overall, legislation was characterized by penalties and few rewards for married women entering the labour market, encouraging either no participation or marginal participation. In the mid-1960s only around 20 per cent of married women were economically active, and nearly half were family workers. In other words, as recently as 30 years ago only slightly over 10 per cent of Dutch married women held jobs outside the family (calculated from SYN, 1969–70: 284–6).

Clearly, women's place was in the home, and one is struck by the lack of benefits attached to motherhood in the Netherlands. Admittedly sickness insurance provided generous maternity pay. However, women did not have a statutory right to maternity leave beyond the relatively short duration of maternity benefits. Nor was there a maternity grant or benefits for non-working mothers. Entitlement to maternity benefits has been based on labour market status as an employee, and originally sickness insurance only recognized the pregnancy of married women as an illness (SZW, 1982: 31). Because of their low labour market participation rate, only a small proportion of all mothers received maternity benefits – a mere 5 per cent in the mid-1960s (calculated from SYN, 1969–70: 26, 315).

In the late 1960s the Netherlands was a prime candidate as the archetype of the breadwinner model inasmuch as social rights derived almost entirely from the principle of maintenance, and the recipient of benefits was the head of the household. The only benefit that could be ascribed to the principle of care, but is probably more accurately attributed to the absence of the male breadwinner, was the widow's pension where a wife's duties in the home were assumed to have disadvantaged her re-entry into the labour market. The sphere of care was overwhelmingly private, and childcare outside the home was regulated by the Poor Law until the mid-1960s (Gustafsson, Chapter 4 in this volume).

The UK: discrimination against married women as choice
Several distinctive features of the postwar British welfare state have been associated with the ideas of William Beveridge; and as feminist scholars have documented, the breadwinner ideology was an integral part of Beveridge's thinking (Lewis, 1983: 33, 44–6, 67, 90–92). His ideas were especially important because it was the postwar reforms that incorporated all women into the British welfare state.

The breadwinner ideology left its imprint on postwar reforms – especially the national insurance scheme and the national assistance programme – in four ways. First, the national insurance scheme allowed married women to choose not to pay full contributions and instead rely upon their husband's contributions, but in the process they forfeited their claim to benefits in their own right. Because of the unified approach inherent in the national insurance scheme, the married woman's option operated to exclude them from *all* social insurance benefits – except the industrial injury benefit and the dependant's pension. Thus utilization of the option resulted in the loss not only of a full individual pension but also of other benefits, such as sickness benefit, invalidity benefit, unemployment benefit, and the maternity allowance. Second, married women who remained in the national insurance scheme paid full contributions but received lower benefits than married men and single persons unless they were the main breadwinner (Groves, 1983). A third feature of the national insurance scheme – adult dependant allowances – provided an incentive for women to stay in the home, thus reinforcing the traditional division of labour in the family. Unlike Dutch benefits, the system of dependant allowances took into direct account the wife's economic activity. The allowance was paid only for dependants without an income or with earnings less than the allowance. Furthermore, married women were not eligible to claim child additions. Fourth, in married couples only the husband could apply for means-tested assistance.

In Britain married women on the labour market were not entirely stripped of their rights to a pension and other benefits as in Holland. Instead they were denied equal rights, and the married woman's option encouraged them to renounce their rights. The option was widely used, and in the early 1970s three-quarters of married women had opted out of the national insurance scheme (Land, 1985: 56–7).

Given that the option was really between no individual rights and minor obligations (contributions) versus only half-rights and full obligations, it is hardly surprising that so many married women made use of the option.

Family allowances, as distinct from in the Netherlands, have been paid to the mother. However, the father retained the right of child tax exemptions, which was arguably the most generous form of family support (Land and Parker, 1978: 345) in terms of cost to the public purse. Beveridge's proposal also excluded the first child from the family allowance scheme, while tax exemptions could be claimed for all the children. Contrary to most other countries, the family allowance was subject to tax. One effect of this arrangement was a redistribution of resources within the family from the wallet to the purse.

The norm of the traditional family with the husband as the keeper of his wife's income and as the financial head of the household also influenced tax legislation. Joint taxation of spouses was obligatory. However, in contrast to her Dutch counterpart, the British working wife received a tax allowance which was identical to a single earner's tax relief. Furthermore, irrespective of whether or not he had a 'dependent' wife, the husband received a married man's allowance (Wilkinson, 1982), which has been roughly one and a half times the single earner's allowance.

Perhaps because of the married woman's earnings allowance, British women's labour participation rates have been considerably higher than Dutch women's. At the end of the 1960s nearly 50 per cent of married women were economically active (Lewis, 1992b: 65; Land and Parker, 1978: 338). On the whole, the tax system furnished incentives for married women to seek employment, while the structure of insurance benefits pulled in the opposite direction. If the married woman used the married woman's option, she received no benefits, and employment meant that her husband lost the adult dependant allowance.

A further obstacle to economic activity has been the poor availability of daycare facilities. Only in wartime has public childcare provision been regarded as a service that should be made available to all working mothers in Britain. Otherwise public childcare services have been targeted on the basis of need, and in the mid-1960s the number of places had dropped to one-third of the wartime figure (Cohen and Fraser, 1991).

At first glance, the UK seems to fit the breadwinner model less than the Netherlands. British policies deviated in three ways. Payment of family allowances was made to the mother, which can be interpreted as an initial recognition of the principle of care. Second,

British married women received a more generous tax allowance. Third, the unit of contributions and benefits in the UK has been the individual. As a beneficiary the husband received an adult dependant allowance, and his wife was entitled to a dependant's pension. Since benefits were tied to the individual, the wife's dependant pension was hers. In one respect, the British system was stricter than the Dutch. The husband collected an adult dependant allowance only when the wife had no earnings or when her earnings were less than the allowance, whereas the Dutch household received benefits irrespective of the wife's employment status. The British case was also stricter in that legislation of the 1970s reinforced the notion of the wife's duty to provide care and service in the home without remuneration. Married women were ineligible to receive the invalid care allowance, which had been introduced to compensate people for having to give up employment to care for the disabled and elderly. The housewives' non-contributory invalidity pension also imposed more rigorous qualifying conditions than the regular non-contributory pension.

The US: two tiers of welfare and women's dependency

The minimalist approach to public provision of welfare in the US might seem to suggest a smaller role for the breadwinner ideology. Nonetheless it has exerted a major influence on legislation affecting the two tiers of public provision of welfare and taxation. In the social security tier, married women's claims to benefits have been heavily dependent upon their husbands' rights and earnings, while women's claims in the welfare tier have often been based on their lack of social security benefits and their poverty.

The breadwinner ideology's most visible impact on the social security tier has been the spouse benefit of the Old-Age, Survivors and Disability Insurance (OASDI) programme. In the 1960s the spouse benefit corresponded to 50 per cent of the insured worker's old age or disability pension, and old age survivor benefits amounted to 80 per cent. As married women have entered the labour market, they have been covered by social security in their own right. Upon retirement, working wives have been able to choose between a spouse benefit or a benefit based on their own earnings – but not both, that is, the spouse benefit plus a benefit based on their own earnings. Married women with social security benefits based on their own earnings which were less than their spouse benefit have had dual entitlement. They have received a secondary benefit which has made up the difference.

The spouse benefit has generally worked to the advantage of the traditional family with a single breadwinner and to the disadvantage of the dual-earner family. In many cases when these two types of families have had roughly the same earnings the family with the single breadwinner has received a larger pension, and the wife has ended up with more generous survivor benefits (Bergmann, 1986: 223. Cf. Miller, 1990: 122; Lopata and Brehm, 1986). The single-earner family has won additionally because the spouse benefit is a non-contributory benefit. In other words, the traditional family has often enjoyed a larger pension and survivor benefits but paid lower social security taxes.

A pattern of favouring the traditional family, particularly to the disadvantage of working wives and single parents, has characterized income taxation in three ways. First, although married couples have been able to choose between individual and joint taxation, the system has actually encouraged joint taxation of spouses. Joint returns have been subject to preferential tax rates, and tax relief has been less beneficial to dual-earner families in relation to families with a sole provider. Second, the single earner family has received the same tax exemptions as the dual-earner family, which virtually amounts to deduction for a dependent spouse. Third, single parent families have not enjoyed the same advantage as a sole provider with a spouse. These three features of the tax system have been aptly described as (1) the dual earner marriage penalty; (2) the housewife bonus; and (3) the single parent penalty (Bergmann, 1986: 218–20).

Despite the disincentives for the dual earner family, it needs to be stressed that the social security system provided incentives for women as individuals. Their social security benefits as workers in all likelihood would be greater than the spouse benefit. Married women's labour market participation rate was much higher than that of their counterparts in the Netherlands and approached that of the UK. In the mid-1960s 35 per cent of married women were working outside the home (SIT, 1968: 128), and the number of women entitled to social security benefits in their own right grew dramatically. Nonetheless, the majority of women still made their claims as wives (Polinsky, 1969: 15–16).

Finally, liberal tenets stressing individual responsibility and the sanctity of the private sphere – home and family – have held enormous sway in the US. As distinct from the other three countries, the US lacks a system of family allowances, although there are tax deductions for children. The major semblance of a programme related to family policy is Aid to Families with Dependent Children in the 'welfare' tier. Accordingly, it has all the disadvantages associated with this tier: meagre means-tested benefits, stigma and intrusive administration. In other words, women's dependency is differentiated in the two tiers of public provision. In the social security tier, entitlement has been based on the strength of one's attachment to the labour market and contributions, benefits are earnings related, and claims for benefits have been heavily dependent upon men's earnings. In the other tier, need determines entitlement, and claimants have overwhelmingly been women (Sainsbury, 1993a).

Sweden: citizenship and the principle of care

A distinguishing characteristic of the Swedish welfare state has been a strong emphasis on entitlement to benefits and services based on citizenship or residence (Elmér, 1975: 252–8; Epsing-Andersen and Korpi, 1987). This basis of entitlement has resulted in less dependency upon one's market position and a de-commodification of wants and needs (Esping-Andersen and Korpi, 1987: 40–1). Another aspect of de-commodification, not touched upon in the other chapters of this volume, has been the availability of a wide range of services which have largely assumed the character of public goods. The centrality of public services in the Swedish welfare state has given rise to its label as the 'social service state' (Siim, 1987a: 3).

Entitlement to benefits on the basis of citizenship has weakened the influence of the breadwinner ideology. In the area of social benefits the influence of the breadwinner ideology has mainly been limited to a wife supplement in unemployment insurance (1941–64) and widow benefits in the public pension schemes (Sainsbury, 1990). In contrast to the other three countries, married women were incorporated in major social insurance schemes with individual entitlement to benefits. Sweden's first national old age insurance, adopted in 1913, included all women irrespective of marital status. The importance of this arrangement in the long term was to establish the principle of individual entitlement to a pension regardless of sex, marital status or labour market status. When compulsory insurance providing sickness benefits was introduced in 1955 coverage was not restricted to the working population, as in the Netherlands and Britain. In addition, spouses at home and single parents at home with children under 16 years old were entitled to minimum cash benefits. In other words, the compulsory insurance system incorporated all women, and they were included as beneficiaries in their own right – and not as the *raison d'être* of benefit supplements for men, as in the UK. Furthermore, under the same programme, maternity benefits were not limited to working women but included a fairly generous flat-rate grant to all mothers. These measures can be interpreted as a modest recognition of the principle of care and that work in the home qualified for entitlement to social benefits.

The principle of care as a basis of entitlement to social benefits and the origins of the 'social service state' can be traced to the population policies of the 1930s. The major breakthrough of the principle of care were means-tested child allowances and public maintenance allowances introduced in the late 1930s along with a series of other benefits attached to motherhood. Maternity grants (*moderskapspenning*) were introduced in 1937 followed by maternity assistance in kind (*mödrahjälp*) in 1938. These reforms extended coverage in relation to subsidized voluntary maternity insurance so that nearly all mothers received maternity benefits (Elmér, 1963; Abukhanfusa, 1987).

Population policy instruments consisted of both individual and collective benefits in kind as well as cash benefits. Collective goods in kind formed the nucleus of what was to develop into the 'social service state'. They consisted of free child delivery, pre- and postnatal medical check-ups, and free vitamins and minerals for mother and child. Collective goods aimed at families and children expanded during the 1940s to include free school lunches, school medical services, social services for families, and day nurseries. In retrospect, cash benefits and collective benefits in kind gradually supplanted individualized means tested benefits in kind, which were eventually phased out in the late 1950s and early 1960s.

The Swedish tax system, prior to the 1970 decision to eliminate joint taxation of spouses' earnings, combined aspects of the breadwinner model and the principle of care. Married couples, irrespective of the wife's employment status, were entitled to a tax allowance which was double the amount of that of a single earner. Accordingly, the Swedish single-earner couple enjoyed a larger housewife bonus than in the UK but comparable to that in the US. On the other hand, the Swedish tax system had traditionally allowed relief for families where the wife had her own income from employment (1919–38, 1947–86). The 1952 tax reform entitled working wives with children who were minors to a larger allowance than other working wives. This allowance was successively raised so that on the eve of the 1971 tax reform, a working wife with children received a standard tax allowance which amounted to nearly twice the amount that her husband received. Finally, tax reforms of the early 1960s benefited single parents by granting them the same conditions of taxation as a married couple – in effect a double tax allowance and the same preferential rate of taxation (Elvander, 1972; SOU, 1964: 25). In short, despite the generous housewife bonus, the Swedish tax system entailed neither a single parent penalty nor a dual earner marriage penalty (however, two-job marriages where each spouse had high earnings did confront a marriage penalty because of progressivity in the tax rates). Tax exemptions for children were abolished when universal family allowances for each child were introduced in the

1940s. Thus wives – and especially mothers – had more tax advantages and fathers had fewer, compared to their counterparts in the other countries.

The Swedish tax system offered incentives for married women to enter the labour market, but lingering influences of the breadwinner ideology on wage and employment policies worked in the opposite direction. Special women's wages had been widespread in manufacturing, but in 1960 labour and management reached a decision to abolish them over a five-year period, which eventually led to decreased wage differentials (Qvist, 1975: 28–9). The active labour market measures of the late 1950s and 1960s were primarily geared to men, who were the main participants in training programmes and recipients of mobility grants. Training allowances were also subject to an income test of a spouse's earnings. Married women's rate of labour market participation was roughly on a par with that in the US and the UK in the 1960s. A major difference, however, was a higher rate of employment among mothers with small children (Rainwater, 1979).

Socal rights compared

To summarize this discussion of social rights and policy patterns, let us compare the countries using the dimensions of variation in Table 10.1. In the late 1960s the prevalent familial ideology reflected in legislation emphasized a traditional division of labour between husband and wife in all four countries. Swedish policies, however, diverged from those of the other countries in significant ways. First, the basis of entitlement to a number of benefits was citizenship or residence. This basis of eligibility resulted in uniform and personal entitlement within marriage. Married women had individual rights to a basic old age pension, disability and sickness benefits. By contrast, the basis of entitlement of married women and men in the other countries was highly differentiated. Married women's entitlements largely derived from their husbands' rights, and especially in the Netherlands and the UK they lacked individual rights. Second, as a result of social rights based on citizenship, the privilege status of the breadwinner was not translated into social legislation to the same extent as in the other countries. Third, the traditional division of labour in the family – with the mother as carer – shaped legislation through incorporating the principle of care in a way which did not occur in the other countries. In fact, around 1970 the Netherlands and Sweden represented polar opposites in terms of benefits attached to fatherhood and motherhood respectively. Dutch benefits were almost entirely attached to fatherhood; even family allowances and child delivery were covered by the father's insurance. The Swedish reforms of the 1930s introduced maternity benefits paid to nearly all mothers. Similarly, child allowances were paid to all mothers – even unwed mothers, and advanced maintenance allowances aided single mothers. This contrasts with the Dutch experience, where unmarried mothers were originally not entitled to either family allowances (Roebroek and Berben, 1987: 692) or maternity pay. As distinct from the other three countries, the Swedish tax system also granted women workers with children, especially solo mothers, considerable tax relief. Fourth, benefits to single mothers ran counter to preferential treatment of marriage.

On the dimension of familial ideology, the other three countries are grouped together with respect to the breadwinner ideology and its effects on policy, although the policy constructions differed. In the Netherlands the family minimum has been the norm, and minimum benefits for single individuals have been calculated as a portion of the standard family benefits. In Britain and the US the *individual* was the unit of benefit but the principle of family maintenance resulted in supplements to cover the additional costs of family members – often both wife and children. In Britain the husband was entitled to the supplements with the exception of the dependant's pension, whereas in the US benefits were generally conferred upon the wife. The British adult dependant's allowance has been fairly generous in relative terms but not in absolute terms. The allowance has provided 60 per cent of the benefit of a single person. The US spouse benefit amounted to 50 per cent of the husband's benefit and in absolute terms has been quite generous, and the survivor's benefit was even more generous, totalling 80 per cent of the husband's benefit.

The husband's duty as family provider resulted in special tax relief in the form of a housewife bonus in all four countries. The treatment of wives' earnings, however, varied across the countries. As in the case of entitlement to social benefits, Dutch married women suffered the most inequitable treatment; they were not entitled to a tax allowance. British working wives received a tax allowance comparable to that of single earners – but one which was only around two-thirds of their husbands'. In the US a dual earner couple divided the marital tax relief equally between husband and wife. Finally, Swedish working wives received the same general allowance as their husband, and those with children were entitled to an additional allowance – the rationale being that an allowance would compensate for extra costs related to childcare.

A final dimension of variation which requires consideration is the sphere of care and family policy. In the US care has remained essentially in the private sphere. Liberalism has enhanced beliefs in the sanctity of the family and a doctrine of minimal intrusion by the government. Public intercession has been condoned in the case of family break-ups and the absence of a family provider. The UK by virtue of its introduction of universal family allowances in 1945 seems markedly different. Yet the liberal traditions of the two countries have had a similar impact: family services have been targeted to families in need. Universalism has not pertained to services for families, reinforcing the norm of care in the private sphere for the vast majority of British families. Dutch 'family policy' has consisted of cash transfers, with the father rather than the mother as recipient, and as in the US and Britain daycare fell within the realm of poor relief. In all three countries, the division between daycare and preschool education has also hampered the expansion of public daycare facilities.

Swedish family policy has comprised not only cash benefits but also collective goods and services. As early as the 1940s the government through state grants encouraged the local authorities to provide services to families, and to do so by training and employing staff to assist in the home. In these instances care in the home was paid work performed by public employees. Although family services were in limited supply, the goal was that they should be available to all families. The services were not means tested but service fees were often graduated according to income, and certain categories of users had priority. In two respects, through benefits based on the principle of care and through transferring tasks in the home to public sector jobs, we can detect the beginnings of care being converted into paid work and the blurring of the boundary between the private and public spheres.

Conclusions

This concluding discussion deals with the implications of the preceding analysis for the original models outlined in Table 10.1 and places the analysis in the larger context of efforts to gender welfare states. The analysis suggests the need to revise the original models in two respects. First, although the breadwinner model strongly influenced the policies of the Netherlands, the UK and the US, the differences in policy constructions between the Netherlands with the family as the unit of benefit and obligations and the other two countries with benefits and obligations tied to the individual suggest two variants of the breadwinner model. The fact that benefits have been attached to the individual has had important consequences for married women. Even if their entitlement was based on their husbands' rights, pensions have been paid to women, providing them with a source of income which Dutch wives did not receive. On the other hand, the Dutch policy construction may be more amenable to change through gender equality reforms and 'individualization' – changes in legislation making the individual the unit of entitlement and obligations (Sainsbury, 1993b).

Second, and more importantly for revising the models, Swedish policies in the 1960s deviated from the breadwinner model but did not fit the individual model either. Swedish women did have more individual social rights but several of these entitlements were rooted in a traditional familial ideology and a strongly gendered division of labour which is the antithesis of the individual model. To accommodate the Swedish case we can conceive of a traditional family model of social policy encompassing two types: (1) the breadwinner variant; and (2) the traditional roles variant.

Both variants share a familial ideology which prescribes a strict division of labour between husband and wife, and entitlement is differentiated. In the breadwinner model the principle of maintenance prevails and married women's social rights are via their husbands. In the traditional roles variant there are two bases of entitlement – the principle of maintenance underpinning men's social rights and the principle of care enhancing women's social rights. Both principles shaped social benefits and the tax system, whereas the principle of maintenance exerted considerable influence on labour market policies. The sphere of care was still largely private, but benefits based on the care principle altered notions of private and public responsibilities and set in motion a new dynamic of interdependence of the private and public spheres.

What are the implications of this analysis with respect to studying gender and welfare state variations? Let us initially contrast our analysis with the results of mainstream scholarship. Mainstream typologies have often distinguished between three bases of entitlement: need, market work performance, and citizenship. These bases of entitlement also underlie Esping-Andersen's regime typology. In the traditional family model two other bases of entitlement are central: the principles of maintenance and care. This model has allowed us to uncover variations between welfare states that mainstream typologies have not revealed. Mainstream scholarship has often emphasized the commonalities of the Dutch and Swedish welfare states, especially when using quantitative indicators, such as social spending, benefit levels, and de-commodification. Britain and the Scandinavian countries have also been grouped together as similar types of welfare states because of their emphasis on universalism and social citizenship. The analysis here discloses sharp divergences in women's and men's social rights between Sweden and the other three countries, calling into question earlier mainstream categorizations.

Turning to feminist scholarship, a major approach in the fledging efforts to gender welfare state analysis has been to devise alternative models and typologies. A key point of departure for these efforts has been the breadwinner model, and Jane Lewis and Ilona Ostner's work has been very influential. One of their important contributions has been to argue that the strength of the breadwinner model varies across welfare states (Lewis and Ostner, 1991; cf. Sainsbury, 1990, 1994), as distinct from earlier feminist writings which viewed the breadwinner model as an inherent feature of the welfare state. However, a major problem of the breadwinner model is its failure to come to grips with motherhood and mothering as a basis of entitlement.

A special difficulty in Lewis and Ostner's scheme is that they concentrate on primarily two bases of entitlement: as breadwinner or earner; and as the dependant of the breadwinner. For women this boils down to social rights based on either their dependent status as wives or mothers within the family *or* as workers. Lewis and Ostner further argued that 'it has been as wives rather than as mothers that women have qualified for benefits in most state social security systems' (1991: 25–6). What Lewis and Ostner see as the essential variation between welfare states is the extent to which women have also been recognized as workers (1991: 9; cf. Lewis, 1992a). They also downplay the principle of care by stating that 'no government has ever succeeded in attaching a significant value to the unpaid work of caring that women do in the family' (1991: 27).

These assumptions have important implications for their analysis. First they fail to explore social entitlements based on motherhood or the principle of care as a variation across countries. Second their emphasis on care as unpaid work causes them to depreciate the trend towards payment for care as an important welfare state variation, while others claim this trend is one of the major innovations of postwar welfare states (Daly and Scheiwe, Chapters 7 and 9 in this volume). Third, their concentration on the social entitlements of workers leads them to neglect entitlements based on citizenship and need. These omissions also result in a misreading of the history of women's social rights in Sweden. The contrast between Swedish women's social rights and those of women in other countries in the 1990s is interpreted as the effect of women's recent entry into the labour market in unprecedented numbers. According to Lewis, it was post-1970 governmental efforts to bring all adult women into the workforce which transformed the basis of Swedish women's entitlement from that of dependent wife to worker (1992a: 168–9). As this chapter has shown, before the 1970s social entitlements based on citizenship and the principle of care had already altered women's social rights so that they were not derived from their dependent status within the family as wives.

In summary, the analysis here affirms that the breadwinner model is crucial to an analysis of gender and welfare states. It also makes clear that the task of gendering welfare states cannot be limited to a typology based on this model. Gendering welfare states requires that women's entitlements not only as *wives* and *workers* but also as *mothers* and *citizens* be built into the analytical framework and investigated as cross-national variations.

Notes

This chapter is part of a larger research project funded by the Swedish Council for Research in the Humanities and Social Sciences and the Swedish Council for Planning and Co-ordination of Research.

1 For an assessment of the impact of gender equality reforms introduced since 1970 in the four countries, see Sainsbury, 1993b.

2 For a more detailed analysis of the four countries using mainstream dimensions of variation, see Sainsbury, 1991.

11

Solo Mothers, Social Policy Regimes and the Logics of Gender

Barbara Hobson

Over the past years, there has been a burgeoning in gender research that addresses citizenship, social rights and welfare statism. This phenomenon can be seen as an extension of the broad research agenda to bring the state back into the analysis of social politics and welfare state development (Evans *et al.*, 1985 and more currently Esping-Andersen, 1990). I would suggest, however, that it also represents a growing awareness among feminist scholars of the need to construct theories and develop paradigms that incorporate a range of policy dimensions sensitive to gender that are not considered in mainstream studies of welfare statism: the politics of time (see Scheiwe, Chapter 9 in this volume); the politics of the body (Shaver, 1992); and the politics of care (Waerness, 1990). These facets of welfare states so crucial to women's citizenship have not been considered areas relevant to the analysis of welfare state variation. Instead they were placed in a nether region, often noted as the private sphere, or civil society. In effect they have been decoupled from the central axis of welfare state theorizing that revolves around the policy sphere of state and market.

In analysing the gendered boundaries in welfare state theorizing, feminist scholars have posed challenges to categories and assumptions. They have revealed gendered constructions of the key concepts of dependence and independence, which they contend are grounded in the notion of one's ability to earn market income instead of one's ability to care for oneself (Knijn, 1991; Saraceno, 1994). By delineating certain spheres as public and others as private, feminist scholars claimed that dominant theories of citizenship failed to confront inequalities and injustices in the family (Hobson, 1990; Okin, 1989; Pateman, 1989a).

In this chapter, my goals are threefold. First, I want to discuss a range of feminist critical perspectives on policy regime theorizing. Then I consider some alternative currents in the research on gender and the policy regime paradigm. Third, I will suggest some criteria for constructing a social policy regime paradigm sensitive to gender differences in citizenship rights that can be used in comparative analyses. Here I take solo mothers as a litmus test group, or indicator of gendered social rights; I analyse the income sources and poverty rates of solo mothers in five countries. In the conclusion I map out the dilemmas for devising social policies attuned to women's social rights.

Critical perspectives of welfare state policy regimes

Feminist researchers have been attracted to welfare policy regime analysis because it supposes that the state is not a neutral arbiter, that the welfare state is a system of stratification in its own right (Esping-Andersen, 1990: 23). Although there exists a range of strategies for developing policy regimes that incorporate gender, I would like to suggest that one could divide them into two general categories. One category seeks to stretch the existing framework in policy regime analysis, gendering the mainstream paradigm. The other proposes alternative typologies with different criteria for clustering welfare states into policy regimes.

The concept of de-commodification has proved to be the most problematical for feminist researchers concerned with incorporating a gender dimension into policy regime analysis. Coined by Gøsta Esping-Andersen, de-commodification is the degree to which welfare states weaken an individual's market dependence. De-commodification does not apply to women who have not been commodified, but even more importantly, it occludes the fact that for many women labour market work has weakened women's economic dependence on husbands, and consequently enhanced their rights to make claims in the family. Not to be ignored is the fact that labour market work has enabled some women to exercise a basic civil right to leave an oppressive relationship, literally to vote with their feet (Hobson, 1991). Moreover, labour market work has allowed never-married or divorced women to become consumers of social services rather than clients on social assistance (Siim, 1993b).

Yet commodification in itself has not resulted in equalizing power relations in the family, since women tend to get lower wages than men; women confront labour markets with multiple levels of discrimination (Folbre, 1994; Morris, 1987). The decommodifying policies that do exist in welfare states are likely to have gendered uses and gendered effects. Men often take educational leave from work to improve their labour market situation. Women are most likely to take child leave that interrupts their working life to care but that has few payoffs for job advancement and can often hinder careers (Hobson, 1991).

De-commodification has become the whipping boy for feminist criticism of welfare regime theory, and perhaps rightly so. Recognizing the need to extend the boundaries of policy regime theorizing, some feminist scholars have suggested a gendered dimension beyond de-commodification. Julia O'Connor has argued for supplementing de-commodification with a concept of non-dependency in personal life, insulation from personal and public dependence as well as from market pressures (O'Connor, 1993). In a similar vein, Ann Orloff (1993) has suggested that de-commodification be subsumed under a more generic concept of independence that would encompass individuals' freedom from a compulsion to enter potentially oppressive relationships in a number of spheres. This would include the role of the state in mediating a range of relations, from the market to family to race relations in communities.

One obvious question that emerges from these endeavours to broaden the terrain of policy regime theorizing is whether going beyond de-commodification implies discarding the dominant welfare state regime paradigm (Orloff, 1993). But another more practical question is how do we apply concepts like non-dependency and freedom from oppressive relationships: can we define regime types or construct sets of measures to capture variability with such all-encompassing definitions?

Gender cuts across policy regime typologies when one considers the division of paid and unpaid work among men and women in society; in effect, who does the care work. I use a standard measure of dependency level in this analysis, which is the difference in the wage contributions of the husband and wife to the family economy (Hobson, 1990; Sørensen and McLanahan, 1987). Comparing the levels of economic dependency in several welfare states, I found that there is no real fit with the welfare policy regime clusters in Esping-Andersen's model (Table 11.1). Within all three clusters, the liberal, corporatist conservative and social democratic regime types, there are wide variations in dependency levels among the countries assigned to a regime type. Compare the patterns of economic dependency in the US and Britain in the liberal cluster, or France and Netherlands in the corporatist conservative group. If one considers wives totally dependent on husbands' income (Table 11.1), again one finds the same varied patterns of economic dependency among countries in regime types, which suggests that social policy shaping women's paid and unpaid work cannot be incorporated into the model.

Research has shown that there exists a hidden poverty among

Table 11.1 *Women's economic dependency in several Western societies*

Country	Dependency level	Dependency working women	% Total dependent	% No dependency
Liberal				
Australia				
(1981)	60.7	27.4	46.0	7.2
Australia				
(1985)	59.3	32.6	39.6	7.8
Canada (1981)	59.0	36.3	35.9	7.5
UK (1979)	60.8	42.0	32.6	5.7
USA (1979)	58.8	36.6	35.5	6.7
USA (1986)	49.8	29.3	29.4	9.6
Corporatist/				
Conservative				
Germany				
(1984)	62.9	27.0	49.2	6.2
Holland (1984)	74.7	20.3	68.2	3.4
Switzerland				
(1982)	77.0	51.4	52.9	2.6
Social				
Democratic				
Norway (1979)	55.7	41.5	25.0	8.3
Sweden (1981)	40.6	33.4	11.2	11.6

Note: The results in Tables 11.1 to 11.5 are based on data from the Luxembourg Income Study. % No dependency, represents those in economically egalitarian marriages, where the income gap is less than 10 per cent of the total family earnings.

wives who do not show up in poverty studies because they are members of families listed as having substantial incomes (Pahl, 1988). These findings call into question the assumption that resources are shared equally. Moreover, the competition for resources other than economic ones can result in inequalities. Here I am thinking of time resources, how time outside employment is organized in the family: this includes the division of paid and unpaid work as well as the freedom to take job opportunities that require long commuting times. Few would disagree that in a work organization, the man who had a housewife taking most of responsibilities for care work would have a competitive edge over the solo mother who had the double role of breadwinner and main carer in the family.

To gender welfare state regimes, therefore, implies more than just rearranging clusters or inserting qualifiers to the regime typologies. Instead it requires that we take a new point of departure, to postulate how and in what ways welfare state regimes promote certain types of family forms. Taking this formulation one step further, we have to let go of some of the theoretical levers in welfare state regime typologies. First, in considering family formation, it is not useful to divide welfare states into proactive and reactive. All welfare states take policy stands that assume a typical family and organize benefits to reflect these norms, penalizing economically and socially those who deviate from them. Tax structures in Western societies often favour a single-breadwinner family, but in Scandinavia the reverse in true: individual taxation makes it very costly for a wife not to work (Gustafsson and Bruyn-Hundt, 1992). Whether benefit levels are linked to contributions, to earnings or labour market status also shapes decisions on paid and unpaid work in the family. Thus one could say that welfare states stratify by gender in diverse ways, but that does not bring us any closer to constructing a barometer of social rights attuned to women's life experiences, nor does it provide a framework for creating alternative bases for policy regime analysis sensitive to gender.

Alternative models

Over the past decade there have been many studies of welfare states and policy-making that implicitly challenge the historical analysis and theoretical suppositions behind the clustering of welfare states in different policy regimes (Skocpol, 1992; Gordon, 1990b; Koven and Michel, 1990). Yet the recent work of Jane Lewis and Ilona Ostner (1991) poses a more direct challenge to the premisses of Gøsta Esping-Andersen's policy regime typology. These authors offer a strategy for developing an alternative gender policy regime paradigm that proposes a different set of criteria for constructing social policy regimes based upon variations in attachment to the male breadwinner ideology. This is an important contribution for several reasons: (1) it aims towards a model that reveals the inter-meshing of public and private spheres of life in the organization of welfare; (2) it attempts to find a framework that addresses the role of women's unpaid work, as providers of welfare; (3) it strives to comprehend the mosaic of women's lives, which have been shaped by social provisioning and welfare state policies – not only levels of benefits, but entitlement structures and the organization of services for care work.

Lewis and Ostner imagine a gender policy regime based upon the strength or weakness of the male breadwinner outlook: how ideas of the bourgeois family form and appropriate male and female roles and how this structures social policies in welfare states. They break down these regime types into three categories:

- strong breadwinner outlook: representative of this type are Germany, Britain and the Netherlands;
- moderate breadwinner outlook: a typical case is France;
- weak breadwinner outlook: Sweden is the paradigmatic case.

By articulating a policy regime model based upon the centrality of the family wage ideology, Lewis and Ostner have highlighted the ways in which gender cuts across typologies in the mainstream discussion. However, though the breadwinner outlook is deeply embedded in the formation of welfare states, it is difficult to devise a policy regime paradigm that could incorporate the many facets of this ideological concept. In fact, the measures used to predict which welfare states are strong, moderate or weak are themselves expressions of the family wage ideology; so we are caught in a tautological bind. For example the variations in breadwinner model can be found in how women are treated in social security systems, in the development of childcare, and in women's labour market participation. The weak, moderate and strong categories conflate the different bases upon which women's care work is incorporated into policy regimes – whether welfare states socialize some of the costs of care or approximate a social wage for mothering; whether the sources of women's claims in welfare states are linked to their status as workers, as wives, or as mothers who service the needs of children.

Besides the fundamental question of how to delineate policy regime types based upon this kind of ideological construct, I find the male breadwinner typology problematical in one crucial respect. Basically it does not capture a core feature in the variability of welfare states: that they redistribute resources and services that affect women's economic well-being, particularly those women who are the only breadwinners in their families. Both women and men are more and less poor in certain welfare states because of the fact that welfare regimes are systems of stratification (Esping-Andersen, 1990; Esping-Andersen and Korpi, 1987; Palme, 1992). Consequently to cluster Britain, the Netherlands and Germany into a strong breadwinner model is to ignore the differences in poverty among solo mothers, who are the residuum in the male breadwinner ideology.

Solo mothers and policy regimes

In this section, I consider the situation of solo mothers as reflective of a family blueprint in divergent policy regimes. I have selected solo mothers for this analysis because they allow for a discussion of different dimensions in welfare states: claim structures; the organization of care; and more generally the unstated assumptions about dependency and independence in welfare states.

Solo mothers are not a homogeneous group, nor is solo motherhood a status, but rather it is a shifting pattern in a life course. For this reason, I have consciously chosen to call this group solo mothers, rather than lone mothers or single parents, since solo parents often do not live alone, but with kin, friends or even lovers. In some countries these mothers are classified as solo mothers and are entitled to benefits as solo mothers, while in other countries they are not. Furthermore, solo mothers may often move in and out of coupled relationships (Morris, 1987). Nevertheless I do not view solo mothers as a border case (O'Higgins, 1987), but as an analytic category for understanding gendered dimensions in welfare states.

There are many justifications for viewing solo mothers as an analytic category in welfare state regime studies. One obvious reason is that they appear as a category in policy discourse, most often as a problem or risk group, and in the US the solo mother is the welfare mother, a trope for dependency or family breakdown. In some cases, policy for solo mothers and definitions of a solo mother are bound up with one another.[1]

But I would add another theoretical justification for including solo mothers as a category from the standpoint of justice and citizenship rights. Solo mothers could be viewed as a highly disadvantaged group in terms of their resources, which include money, time and social networks. If one assumes that all married mothers are potentially solo mothers (given the rises in divorce in all Western industrial societies over the last decades), then the kinds of state support solo mothers receive indirectly shape the equality in families. Solo motherhood is the reflector or rearview mirror for the dynamics of power and dependency – the more difficult and stigmatized solo motherhood is in a society, the greater the barriers against opting out of a bad marriage. From this standpoint, the kinds of state support solo mothers receive can be employed as a barometer of the strength or weakness of social rights of women with families.

Most relevant to this discussion of policy regimes is that a focus on solo mothers can also reveal policy logics around the organization of paid and unpaid work. Beginning with this assumption, we can see patterns in welfare states in which social provisioning, services and protective legislation are aimed at a mother who works outside the home. Others are built around a mother carer in the home; and some have contradictory policies that divorce the experiences of married mother and unmarried mother and produce separate systems or tracks of welfare and work.

In order to capture the various dimensions of solo mothers and their potential for constructing policy regime typologies, I have divided the analysis into three parts. First, I examine the variations in poverty rates in five countries; next I compare the income packages of solo mothers in these countries; and finally I employ a model of different solo mother groups, those whose main source of income is from earnings, social transfers, and private transfers. Finally, I consider the poverty rates of these groups.

The data for this analysis of solo mothers are from the Luxembourg Income Study (LIS).[2] For purposes of comparability, I have selected five countries which represent different types of welfare policy regimes within the dominant paradigm: the United States and Britain as liberal policy regime countries; Germany as the conservative corporatist; Sweden as the social democratic; and the Netherlands because it has been aligned with the social democratic regimes in some studies, and corporatist Christian Democratic alongside Germany in other analyses (see Gustafsson, Chapter 4 in this volume).

All solo mothers between the ages of 20 and 50 and with children under 18 are in the sample. The strength of the LIS is its highly comparable income and social transfer data, so this analysis will exploit these sources of income. I use a standard convention for calculating relative poverty rates; all solo mothers with incomes below half the median income, adjusted for family size, are defined as poor.

If we look at Figure 11.1 we can see that, as expected, Sweden and the US represent the opposite ends of the poverty rates of solo mothers (Sweden having the lowest rate and the US the highest). Less obvious are the variations in poverty rates among the other three countries. Though the Netherlands and Germany are examples of the strong male breadwinner outlook, according to Lewis and Ostner's schema, German solo mothers are three times more likely to be poor than their Dutch counterparts. Britain, paired with the US as a liberal policy regime type in Esping-Andersen's typologies, does not show the same high rate of poverty for solo mothers. They have a much lower risk of poverty than either American or German solo mothers.

In comparing the income sources of solo mothers (earnings, social transfers and private transfers), I sought to apply some criteria for the hegemony of the male breadwinner outlook: the greater the proportion of earnings among solo mother earners, the weaker the male breadwinner outlook.[3]

But even the Swedish case does not fit this hypothesis (see Figure 11.2). Often characterized as the prototype of the citizen worker model among Western industrialized countries (Ruggie, 1984; Esping-Andersen, 1990), Sweden is the country with the highest

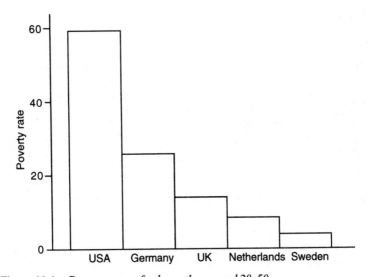

Figure 11.1   *Poverty rates of solo mothers, aged 20–50*

Source: Data for Figures 1–4 are from the *Luxembourg Income Study*.
The years included are: US 1986; Germany 1984; UK 1986; Netherlands
1987; Sweden 1987.

proportion of women in the labour force and has the most extensive
daycare services, among our five countries. Yet solo mothers are
dependent on social transfers for a significant portion of their income
package. Whereas social assistance is the form of transfer payments
most solo mothers receive in other countries, in Sweden they are
more likely to make up their income package with supports from
housing allowances, daycare subsidies and income maintenance
payments (Gustafsson, 1990)

Private transfers (see Figure 11.2) comprise a very small proportion of solo mothers' income. One might expect that in those
countries said to represent the liberal and corporatist policy regime
types, where the family is supposed to be the main source of welfare,
a substantial portion of solo mothers' income would derive from
private transfers. However, not more than 7 per cent of solo mothers
got the main part of their income from private transfers even in
Germany, Britain and the US (see Figure 11.3).

The income packages of solo mothers may not fall into neat
clusters of welfare policy regimes, but they shed light on how policy
regimes can structure women's choices around paid and unpaid
work. Furthermore they can tell us something about the degree to
which welfare states display a two-track system of work or welfare. In
order to reveal how the income sources of solo mothers in the five

50% Earnings

45% Social transfers

4% Private

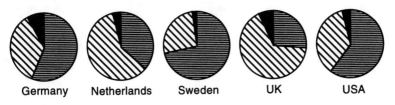

Germany   Netherlands   Sweden   UK   USA

Figure 11.2   *Size of solo mother groups based on main income source*

countries reflect different policy options, I have classified solo mothers into three categories. My purpose is to identify the main source of income of solo mothers, and I differentiate three groups: the earnings group composed of those with wages as their main income source; the social transfer group whose main source of income is government transfers, both means tested and universal: social assistance, child allowance, housing allowance, income maintenance, unemployment, maternity allowance and so on. The third group is dependent on private transfers for their income, which includes alimony or child support or other income.[4]

If we compare the size of these groups, we see that Sweden is the country with the highest proportion of earners; the UK, the lowest. These two cases exemplify the constraints and opportunities for mothers to be in or out of the labour force. Daycare facilities, employment possibilities, and the general extent to which welfare states have socialized the costs of care compose one side of the constellation of solo mothers' universe of choices; the ways in which types of benefits and levels are defined compose the other side. For example, Heather Joshi (1990), asking if British solo mothers have alternatives to living on social assistance, considers the gross wages of mothers with and without jobs, and concludes that social assistance, tax structures and daycare facilities are barriers against solo mothers increasing their economic activity. For Swedish solo mothers, the reverse is true: tax systems, daycare places and parental leave allowances favour women who are wage-earners (Gustafsson, 1990).

Not surprisingly, in all five countries earners are the category of solo mothers who are the least poor. This can be seen as an effect of the rules of entitlement in some welfare states – where benefits are means tested and often eliminate wage-earners. Another explanation for the lower poverty rates of earners is that social assistance

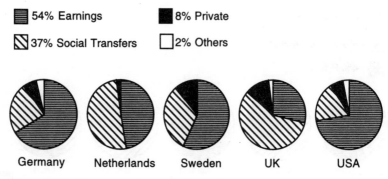

Figure 11.3   *Income packages of solo mothers*

benefits are often set low enough to discourage workers from going on the dole. So in order to capture the ways in which social policies might shape decisions about paid and unpaid work, it makes sense to examine the poverty rates of solo mothers whose main source of income is social transfers.

Looking at Figure 11.4, we see that among solo mothers who rely on social transfers for most of their income, American women and German women are the poorest; 89 per cent of American women in this group have incomes below half the median income; 49.5 per cent of German solo mothers who are dependent on transfers for their main income source are poor compared with only 10 per cent of those in the earning category. This group is less disadvantaged in Sweden, considered the paradigm worker citizen model in policy regime analyses; there is actually a smaller gap between earners and social transfer groups. In the Netherlands the poverty rates are the same (9 per cent) among solo mothers who depend on earnings and those who depend on transfers as their main income source.

What is emerging from this preliminary analysis is that the income packages of solo mothers seem to confound our expectations about models of motherhood in different social policy regimes. Leibfried (1990a) has argued that citizens make claims upon welfare states in the spheres or work or need, and feminist scholars have extended citizen claims to include motherhood (Skocpol, 1992; Gordon, 1990b). When analysing the situation of solo mothers, it is also important to consider that the basis of entitlement may differ for married mothers and solo mothers.

To say that welfare regimes stratify by gender therefore requires a careful examination, not only of the forms of entitlement solo mothers have around work, need and motherhood, but of how policies are fitted together: are solo mothers detached nebulae in a

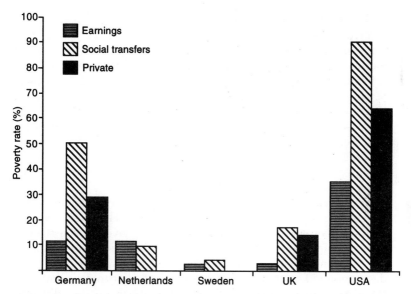

Figure 11.4   *Poverty rates of groups of solo mothers*

policy universe not connected to care-giving through marriage or wage-earning in the labour market? Are they a deviant category in the everyday life patterns of mothers with children? Finally, is there a logic or consistency in the treatment of solo mothers in relation to married mothers in a policy regime?

To view solo mothers in this context is to make sense of the high rates of poverty in two countries, Germany and the United States, which are supposed to represent different types of welfare regime. In both countries solo mothers exist in a black hole within a policy constellation where benefits revolve around worker status, and where entitlement is grounded in the notion of contribution. But there are few provisions to support working mothers or non-working mothers (who are not wives). Wives and widows are privileged in both systems. This bifurcation in policy between worker and non-worker, married mother and unmarried mother, produces extreme levels of poverty among solo mothers who are dependent on social transfers.

In Germany, social policy has a gender logic which assumes that mothers are claimants through their status as wives (Esping-Andersen, 1990; Ostner, 1993). Both taxes and social transfers are built around a breadwinner with a dependent wife with or without children. For solo mothers, this has translated into a low level of benefits; around 49 per cent of German mothers who have social transfers as their main source of income are poor. All German mothers receive a care benefit for children, but it is not a care wage; instead it is a supplement to husbands' earnings. The disincentives for married mothers to work can be seen in the gap between married women's and solo mothers' labour force participation: 57 per cent of solo mothers versus 41 per cent of married mothers claimed to be employed in the recent EC survey on lone mothers (Pieters *et al.*, 1992: 72). Although there is a parental leave benefit, there are minimal facilities for daycare, particularly for children under the age of three (Kulawik and Riedmüller, 1991). Some of the greatest impediments to combining employment and parenting appear in the organization of everyday life, when schools are in session and shops are open.

Never-married solo mothers in Germany are most vulnerable in a system that supports the wives of working men. However, divorced mothers also fare poorly in that they do not have a social right to income maintenance. In theory a former husband is bound to support his children; yet it is a discretionary judgment based on a court decision, and failure to pay again requires a court proceeding. The state will provide income maintenance payments for divorced mothers when husbands fail to support their children, but only for a short period, usually about three years. Solo mothers have no policy domain either as full-time carers or as paid workers. Within the gender logic of the German policy constellation that is organized around marital status or paid work, solo mothers are a residual category.

Within the US policy matrix of welfare or work, solo mothers fit uneasily into either track. As recipients of Aid to Dependent Children, they are not provided with a living wage, so many mothers supplement welfare benefits with shadow labour market work (Amott, 1990). Solo mothers who are dependent on social transfers are extremely poor: 89 per cent of those in this study. Nor can solo mothers readily combine work and caring responsibilities. As labour market participants, they lose their welfare benefits and state health care benefit. At the same time they lack the basic supports necessary to sustain working mothers: affordable daycare and part-time jobs that provide minimum wage or job security. American working mothers have some of the weakest mandated job protection or maternal leave benefits in Western industrialized countries (Kamerman and Kahn, 1991). Only recently has a national policy been passed (1993) that allows for unpaid maternal leave. Individual workplaces often have maternal leave policies and some have daycare facilities, but these are more likely to be firms or organizations with skilled and professional full-time workers. In a market-based system of care provision, the solo mother, with fewer time resources and social supports, is very disadvantaged (Kamerman and Kahn, 1991).

In the US solo mothers have no legitimate place in the discursive universe of social policy. As full-time carers supported by public assistance, they are condemned as welfare dependants, non-contributors to society, and as full-time workers, they have been censured as neglectful mothers. Solo mothers as widows, however, are defined as deserving; not welfare dependants, but entitled to a survivor's benefit, through their husband's social insurance contributions (Fraser and Gordon, 1994). Aid to Dependent Children emerged from a mother's pension movement and was constructed around a mother's need to care for her children (referred to as welfare in American social policy) (Skocpol, 1992). However, the current wave of welfare reform seeks to force welfare mothers to join the labour force (referred to as workfare), and what is evolving is a single-track system of a worker mother who supports her family. This attempt to undermine the welfare dependency of solo mothers, has not led to changes in the framework or policy logic: there are few caring services for working mothers; few benefits or job protection for part-time workers; and the labour market sustains discriminatory wage patterns for women and blacks.

Having discussed the lack of fit or logic in welfare states where solo mothers are likely to be poor, I want to turn to policy frameworks where solo mothers seem to be integrated into what I will refer to as gender policy regimes in which mothers are compensated for care work. Here we might consider criteria for constructing gender policy regime typologies: whether benefits are in the form of social wage, socials services or income supports; and more generally whether the claim structures or forms of entitlement for solo mothers are constructed around their roles as workers, as mothers, or as citizens.

From these perspectives, Sweden appears as a parent-worker citizen model where benefits are linked to labour market participation but also to solo parenting. Swedish solo mothers are mainly wage-earners, but receive benefits – such as daycare subsidies and child allowances – on the basis of motherhood/parenthood. They also receive benefits as solo mothers; when fathers are unable to or do not pay child support, they are given income maintenance payments. Working parents are entitled to daycare if there is a daycare place, but solo working mothers have priority in the queue, and in many municipalities have reduced fees. As citizens, they receive child allowances; as low-income earners, they are entitled to housing subsidies. They are also accorded rights on the basis of worker status, job protection after parental leave and the right to work part time for six years of child-rearing.[5]

Holland, on the other hand, exemplifies a mother–carer–citizen model. In practice solo mothers in Holland are given a social wage, a benefit that has allowed them to remain at home as full-time carers. Although they receive some benefits as solo mothers, their main income source is a general benefit that all persons without work are entitled to, based on a minimum wage level for a family (Knijn, 1994). The benefit levels are high and approximate a social wage; more than 95 per cent of Dutch solo mothers mainly dependent on social transfers for their income would be poor if they did not receive them. [6] In the Dutch policy framework, solo mothers have not had to look for work as unemployed workers nor have their benefits been reduced if they were living with a man not their husband who earned income (Knijn, 1994). Their payment in fact has been a care wage, and they have had the social right to be a head of household.

In both cases married and unmarried mothers display similar patterns. In Sweden over 90 per cent of women between the ages of 25 and 55 are in the labour force; and married mothers and solo mothers have nearly equal rates of labour force activity (Gornick, 1992).[7] Mothers in Holland, both solo and married, tend to be outside the labour force: only 24 per cent of the former and 28 per cent of the latter are in market work, according to the recent lone mothers survey (Pieters *et al.*, 1992).

British solo mothers are like their Dutch counterparts in that they tend to be full-time carers. Although benefit levels are not as high as in Holland – they do not approximate a minimum wage for a household – supports for solo mothers and their children are relatively generous compared to treatment of other vulnerable groups in society. Solo mothers in Britain are entitled to a means-tested benefit as non-earning mothers who lack a breadwinner.[8] If they become wage-earners, they lose their benefits. If they cohabit with another man, it is expected that he will take over the responsibility of breadwinner. I would refer to this variant of policy regime in relation to solo mothers as mother-needs.[9]

Rather than propose a social policy regime paradigm, my purpose in this analysis has been to put forward a set of criteria and dimensions on which to build a theory of gendered social rights that can be deployed in comparative studies of welfare states.

I use solo mothers as an analytic category because they are a disadvantaged group, and in nearly all societies policymakers treat them as the border or deviant case although the numbers of solo mothers are increasing exponentially. However, suppose those making policy assumed that all mothers might be solo mothers at one time during their life course. More broadly, suppose we as citizens began with Rawls's veil of ignorance, that none of us can know whether we are to be a solo father or mother. Such an *a priori* position might produce more equal distributive systems of services and incomes than now exist in any of the countries in this analysis.

This standpoint allows us to take the analysis of social rights within gender policy regime theorizing one step further: beyond the male breadwinner outlook model, which does not take into account the outcomes of policy regimes and where solo mothers are a border case in the construction of policies. It also enables us to analyse what it means in actual policy to permit women the 'independence or freedom from compulsion to enter potentially oppressive relationships' (Orloff, 1993). Or how we assess what value welfare states place on women's unpaid caring work.

As this analysis reveals, solo mothers are least disadvantaged when they are fitted into a policy frame that recognizes them as the heads of legitimate households, within a policy logic of care as service or care as facet of citizenship. Taking this as our point of departure, we can suggest a set of strategies for decoding the logic in a policy frame. Are solo mothers a deviant or residual category in the construction of care and parenting within welfare states? How do welfare states stratify the distribution of benefits and services through various claim structures of work, need and parenting? Are solo mothers mainly dependent on transfers as poor as those dependent mainly on earnings? Are there specific policies both on services and on income support that address solo mothers?

Policy regimes can be likened to ecosystems; to disturb one habitat can upset the equilibrium and cause radical changes. Thus in Holland recent proposals that seek to compel solo mothers to find employment implies a change in systems of care and a policy frame that constrains women from combining work and family life.[10] A less sanguine scenario is that forcing solo mothers to obtain labour market work would mean an increase in their poverty since they probably will not find market work with wages high enough to enable them to hire private carers. In Sweden, an intense policy debate over a form of care subsidy for mothers raises similar concerns, from the opposite side. This benefit gives mothers the option to stay at home, or to purchase as many hours of care – public or private – as a family chooses. Though these subsidies are not a replacement for wages (they assume a breadwinner earner to be the main source of income), they require large outlays from the state budget and will be funded through reductions in provisions for public care. These initiatives portend the dismantling of a policy structure that has supported parenting and working. Since the public sector has been a provider of both social services and jobs, a circular effect operates. The fewer women who require a daycare place, the fewer jobs; the fewer jobs, the fewer places. As one module is removed from the policy framework, others tend to fall away, such as generous paid parental leave, paid sick days to care for children, and other social rights related to parenting.

Concluding remarks

In thinking about gendering welfare state regimes, it is obvious that we need to construct other barometers of social rights to those that form the basis of the dominant paradigm in welfare policy regimes. Instead of posing the question of how much the state socializes the cost of care (Esping-Andersen, 1990), a more inclusive strategy for a gendered analysis of policy regimes is to ask, what are the compensatory policies for caring? Public provision of care is only one type of compensatory policy for caring. Such policies can include paid parental leave, time off from employment with wage replacement to care for sick children, as well as caring benefits to mothers who take the role of full-time carers for their small children. It should not be forgotten that even in countries with highly developed public care systems, women bear the main responsibility for taking care of children and elderly parents (Waerness, 1990).

No pure model of social policy regimes organized around paid work or unpaid domestic care work exists in Western industrial societies, which is a reflection of the growing numbers of mothers who now participate in market work and the increase in solo parent families.

At this stage in the discussion of gender and social policy, the question of choice comes to the fore. Many of the current feminist analyses of social rights have advocated both women's right to choose not to care (Land, 1983) and the right to care (Orloff, 1993; Ungerson, 1990). Yet the rollback or retreat of welfare states in providing services and benefits apparent in Western countries, even more dramatic in former socialist states, heightens the dilemma of having it both ways: is it realistic to imagine a social policy regime that supports equally a mother's wage for caring that would allow her to form an autonomous household, and a system of services and provisions that would allow mothers to be integrated into working life?

Notes

This research has been supported by a grant from the Swedish Social Science Research Council and Swedish Work Environment Fund. I would like to thank Joakim Palme for all his help with the LIS data and for his invaluable suggestions for this chapter. I would also like to thank Teresa Kulawik and Diane Sainsbury for their comments.

1 This is the case in the UK, where lone parents are eligible for supplementary benefit until their children can claim income support benefits themselves, which is interpreted to mean that they are no longer dependent on their mothers for money or care (Pieters *et al.*, 1992: 35).

2 For a description of the data source and its applicability to gender regimes, see Hobson (1990).

3 Lewis and Ostner (1991) allude to the difficulty of applying their typology to the experiences of solo mothers in the respective countries.

4 These categories are based on similar groups in Joakim Palme's comparative study of the poverty of the pre-retirement elderly (1992).

5 In the formative stages of Swedish welfare state development, policy makers addressed women's roles as mother and worker in the public debates around population decline. The legislation that supported married women's rights as workers in the 1930s was embedded in a discourse of motherhood, i.e. working women's right to be mothers (Hobson, 1993).

6 I estimated this poverty rate for Dutch mothers without social transfers by conducting some hypothetical experiments in which I took away sources of income for each group: earnings, social transfers and private transfers.

7 Married mothers are more likely to work part time than solo mothers, but that usually means a 30-hour week, and married women may have increased care work for husbands and children.

8 The current policy shift towards solo mothers is towards making the father pay back the state. This has caused a storm of protest by middle-class fathers who now support new families and by solo mothers who refuse to give the names of fathers to social authorities (Lister, 1994).

9 Within the policy constellations around caring and earning, there is a tradition and an orientation toward mothers' entitlement as carers,which can be seen in the policy decision to pay child allowance benefits directly to mothers (Lewis, 1991b).

10 Current procedures require that they must work if there is a daycare place or a care substitute.

12

Social Policy and Gender in Eastern Europe

Toni Makkai

Although this chapter is speculative to a degree, its primary purpose is to examine the embryonic developments in welfare policy in Eastern Europe and the extent to which these changes are affecting male and female labour force participation and gender roles generally. It will show that in these terms the former state socialist welfare regime of Eastern Europe appears to be following the continental model of welfare provision. Fundamentally, the state is seen to have a subsidiary role emphasizing a traditional patriarchal family structure.

The breakdown of the state socialist order and the move toward a market economy has resulted in an 'institutional vacuum' (Stark, 1992: 299), and it is within this vacuum that social policy is undergoing change as it moves from a 'monistic' to a 'pluralistic' system (Mishra, 1977). It is highly likely that women's lives will be as dramatically affected as they were when the command economy was instituted. The high labour force participation of women means that any restructuring of the economy and social policy will differentially impact on them as workers and as consumers (Buckley, 1992). The types of welfare regimes that develop will be most critically defined by the way in which the state mediates the relationship between men and women and the relationship between men and women and the labour market.

The welfare mix that is evolving is dependent to a certain extent on two factors. The first is the different historical, political and cultural roots that characterized these countries prior to the Second World War. The second is the economic, social and political circumstances in which these countries find themselves. As a result welfare policy across the region will have both commonalities and diversity (Deacon, 1992b). Before moving to contemporary patterns, it is therefore important to provide an overview of the inherited system.

Social policy pre-1989

The advent of state socialism in Central and Eastern Europe resulted in a fundamental change in the structure of society and in the role of women. Where previously these societies had been peasant based with low industrial development, the post-1945 regimes set about building up an extensive industrial basis. This industrial basis was intended to provide workers with better living standards than was possible under a capitalist system, and was based on two important principles. The first was that all people, regardless of sex or race, were equal politically, economically and socially. The second was that all those capable of working in the paid labour market should do so and rewards in the new society were to be based on this form of worker participation. Both of these factors directly impacted on women: not only were women regarded as equal, at least at an ideological and formal level, but they were also now expected – and actively encouraged – to participate in the paid labour market.

The model of state socialism that was imported into these countries was almost universally similar – the Soviet model of a command economy that stressed collectivization so that production and consumption could be centrally planned and controlled. This also included the provision of welfare services with the state acting as the provider, on egalitarian principles, for each individual from the cradle to the grave.

The ideological premiss that underlay the new state socialist order was that only market economies required social welfare provisions in order to bolster support for a capitalist system that was inherently crisis ridden. These crises would lead to longer and ever worsening recessions and all of the associated social problems that accompany such cycles. In a one-party state, it was argued, the economy could be efficiently managed and directed so that such recessions did not occur and paid employment was guaranteed for all able-bodied citizens who were expected to work full time. Social policy was not viewed as distinct from politics and any discussion of social policy as a separate issue was regarded as unnecessary. The official view was that social problems, such as the 'woman' question and unemployment, would cease to exist as the state socialist system became an even larger producer of goods.

Writing in the late 1970s Mishra (1977) referred to the state socialist countries as 'normative' welfare systems based on an ideology of 'each according to their need'. To illustrate the normative welfare type he used the USSR as a case study. His work, in a classical gender-blind approach, examines social policy in the areas of income maintenance, medical care, housing and education. There are no references to the inherently discriminatory nature of a social insurance system linked to a labour market in which women were channelled into the lowly paid sectors or to the overwhelming responsibility that women had for caring work within the family under state socialism.

During the 1980s, the East European countries spent over one-fifth of their GDP on social programmes and on the subsidization of many goods and services (Holzman, 1992). However, the provision and financing of social programmes was closely linked to the structure of the command economy and most welfare payments were linked directly to employment status. The type and duration of employment were the most important factors in determining eligibility for welfare and the level of payment. There were, of course, variations between the different East European countries in eligibility criteria, the structure and type of benefits, and in the levels of payment (Holzman, 1992). However, analyses of cash social transfers in 1988 for Hungary, Czechoslovakia, Poland and Bulgaria indicate that the size and distribution were relatively similar across the four countries, accounting for between 21 and 25 per cent of gross national income (Milanović, 1992).

Unemployment was unknown, or at least unacknowledged, and retirement benefits were related to work history. This was not, then, a system based on universal citizenship rights but one based on work performance. Those who had long work histories in the industrial sectors received the largest benefits, as they were seen as the most productive workers. The distortion in wages and its flow on to pensions thus ensured that certain sectors received much lower wages and consequently lower pensions. The statutory replacement rate of pensions was low and many pensioners either lived in poverty or found jobs to supplement their pensions. There was no automatic indexation of pensions, and widows' pensions were a proportion of the pension of the deceased spouse. Given the low level of wages, widows who did not work in the paid labour market were and remain one of the most economically underprivileged groups in the community.

Non-cash benefits associated with labour force participation were important social goods. Via the enterprise within which they worked, individuals obtained subsidized meals, holidays, transportation to work and childcare. The state provided most housing, and rent and food prices were subsidized so that basic subsistence items like bread and milk were available to all at very low prices. With a commitment to universal benefits, education and health services were, on the whole, provided free. These provisions were seen as being more equitable than cash benefits, and they supplemented low wages.

In their drive to achieve equality before the law for all sections of the society East European countries moved to introduce a variety of mechanisms that would enable women to enter the labour market while still having children. Maternity benefits and maternity leave with the guarantee of returning to their original occupational position, child benefits, and equal rights before the law for both legitimate and illegitimate children were also introduced. The principle of equal work and equal pay was enshrined in law. The premiss underlying these provisions was that the exploitation of women would be overcome once they were proletarianized (Meyer, 1985; Swain, 1992).

Despite state socialist intentions, the longer-term outcomes that became apparent indicated that, although income inequality had been greatly reduced, capricious and selective redistribution of social goods had 'the effect of making overall social inequality greater than inequalities of income' (Swain, 1992: 186). The net result was that 'socially valued groups continued to receive a disproportionately large share of the cake, even after socialist income policies had significantly reduced inequality' (ibid.).

This system has led Wnuk-Lipinski (1992: 185) to talk about the development of 'an equality of conditions rather than equality of opportunity'. Although social policy was part of an integrated package that was supposed to result in a humane, efficient, in-dustrialized society with full employment, Wnuk-Lipinski has noted, as have others (Swain, 1992; Deacon, 1992a, 1992b), that social inequality did not disappear but manifested itself via other mechan-isms. Certainly, there was no differentiation on the basis of property rights, and upward mobility occurred for workers and the peasantry in the early days of state socialism. Also women entered the labour market in such large numbers that by the 1980s they represented just under half of the active labour force – a much higher rate of participation than that found in most Western countries.

Although women represented almost half of the workforce they still failed to gain significant representation in the top earning occupations.[1] The heavy industry and construction sectors were prioritized for higher wages and it was in these sectors that women were especially under-represented. As a consequence, women's wages were lower than men's (Siemieńska, 1985; Einhorn and Mitter, 1991; Heinen, 1990; Hubner *et al.*, 1991). For example, data from Hungary in 1967 showed that women's earnings as a proportion of men's was 66.7 per cent, increasing to 69.1 per cent in 1972 and 71.2 per cent in 1977 (Kulcsár, 1985; Swain, 1992). Recent data indicate that the average gap in official earnings between men and women was 25 per cent but more commonly around 30 per cent or more (Eberhardt and Heinen, 1993).

Even in occupations dominated by women few were found in senior managerial positions (Einhorn and Mitter, 1991; Heinen, 1990).[2] Eberhardt and Heinen (1993) estimated that in large companies the proportion of women at managerial level never exceeded 8 per cent, and was usually much lower. The under-representation of women in the occupational structure was also mirrored within the trade unions and the political organs of the state, particularly in the higher decision-making bodies where policy debate and agenda-setting occurred (Wagnerová, 1983; Siemieńska, 1983; Castle-Kanerová, 1992).

Political affiliations were important for obtaining access to scarce and valuable goods. This impacted directly on the household's well-being and women were significantly less likely to belong to households which had such connections. It is difficult to quantify the impact of such non-monetized activity, and surveys asking about such issues are rare. More recent data from seven East European countries indicate that 30 per cent of people reported that someone in their household had gone to somebody to get things done that they could not get done in an ordinary way.[3] Yet only 27 per cent of women reported this as compared to 33 per cent of men. Given that this question refers to households and not individuals it is more than likely that the discrepancy between women and men is an underestimate.

Income, although important, was by no means the most important factor in fulfilling unmet needs. Having access to the black market or to circles in which illegally obtained goods and services could be bartered provided differential access to material assets. This is why inequality measures on income are less relevant in the East European context. Twelve per cent of East Europeans reported in the 1992 New Democracies Barometer that someone in their family had been able to buy things with foreign currency. Again, women are less likely to be located in households engaged in such activities. Ten per cent of women as compared to 14 per cent of men reported such activity within their household. Similarly, access to land to raise small animals or grow vegetables that could then be stored throughout the winter eased the burden of food shortages and endemic queuing (Wnuk-Lipinski, 1992; Rose, 1992a). The endemic consumer shortages meant that citizens had to spend long hours queuing. This role was, however, the responsibility of women. Analysis of the 1992 New Democracies Barometer data showed that women across seven East European countries were significantly more likely to report that they spend more than an hour a day queuing in shops. The level of such activity varies enormously across countries and the extent of the male/female difference also varies. However, in none of the countries did men undertake more queuing. Not only does such activity extend the working day; there is no monetary compensation for the activity.

Access to social security was not a universal benefit and it was

Table 12.1 *Crèche and nursery school coverage in Eastern Europe, 1989–90 (%)*

Country	Crèches	Nursery schools
Albania	21.0	71
Bulgaria	12.6	67
Czechoslovakia	16.0	90
East Germany	80.0	90
Hungary	8.6	86
Poland	5.0	48
Romania	5.5	85

Sources: Eberhardt and Heinen (1993: Table 4); Szalai (1991: Tables 4a and 4b)

distorted by location in particular status groups. In Czechoslovakia, for example, 'social security was degraded from a legal right to a political award, subject to ex-post facto whims of the state' (Ulc, 1974: 50, quoted in Castle-Kanerová 1992: 98). While in Hungary, for example, the nomenclatura received up to five times the average pension (Szeman, 1992) and in Poland the ruling strata were exempt from taxation (Clark and Wildavsky, 1990). Aggregate figures of the amount of GDP spent on social welfare obscure the distortion in access to social welfare. Although women represented half of the labour force they were by no means half of the nomenclatura. As a consequence access to privileges was greatly reduced, or women were dependent on such privileges being granted via their husbands.

State socialist policies were designed in such a way that women were not forced to choose between paid work and raising children. However many of these policies reinforced the traditional view that caring was a woman's and not a man's role. As a consequence, provision of crèches and nursery schools was not as widespread as it was claimed, with the exception of East Germany (Eberhardt and Heinen, 1993). Table 12.1 shows the percentage of children who were in crèches for children generally, aged one to three years and the percentage of children in nursery schools generally, aged between 4 and 6 years. Eberhardt and Heinen (1993) point out that the percentage of crèche places ranged from a low of around five per cent for Poland and Romania to a high of 80 per cent for the former GDR.

Of the policies that were directed towards the care of children – maternity leave, childcare facilities, leave to care for sick children – they were generally used by women and there was no attempt to reallocate responsibilities for caring within the home so that men assumed an equal share of the burden. In other words, the traditional patriarchal family model dominated the lives of East and Central European women (Meyer, 1985). This is most clearly demonstrated by the time use surveys conducted in a variety of countries. Data from the mid-1960s showed that under state socialism women were not only more likely to be engaged in full-time labour activity than women in France or the United States but that they undertook more housework and had less free time than western female counterparts (see Lupri, 1983: Table 4). In the GDR women performed 50–75 per cent of all domestic labour and three out of five women said that they were satisfied with this arrangement (Dölling, 1991; Einhorn, 1991; Swain, 1992). Similar findings were reported for Hungary and Poland (Einhorn, 1991).

The basic contradiction under state socialism was that women were defined as workers and mothers while there was no similar redefining of men's roles (Dölling, 1991; Einhorn, 1991). The state had poor provisions for other forms of welfare such as aged care, health care and housing. This was a direct result of spending priorities; industrial production was allocated the major share of resources while unproductive sectors such as health provision were left with a residual amount (Swain, 1992).

Within the welfare budget, the share of expenditure on health care and education was smaller than in West European countries (Smeeding, 1991). The lower status allocated to these functions disproportionately affected women. In terms of health care, women are greater consumers both for themselves and their children. Poor health provisions are most dramatically evidenced by the higher rates of infant mortality in Eastern than in Western Europe. With the exception of East Germany, all the East European countries have infant mortality rates higher than Portugal's rate of 11.0 per thousand (Rose, 1992b). Similarly, women not only disproportionately make up the old-aged population but they are also the ones who carry the burden of caring for elderly parents.

Aggregate statistics demonstrate a lower overall level of inequality in state socialist societies than the market economies (Milanović, 1992) but these clearly mask the additional burden that was placed on women in these societies. Such statistics do not include the level of unpaid care that women provided and their contribution to the family in other non-monetized forms such as queuing. Women were also much more likely to be affected by poor funding of social programmes in the areas of health and aged care. The question that now arises is, what impact is the transition from a command to a market economy having on women and men?

The gendered nature of social policy in the transitional phase

Unemployment represents one of the most serious economic problems facing transitional societies; another is inflation and high prices (inflation has increased dramatically and as a consequence real incomes have declined in value and prices have increased). For example, in Poland real incomes were estimated to have dropped 35 per cent during the first nine months of 1990, while the proportion of household income spent on food increased (Księżopolski, 1992). This is compounded by the already low level of wages. Ferge (1992a) points out that an average wage in 1991 in Hungary was equivalent to US\$200 a month. Given that women are located in the poorer-paying sectors of the economy, they are differentially affected. Castle-Kanerová (1992: 110) noted in 1992 that only 3 per cent of workers in Czechoslovakia were paid at the minimum wage, but 80 per cent of these were women. One consequence has been the steady increase in poverty rates. Poverty rates in Poland showed that in 1980 8 per cent of workers' households and 23 per cent of pensioners' households were classified as having incomes below the subsistence level. By 1990 the figures were 30 per cent of workers' households and 31 per cent for pension households (Księżopolski, 1992: 235).

One of the problems with focusing on income from the official economy is that hidden income from the informal economy or from illegal activities is difficult to determine.[4] Participation in the informal economy is gender biased, with men having higher participation rates than women (cf. Hubner *et al.*, 1991). Hungarian research has suggested that if hidden incomes are taken into account it is those in the higher incomes who earn more from such activity and 'that the relative deprivation of the vulnerable groups in most societies (single-parent families, retirees and women in general) who have lower reported income than the average is likely to be underestimated by official statistics' (Smeeding, 1991: 4). Sik (1992) has argued that increasing unemployment will result in growth in the informal economy, so its impact during the transition phase will probably increase rather than decrease.

Rising unemployment has led the East European countries to institute earnings-related unemployment schemes.[5] By the end of 1991 the average rate of unemployment across all these countries was higher than the OECD average (Holzman, 1992: 10). The expectation is that unemployment will continue to grow. Holzman points out that Western countries that have undergone restructuring have experienced high rates of unemployment in the process. He cites the example of Spain, where unemployment reached 21.4 per cent in

Table 12.2 *Unemployment data for East European countries, 1992*

Country	Per cent of unemployed	Per cent of women in total unemployed pool
Albania	20.0	–
Bulgaria	14.0	54.3
Czechoslovakia	6.6	54.0
East Germany	17.0	61.6
Hungary	10.0	42.0
Poland	13.0	53.0
Romania	4.0	61.0

Source: Eberhardt and Heinen (1993: Table 3)

1985. Unemployment figures show that women represent a higher percentage of the pool of total unemployed across Eastern Europe, except for Hungary. Table 12.2 indicates that in 1992 unemployment ranged from 42 per cent in Hungary to almost 62 per cent in the former East Germany.[6] Given that women represent slightly less than 50 per cent of the employed workforce, unemployment is having a much stronger impact on female labour force participation rates (Eberhardt and Heinen, 1993).

As the restructuring of the economy in these countries continues it is the sectors most under threat in which women are located (Einhorn and Mitter, 1991). For example, redundancies are high in sectors such as textiles which are characterized by old technology (Einhorn, 1991). Even where new technology has been introduced, men are displacing women in the training schemes; at present retraining schemes do not make allowances for female responsibility for children. This is particularly problematic given that childcare provisions are being reduced by the state and by private enterprises (Einhorn, 1991; Eberhardt and Hienen, 1993). Others have confirmed that the pool of jobs available to women is smaller (Księżopolski, 1992).

As enterprises attempt to become more efficient and profit oriented in the newly emerging market economy, it is the various 'fringe benefits' that have come under attack first. Although some subsidized benefits affect both men and women, such as meals, the burden is greater for women. For example, in regard to meals these now have to be supplied by the family and it is women who are disproportionately responsible for this activity within the household. Some benefits do not simply place greater strain on women; they directly affect their ability to continue participating in the paid labour market or, if they are unemployed, to be able to re-enter the paid labour market. In Hungary, 30 per cent of kindergartens are attached to the enterprise and many have been closed. The remainder are operated by the central government but as it withdraws from social welfare provision the cost of these services are having to be borne by underfunded, ill-equipped and untrained personnel within local governments (Ladó, 1991; Tausz, 1992).

As women live longer than men, and their retirement age is generally five years earlier than that of men (Holzman, 1992), women are disproportionately more likely to be pensioners. This means that older women are especially vulnerable. Szeman (1992) has written that in Hungary 13 per cent of those in retirement are women who received a widow's pension which is half that of their deceased husband's pension – this particularly disadvantages agricultural workers, as they receive lower wages than industrial workers. There are few retirement or nursing homes for the elderly throughout Eastern Europe. In Hungary in 1988 only 1 per cent of the elderly lived in nursing homes and demand for places was high despite the appalling conditions of these homes (Lévai, 1985 cited in Szeman, 1992). Moreover, there is little provision for homecare; Szeman reports that 3 per cent of the elderly receive such care but it is estimated that 30 per cent are in need.

Under state socialism abortion was available throughout Eastern Europe from the mid-1950s (Mieczkowski, 1985). A subsequent drop in fertility levels led to mild restrictions in Czechoslovakia, Bulgaria and Hungary, with legal abortions being eliminated in 1966 in Romania (McIntyre, 1985).[7] Under post-state-socialism there has been a concerted attack on reproductive rights, with abortion being outlawed in Poland, a two-year reprieve in East Germany, and abortion as one of the first issues discussed for reform in Hungary after 1989. As Kiss (1991: 53) notes: 'It is rather intriguing that in the middle of a deep economic crisis, political chaos and social insecurity, when the very foundations of society are to be reshaped, abortion has become a primary question in almost all post-communist countries.'[8] Restrictions on abortion support the emergent ideology which represents the patriarchal family as the cornerstone of the new post-state-socialist societies. It also helps to alleviate high unemployment by tying women to the role of full-time carer. This accords with 'Catholicism's subsidiarity principle [which] has always insisted that private organisations (mainly the Church) be prominent in social services' (Esping-Anderson, 1990: 134). Esping-Anderson has shown that a defining characteristic of the conservative welfare state is a strong Catholic influence.

The view that a woman's happiness and fulfilment is most likely to be achieved via full-time domestic duties is also exemplified by the poor support for women in the recent elections in Eastern Europe (Watson, 1993). Thus the low level of political representation under the state socialist system has been reduced further in recent elections in Romania, Hungary, Czechoslovakia and Poland. Female members of parliament hold no more than 5–9 per cent of the seats in these countries (Eberhardt and Heinen, 1993; Division for the Advancement of Women, 1991).

Under state socialism, women were not only discriminated against in the labour market but suffered from a triple burden in that they were often expected to involve themselves in public or political activities for the state (Einhorn, 1991). Einhorn (1991: 20) writes that 'the exigencies of this double and often triple burden meant that many East Central European women perceived their right to work rather more as an obligation. This view is understandable, given that access to many social benefits was tied to employment.' The last few years of transition have not altered this situation, and women are increasingly bearing the burden of economic restructuring. As a result they are being pre-commodified, yet there appears at present to be little 'serious feminist challenge' (Watson, 1993: 471) and Dölling (1991: 4) writes that the vast majority of women have rejected 'emancipatory or feminist ideas and practices'.[9]

Feminist writers who have attempted to explain this phenomenon have focused on two aspects of state socialism – its unintended support for traditional patriarchy (Watson, 1993) and the lack of control that women could exercise over their own lives (Einhorn, 1991; Dölling, 1991). The conditions that surrounded their daily experiences were bestowed from above which was inherently patriarchal and paternalistic; more importantly, such rights can be withdrawn (Meyer, 1985). Kiss (1991) argues that because these changes did not result from pressure from below they did not ultimately affect the everyday relationship between men and women – such liberation was not genuine as it was not self-liberation (Meyer, 1985). In the public sphere or at the society level a variety of changes were implemented, albeit imperfectly; but in the private sphere little changed. Hence there was no discussion of personal lived experiences – sexuality, domestic division of labour, violence, alcohol and incest remained silent, unaddressed issues. In the quest for 'normality' in Eastern Europe, women desire to spend more time as mothers and wives, but 'the creation of a civil society and market economy in Eastern Europe fundamentally entails the construction of a "man's world" and the propagation of masculinism in the public sphere' (Watson, 1993: 472). The outcome is the 'domestication' or pre-commodification of women, where women have a lower relative worth than men within a liberal market society (Watson, 1993).

The different welfare regimes in Western market economies has resulted in different outcomes for particular groups. Social democratic regimes have been more successful than other regime types in redistributing wealth and resources within their societies. In these countries women have higher labour force participation rates than their counterparts in other welfare states, and poverty among the old is rare. The move in Eastern Europe is towards insurance-based schemes that are status linked and in which the traditional family is seen as the basis of the moral order. This process is also being facilitated in some countries by the increasing role of Catholicism. Thus the quest for 'normality' by East European women, the role of the church as a provider of both moral and social substance, and the withdrawal of the state from the social policy arena all suggest a move towards the continental model of social welfare provision.

Popular support for welfare values

Current developments indicate that the governments of these transitional economies have weak and poorly formulated social policies. Just as social policy took a back seat under state socialism (Księżopolski, 1992) there is the premiss that the transformation to a market economy will involve substantial social costs but eventually the new system will sort itself out. The direction and strength of public opinion on these welfare issues will be of some importance in determining the final mix. Księżopolski (1992) sees public opinion as divided into three camps. The first camp he calls the 'caring state', which represents those who are currently dependent on welfare provisions and therefore favour retention of the current system. The second group is the 'welfare pluralists' who favour the provision of welfare but who want greater input from non-government organizations. The third group is 'liberalist'. They demand greater privatization, with individuals taking responsibility for the type of service and insurance they want.

With increasing differentiation in wages, inequality between the working class and the middle class will become more apparent as market forces begin to impact. Millard (1992: 141) writes that 'There are indications that women will suffer particularly from unemployment, as well as from the consequences of expected anti-abortion legislation and the erosion of pre-school child care provision.' The extent to which these inequalities are extenuated will depend on government policy, which in turn will be affected by social values and attitudes. As Eastern Europe is in transition the extent to which institutions have legitimacy will be critical in the development of a democratic welfare state. Offe (1992b) observes that if social security and welfare reform are tardy then in the medium term social conflict is a likely outcome.

Ginsburg (1992) has also argued that the welfare state under capitalism was as much a product of forces from below as from above. He points out that popular movements or new social movements have been undervalued when searching for an understanding of the origins and development of social policy. In particular, he argues that feminist movements have been at the forefront in pressuring the state to provide opportunities for women to reduce their economic dependence on men.

Overall, support for the welfare state remains reasonably high across Eastern Europe and citizens clearly differentiate between the state's involvement in economic activities and the provision of welfare services. When asked whether the state or private entrepreneurs should run enterprises, only 33 per cent preferred the state while 67 per cent preferred entrepreneurs.[10] However, slightly more than half (57 per cent) agreed that the state should provide for the family, while the remainder thought that individuals should take responsibility for themselves. Support for state provision for social welfare benefits is favoured by almost two-thirds of East Europeans surveyed. Sixty-five per cent supported the statement: 'Even if it means people like myself paying more in taxes, government should spend more on education, health and pensions', while 35 per cent supported the statement: 'Government should cut taxes even if it means reducing spending on education, health care and pensions.' Data collected in 1991 (Rose, 1991) show that these views are relatively stable despite the transitional nature of the sociopolitical systems in the various countries.

Support for state provision of welfare coincides with a rejection of the command economy; the majority favour a welfare state within a market economy. Males and females equally support the retention of state provision for welfare services, while females are somewhat less likely to support the market (66 per cent) than men (73 per cent). When it comes to state intervention in family policy women (64 per cent) are somewhat more likely to favour state involvement than men (57 per cent). It would seem that support for state involvement in welfare provisions is universally supported while in critical areas that directly impact on women, women are slightly more likely to support state intervention than are men. These differences are significant but not substantial, suggesting that there is little dissention between males and females over welfare provision.

Those whose main source of income is a pension or allowance (excluding the unemployed) are disproportionately more likely to favour state intervention, not just on welfare but in the economy generally. They are the most vulnerable in the community and have been hardest hit by inflation and poor social support. However, there are no statistically significant differences between male and female pensioners in their attitudes and the differences between female pensioners and male non-pensioners are minor.

Esping-Anderson (1990) has argued that the new middle classes have been a critical factor in the shape that the welfare state has taken. In the Scandinavian model the middle classes were incorporated into the welfare state while in the residual welfare states of the Anglo-Saxon countries the middle classes were never 'wooed from the market to the state'. However, in continental Europe a status-based insurance scheme ensured middle-class support for both the political system that introduced this type of welfare system and the welfare state that protected their position within the occupational structure. It is difficult to obtain a comparable measure of class for the different East and Central European countries, and education is used as a surrogate.

The 1992 New Democracies Barometer shows that those with a university education are more likely to favour support for the provision of 'traditional' welfare measures such as education, health and pensions but less likely to support state ownership of enterprises or the state taking responsibility for the family. When the university-educated are broken down by gender, university-educated women are more likely to support state involvement in traditional welfare areas, the economy and family than are university-educated men. Similarly, women without a university qualification are closer to their university-educated counterparts than to their male peers who do not have a university education. However, the largest differences are between those who possess and those who do not possess university qualifications, regardless of gender.

Overall, these data suggest that at present women in Eastern Europe do not, on the whole, see their interests as different to those of men. Data collected in 1993 in the Soviet Union indicate that a staggering 50 per cent of Russians totally agreed that 'A husband's job is to earn money and a woman's job is to look after the home and family'; a further 35 per cent agreed with the statement.[11] The pattern of agreement/disagreement is identical for females and males. Where there is some minor disagreement is on the statement: 'Being a housewife is as satisfying as earning money.' Overall, 22 per cent of Russians totally agreed and a further 40 per cent agreed with this statement. However, 19 per cent more females agreed than males. The strong support for traditional gender roles for both males and females is consistent with the findings of other scholars who have noted the lack of a strong and visible women's movement, support for women to return to the home, and the inheritance of a patriarchal ideology. Watson (1993) has argued that the exclusion of women from the transitional processes that are occurring at this time, coupled with the lack of a 'serious feminist challenge', represents a silent process of masculinism. This process is highly conducive to the formation of a welfare state where the state seeks to maintain a traditional family structure based on a working husband and a full-time housewife.

Recent work by Deacon (1992b) has attempted to classify the countries of Eastern Europe into a series of welfare regimes. His work is necessarily speculative because of the transitional nature of the countries under study. Deacon addresses the erosion of women's rights in the transitional phase as one of the areas in which social policy is changing. In his discussion he focuses on traditional areas such as unemployment benefits, housing policy and medical care; there is an implicit assumption that changes will affect men and women in a similar way and it is only in policy areas specific to women, such as childcare grants, that women are discussed.

Deacon (1992b) has posited that the Czech Republic will be most likely to follow the Scandinavian model of welfare, Hungary the liberal model of welfare, and that the other countries may form bureaucratic socialist welfare states (or post-communist conservative corporatist regimes) where the old nomenclatura will form an alliance with the state to preserve their privileged position within the social structure; this is similar to the continental model of welfare but instead of a liberal democratic political system these countries may have totalitarian political systems. Given that citizens' attitudes and values play a role in determining the shape of the welfare state, we would expect there to be noticeable variations between these countries in terms of their support for various state interventions in the economy, family and the provision of basic welfare.

Table 12.3 examines attitudinal data collected in three of the East European countries – the Czech Republic, Hungary and Romania. Although these data are limited and can only provide some indication of public opinion on such complex matters, there is some support for the welfare regime model proposed by Deacon. Romanians are significantly more likely to support state involvement in the running of enterprises than are either Hungarians or Czechs, while Hungarians are least likely to support state involvement in the provision for the family than are either the Czechs or the Romanians. Support for raising taxes and increasing basic welfare benefits is strongest amongst the Czechs and weakest amongst the Hungarians. Regardless of the country, women do not differ significantly from men in the attitudes they hold.

Table 12.3 *Support for state intervention in three East European countries, 1992 (%)*

	Hungary	Czech Republic	Romania
Agree that state ownership is the best way to run an enterprise	24	17	48
Agree that the state should be responsible for everyone's material security	40	46	46
Agree that even if it means people like myself paying more in taxes, government should spend more on education, health and pensions	55	74	64

Source: New Democracies Barometer II, Rose *et al.* (1993)

Conclusion

In a command economy, social policy is largely built into the structural arrangements of the labour market. Privatization, or the move to a market economy, requires the dismantling of this structure. Popularly elected governments must balance the competing demands of many interest groups and manage the economy effectively. Of necessity, hard choices have to be made about the institutional arrangements surrounding the provision of social welfare, who will benefit from these arrangements, and for how long. However, citizens in Eastern Europe lack the institutions that fought for citizenship rights in Western societies, such as a vocal women's movement, trade unions, a free press and strong political parties. Ferge (1992b) has noted that these groups are either delegitimized, weak or in a state of flux in Eastern Europe.

The *ad hoc* nature of the development of social policy may ultimately undermine the legitimacy of transitional governments as they attempt to reform both the political and economic systems (Millard, 1992). The rejection of state socialism does not necessarily mean the evolution of a democratic welfare system within a capitalist economic system. It is possible that authoritarian regimes may regain power as people look for easy solutions to difficult problems; alternatively war or 'movements of rage' are already visible in many of these societies. However, it is clear that Eastern Europe – regardless of its political configuration – is moving towards a continental welfare system in which the state seeks to preserve the current status hierarchies via insurance-based systems and intervenes in the provision of welfare only as a last resort.

Feminists have noted that the move towards a market economy has unleashed on to the public sphere the patriarchal ideology that has dominated family relations within Eastern Europe. This is resulting in the pre-commodification of women, which is being reinforced by the withdrawal of the state from providing welfare (Einhorn, 1991; Dziewiecka-Bokun, 1992) and incursions into social rights such as the access to abortion. This is being enhanced by a weak women's movement, weak trade unions, high levels of unemployment, economic deprivation, ethnic conflicts and the influx of refugees. The limited public opinion data drawn upon here indicate that women do not differ from men in their attitudes to the role of the state in welfare provision, nor about gender roles generally, all of which will facilitate the implementation of a welfare model based on the principle of subsidiarity.

Notes

This chapter was written while the author was a visiting fellow at the Centre for the Study of Public Policy at the University of Strathclyde. The research was funded by an ESRC grant to the Centre for the Study of Public Policy on Social Welfare and Individual Enterprise in Post-Communist Societies (Y 309–25–3047). An earlier version was delivered at the 1993 Workshop on Gender and Welfare States, Leyden University, the Netherlands. A number of people have provided assistance and comments. My thanks to Lois Bryson, Beverley Bullpit, Margrit Davies, Jacqueline Heinen, Ian McAllister, Frances Millard, Deborah Mitchell, Richard Rose, the participants of the ECPR workshop and especially Diane Sainsbury.

1 In the Soviet Union the percentage of women in the paid labour market increased from 49.1 in 1939 to 54.0 per cent in 1959 (Sacks, 1978). This was in large part due to the imbalance in the sex ratio caused by the high loss of male lives during the Second World War.

2 Heinen (1990) points out the interesting contradiction that in Poland quotas were placed on entry to professional occupations like medicine where the number of female applicants exceeded the number of male applicants but similar quotas were never applied to feminized occupations such as nursing and childcare.

3 These data come from the New Democracies Barometer, a multinational annual survey of Central and East European countries coordinated by the Paul Lazarsfeld Society, Vienna, and funded by the Austrian Ministry for Science and Education and the Austrian National Bank. The data are for seven East European countries – Hungary, Romania, Bulgaria, Czech Republic, Slovak Republic, Slovenia and Poland. The data used here are from the 1992 wave of surveys. For simplicity the figures are not presented separately for each country but for the overall region, with each country being weighted equally. There are country differences but the overall trend remains, regardless of which country is examined individually.

4 Sik (1992:6) defines the informal economy as 'all productive and distributive income-earning activities which take place outside the scope of the public regulation on the macro societal level'.

5 Unemployment benefits were introduced in Hungary in 1989, Bulgaria and Romania in 1990 and Czechoslovakia in 1991.

6 Although the figures for Hungary appear favourable at this time the unemployment rate for women grew faster in 1991 than it did for men (Ladó, 1991).

7 Conditions were often poor, resulting in complications. Heitlinger (1987) reports that 30–40 per cent of abortions in Czechoslovakia result in either early or later complications.

8 Shaver (1992) has argued that within the liberal welfare states civil and social rights to abortion have varied between countries. In those countries where abortion is defined in terms of body or social rights availability of abortion has been much more unstable. In countries where abortion is defined as a medical entitlement access to abortion has been less susceptible to change.

9 Women were significant actors in the heady days of 1989 (Dölling, 1991; Einhorn, 1991) but today they form a silent majority.

10 These data are taken from the 1992 New Democracies Barometer.

11 These data are taken from the New Democracies Barometer conducted in Russia in late 1993 (Rose *et al.*, 1993).

Bibliography

ABS (Australian Bureau of Statistics) (1990) *Measuring Unpaid Household Work: Issues and Experimental Estimates*, Catalogue No. 4111.1. Canberra: Australian Bureau of Statistics.

ABS (Australian Bureau of Statistics) (1992) *Child Care Australia*, November 1990, Catalogue No. 4402.0. Canberra: Australian Bureau of Statistics.

Abukhanfusa, Kerstin (1987) *Piskan och moroten. Om könens tilldelning av skyldigheter och rättigheter*. Stockholm: Carlssons.

Acker, Joan (1989) 'The problem with patriarchy', *Sociology*, 23(2): 235–40.

Affirmative Action Agency (1987) *Annual Report 1986–87*. Canberra: Australian Government Publishing Service.

Amott, Teresa (1990) 'Black women and AFDC: making entitlement out of necessity', in Linda Gordon (ed.), *Women, the State and Welfare*. Madison: University of Wisconsin Press. pp. 280–301.

Andersen, Jørgen Goul and Christiansen, Peter Munk (1991) *Skatter uden velfærd*. Charlottenlund: Jurist-og Økonomforbundets Forlag.

Balbo, Laura (1982) 'The servicing work of women and the capitalist state', in M. Zeitlin (ed.), *Political Power and Social Theory. A Research Annual*. Vol. 3. London/Greenwich: JAI Press. pp. 251–70.

Balbo, Laura (1987) 'Crazy quilts: rethinking the welfare state from a woman's point of view', in Anne Showstack Sassoon (ed.), *Women and the State*. London: Hutchinson. pp. 45–66.

Barrett, Michelle (1980) *Women's Oppression Today: The Marxist/Feminist Encounter*, revised edn. London: Verso.

Becker-Schmidt, Regina, Knapp, G.-A. and Schmidt, B. (1985) *Eines ist zu wenig, beides ist zuviel. Erfahrungen von Arbeiterfrauen zwischen Familie und Fabrik*. Bonn: Verlag Neue Gesellschaft.

Bergmann, Barbara (1986) *The Economic Emergence of Women*. New York: Basic Books.

Berk, S. F. and Berk, Richard A. (1979) *Labor and Leisure at Home*. Beverly Hills: Sage.

Bieback, Karl-Jürgen (1990) 'Mittelbare Diskriminierung der Frauen im Sozialrecht', *Zeitschrift für ausländisches und internationales Arbeits- und Sozialrecht*, 4(1): 1–33.

Bieback, Karl-Jürgen (1992) 'Family benefits: the new legal structures of subsidizing the family', *Journal of European Social Policy*, 2(4): 239–54.

Bittman, Michael (1991) *Juggling Time*. Canberra: Office of the Status of Women, Department of the Prime Minister and Cabinet.

Blaas, Wolfgang (1992) 'The Swiss model: corporatism or liberal capitalism?', in Jukka Pekkarinen, Matti Pohjola and Bob Rowthorn (eds), *Social Corporatism: A Superior Economic System?* Oxford: Clarendon Press.

Blau, David M. (1992) 'The child care labor market', *Journal of Human Resources*, 27(1): 9–40.

Blok, Els (1978) *Loonarbeid van vrouwen in Nederland 1945–1955*. Nijmegen: Socialistische Uitgeverij.

Bock, Gisela and Thane, Pat (eds) (1991) *Maternity and Gender Policies, Women and the Rise of the European Welfare States 1880–1950*. London: Routledge.

Borchorst, Anette (1989) 'Kvindeinteresser og konflikter', *Forum for kvindeforskning*, 3: 21–34.

Borchorst, Anette (1993) 'Working lives and family lives in Western Europe', in Søren Carlsen and Jørgen Elm Larsen (eds), *The Equality Dilemma*. Viborg: Danish Equal Status Council. pp. 167–81.

Borchorst, Anette (1994) 'Scandinavian welfare states – patriarchal, gender neutral or women friendly?', *International Journal of Contemporary Sociology*, 31(1).

Borchorst, Anette and Siim, Birte (1987) 'Women and the advanced welfare state – a new kind of patriarchal power?' in Anne Showstack Sassoon (ed.), *Women and the State*. London: Hutchinson. pp. 128–54.

Brannen, Julia and Moss, Peter (1988) *New Mothers at Work: Employment and Child Care*. London: Unwin Hyman.

Brown, William and Rowthorn, Bob (1990) *A Public Services Pay Policy*. Fabian Tract 542. London: Fabian Society.

Bryson, Lois (1992) *Welfare and the State: Who Benefits?* London: Macmillan.

Buckley, Mary (1992) 'Introduction: women and perestroika', in Mary Buckley (ed.), *Perestroika and Soviet Women*. Cambridge: Cambridge University Press.

Bussemaker, Jet (1991) 'Equality, autonomy and feminist politics', in E. Meehan and S. Sevenhuijsen (eds), *Equality Politics and Gender*. London: Sage. pp. 52–70.

Bussemaker, Jet (1993) *Betwiste zelfstandigheid. Individualisering, sekse en verzorgingsstaat*. Amsterdam: SUA.

Cameron, David R. (1978) 'The expansion of the public economy: a comparative analysis', *American Political Science Review*, 72: 1243–61.

Carlsson, Allan (1990) *The Swedish Experiment in Family Politics. The Myrdals and the Interwar Population Crisis*. New Brunswick: Transaction Books.

Castle-Kanerová, Mita (1992) 'Social policy in Czechoslovakia', in Bob Deacon (ed.), *The New Eastern Europe: Social Policy, Past, Present and Future*. London: Sage.

Castles, Francis G. (1978) *The Social Democratic Image of Society. A Study of the Achievements and Origins of Scandinavian Social Democracy in Comparative Perspective*. London: Routledge & Kegan Paul.

Castles, Francis G. (1985) *The Working Class and Welfare: Reflections on the Political Development of the Welfare State in Australia and New Zealand, 1890–1980*. London: Allen & Unwin.

Castles, Francis G. and Merrill, Vance (1989) 'Towards a general model of public policy outcomes', *Journal of Theoretical Politics*, 1(2): 177–212.

Castles, Francis G. and Mitchell, Deborah (1992) 'Three worlds of welfare capitalism or four?' *Governance*, 5(1): 1–26.

Castles, Francis G. and Mitchell, Deborah (1993) 'Worlds of welfare and families of nations', in Francis G. Castles (ed.), *Families of Nations: Patterns of Policy in Western Democracies*. Aldershot: Dartmouth.

Central Statistical Office of Finland (1991) *Women and Men in Finland*. Helsinki: Central Statistical Office of Finland.

Child Care Advocacy Association of Canada (1993), *Vision*, 16 (Spring).

Chubb, Basil (1992) *The Government and Politics of Ireland*, third edition. Harlow: Longman.

Clark, John and Wildavsky, Aaron (1990) *The Moral Collapse of Socialism*. San Francisco: Institute for Contemporary Studies Press.

Cohen, Bronwen and Fraser, Neil (1991) *Childcare in a Modern Welfare System*. London: Institute of Public Policy Research.

Cusack, Tom and Rein, Martin (1987) 'Social policy and service employment', unpublished paper. Science Center Berlin.

Dahlerup, Drude (1987) 'Confusing concepts – confusing reality: a theoretical discussion of the patriarchal state', in Anne Showstack Sassoon (ed.), *Women and the State*. London: Hutchinson. pp. 93–127.

Dale, Jennifer and Foster, Peggy (1986) *Feminists and State Welfare*. London: Routledge & Kegan Paul.

Dalley, Gillian (1988) *Ideologies of Caring: Rethinking Community and Collectivism*. London: Macmillan.

Daly, Mary (1994) 'A matter of dependency? The gender dimension of British income maintenance provision', *Sociology*.

Davies, Hugh and Joshi, Heather (1990) 'The forgone earnings of Europe's mothers'. Discussion Paper in Economics 24/90, Birkbeck College, University of London.

Deacon, Bob (1992a) 'East European welfare: past, present and future in comparative context', in Bob Deacon (ed.), *The New Eastern Europe: Social Policy, Past, Present and Future*. London: Sage.

Deacon, Bob (1992b) 'The future of social policy in Eastern Europe', in Bob Deacon (ed.), *The New Eastern Europe: Social Policy, Past, Present and Future*. London: Sage.

Division for the Advancement of Women (1991) 'Women's role in making reform work', in *The Impact of Economic and Political Reform on the Status of Women in Eastern Europe*, Proceedings of a United Nations Regional Seminar, Vienna, 8–12 April.

Dölling, Irene (1991) 'Between hope and helplessness: women in the GDR after the "Turning Point"', *Feminist Review*, 39: 3–15.

Döring, Diether, Hauser, Richard, Rolf, Gabriele and Tibitanzl, Frank (1992) 'Old age security of women in the twelve EC-countries – to what extent are Beveridge's two main principles of universality and guaranteed minimum fulfilled?', Luxembourg Income Study working paper 81.

Dziewiecka-Bokun, Ludmila (1992) 'Towards democracy: can the welfare state work in Eastern Europe?', paper presented at the conference on Comparative Studies in Welfare State Development: Quantitative and Qualitative Dimensions, Centre for Social Policy Research, University of Bremen.

Eberhardt, Eva and Heinen, Jacqueline (1993) *Central and Eastern Europe: Women Workers in the Transitional Phase*. Petit-Lancy, Switzerland: International Union of Food and Allied Workers' Associations.

Einhorn, Babara (1991) 'Where have all the women gone? Women and the women's movement in East Central Europe', *Feminist Review*, 39: 16–36.

Einhorn, Barbara and Mitter, Swasti (1991) 'A comparative analysis of women's industrial participation during the transition from centrally planned to market economies in East Central Europe', in *The Impact of Economic and Political Reform on the Status of Women in Eastern Europe*, Proceedings of a United Nations Regional Seminar, Vienna, 8–12 April.

Elmér, Åke (1963) *Från Fattigsverige till välfärdsstaten*. Stockholm: Aldus/Bonnier.

Elmér, Åke (1975) *Svensk socialpolitik*. Lund: Liber.

Elvander, Nils (1972) *Svensk skattepolitik 1945–1970*. Stockholm: Raben & Sjögren.

Esping-Andersen, Gøsta (1985a) *Politics against Markets. The Social Democratic Road to Power*. Princeton: Princeton University Press.

Esping-Andersen, Gøsta (1985b) 'Power and distributional regimes', *Politics and Society*, 14(2): 223–56.

Esping-Andersen, Gøsta (1987) 'The comparison of policy regimes: an introduction', in Martin Rein, Gøsta Esping-Andersen and Lee Rainwater (eds), *Stagnation and Renewal in Social Policy. The Rise and Fall of Policy Regimes*. Armonk: Sharpe. pp. 3–13.

Esping-Andersen, Gøsta (1990) *The Three Worlds of Welfare Capitalism*. Cambridge: Polity Press.

Esping-Andersen, Gøsta and van Kersbergen, Kees (1992) 'Contemporary research on social democracy', *Annual Review of Sociology*, 18: 187–208.

Esping-Andersen, Gøsta and Korpi, Walter (1984) 'Social policy as class politics in post-war capitalism: Scandinavia, Austria and Germany', in John H. Goldthorpe (ed.), *Order and Conflict in Contemporary Capitalism*, Oxford: Clarendon Press. pp. 197–209.

Esping-Andersen, Gøsta and Korpi, Walter (1987) 'From poor relief to institutional welfare states', in Robert Erikson, Erik Jørgen Hansen, Stein Ringen and Hannu Uusitalo (eds), *The Scandinavian Model*. Armonk: Sharpe. pp. 39–74.

Esping-Andsersen, Gøsta, Rainwater, Lee and Rein, Martin (1988) 'Institutional and political factors affecting the well-being of the elderly', in John L. Palmer, Timothy Smeeding and Barbara Boyle Torrey (eds), *The Vulnerable*. Washington, DC: Urban Institute Press. pp. 333–50.

European Commission's Childcare Network (1990) *Børnepasning i de europæiske fællesskaber 1985–1990*. Brussels: EC.

European Commission Network on Childcare (1993) *92 Annual Report*. Brussels: EC.

Evans, Peter B., Rueschemeyer, Dietrich and Skocpol, Theda (eds) (1985) *Bringing the State Back In*. Cambridge: Cambridge University Press.

Ferge, Zsuzsa (1992a) 'Unemployment in Hungary: the need for a new ideology', in Bob Deacon (ed.), *Social Policy, Social Justice and Citizenship in Eastern Europe*. Aldershot: Avebury.

Ferge, Zsuzsa (1992b) 'Social change in Eastern Europe – social citizenship in the new democracies', paper presented at the First European Conference of Sociology, Vienna.

Finch, Janet and Groves, Dulcie (eds) (1983) *A Labour of Love: Women, Work and Caring*. London: Routledge & Kegan Paul.

Flora, Peter and Heidenheimer, Arnold (eds) (1981) *The Development of Welfare States in Europe and America*. New Brunswick: Transaction Books.

Flora, Peter, Alber, Jens and Kohl, Jürgen (1977) 'Zur Entwicklung der westeuropäischen Wohlfahrtsstaaten', *Politische Vierteljahresschrift*, 18: 707–72.

Folbre, Nancy (1994) *Who Pays for the Kids: Gender and Structures of Constraint*. London: Routledge.

Fraser, Nancy (1987) 'Women, welfare and the politics of need interpretation', *Thesis Eleven*, 17: 88–106.

Fraser, Nancy (1989a) *Unruly Practices: Power, Discourse and Gender in Contemporary Social Theory*. Minneapolis: University of Minnesota Press.

Fraser, Nancy (1989b) 'Women, welfare and the politics of need interpretation', in Nancy Fraser, *Unruly Practices: Power, Discourse and Gender in Contemporary Social Theory*. Cambridge: Polity Press. pp. 144–60.

Fraser, Nancy and Gordon, Linda (1994) 'Dependency: inscriptions of power in a keyword of the welfare state', *Social Politics: International Studies of Gender, State and Society*, 1(1): 4–32.

Galler, Heinz P. (1988) 'Familiale Lebenslagen und Familienlastenausgleich. Zu den

Opportunitätskosten familialer Entscheidungen', in Bernhard Felderer (ed.), *Familienlastenausgleich und demographische Entwicklung*. Berlin: Schriften des Vereins für Socialpolitik, Neue Folge 175: 83–112.

Garfinkel, Irwin and McLanahan, Sara (1986) *Single Mothers and Their Children: A New American Dilemma*. Washington, DC: Urban Institute Press.

Gather, Claudia, Gerhard, Ute, Prinz, Karin and Veil, Mechthild (eds) (1991) *Frauenalterssicherung. Lebensläufe von Frauen und ihre Benachteiligung im Alter.* Berlin: sigma.

Gauthier, Anne H. (1991) 'Family policies in comparative perspectives'. Oxford: Centre for European Studies, Nuffield College, Discussion Paper 5.

Gerhard, Ute (1988a) 'Die Verfügbarkeit der Frauen. Arbeitspolitik gegen Frauen', in U. Gerhard, A. Schwarzer and V. Slupik (eds), *Auf Kosten der Frauen. Frauenrechte im Sozialstaat*. Weinheim and Basle: Beltz. pp. 39–78.

Gerhard, Ute (1988b) 'Sozialpolitik auf Kosten der Frauen', in R. Heinze, B. Hombach and H. Scherf (eds), *Sozialstaat 2000. Auf dem Weg zu neuen Grundlagen der sozialen Sicherung*. Bonn: Verlag Neue Gesellschaft. pp. 113–21.

Gerhard, Ute, Schwarzer, A. and Slupik, V. (eds) (1988) *Auf Kosten der Frauen. Frauenrechte im Sozialstaat*. Weinheim and Basle: Beltz.

Ginn, Jay and Arber, Sara (1992) 'Towards women's independence: pension systems in three contrasting European welfare states', *Journal of European Social Policy*, 2(4): 255–77.

Ginsburg, Norman (1992) *Divisions of Welfare*. London: Sage.

Goldin, Claudia 1990) *Understanding the Gender Gap: An Economic History of American Women*. New York: Oxford University Press.

Golonka, S. and Ooms, T. (1991) 'Child care in the 101st Congress: What was achieved and how will it work?'. Washington, DC: The Family Impact Seminar.

Gordon, Linda (ed.) (1990a) *Women, the State and Welfare*. Madison: University of Wisconsin Press.

Gordon, Linda (1990b) 'The new feminist scholarship on the welfare state', in Linda Gordon (ed.), *Women, the State and Welfare*. Madison: University of Wisconsin Press.

Gornick, Janet (1992) 'The economic position of working-age women, relative to men: a cross-national comparative study', paper presented at the Conference on Comparative Studies of Welfare State Development, Bremen.

Graham, Hilary (1987) 'Women's poverty and caring', in C. Glendinning and J. Millar (eds), *Women and Poverty in Britain*. Brighton: Harvester Wheatsheaf.

Groot, Wim and Maassen van den Brink, Henriëtte (1992) 'Labor supply, child care, and consumption', research manuscript, Department of Economics, University of Amsterdam.

Groves, Dulcie (1983) 'Members and survivors: women and retirement legislation', in Jane Lewis (ed.), *Women's Welfare, Women's Rights*. London: Croom Helm.

Gustafsson, Björn and Klevmarken, Anders N. (1993) 'Taxes and transfers in Sweden: incentive effects on labour supply', in A. B. Atkinson and G. V. Mogensen (eds), *Welfare and Work Incentives*. New York: Oxford University Press. pp. 50–134.

Gustafsson, Siv (1984) 'Equal opportunity policies in Sweden', in G. Schmidt and Renate Wietzel (eds), *Sex Discrimination and Equal Opportunity. The Labour Market and Employment Policy*. Aldershot: Gower for Wissenschaftzentrum, Berlin. pp. 132–54.

Gustafsson, Siv (1990) 'The labour force participation and earnings of lone parents. A Swedish case study with comparisons to Germany', in *Lone-Parent Families. The Economic Challenge*. Paris: OECD.

Gustafsson, Siv and Bruyn-Hundt, Marga (1992) 'Incentives for women to work: a comparison between the Netherlands, Sweden and West Germany', *Journal of Economic Studies*, 18: 30–65.

Gustafsson, Siv and Stafford, Frank (1992) 'Childcare subsidies and labor supply in Sweden', *Journal of Human Resources*, 27(1): 204–30.

Gustafsson, Siv and Stafford, Frank (1994) 'Three regimes of childcare', in Rebecca Blank (ed.), *Social Production versus Economic Flexibility: Is there a Trade-off?* NBER and Chicago University Press.

Halsaa, Beatrice (1987) 'Har kvinnor gemensamma intressen?', *Kvinnovetenskaplig tidskrift*, 8(4): 45–56.

Hartog, Joop and Theeuwes, Jules (1993) 'Post-war unemployment in the Netherlands', *European Journal of Political Economy*, 9: 398–448.

Hatje, Ann-Katrin (1974) *Befolkningsfrågan och välfärden. Debatten om familjepolitik och nativitetsökning under 1930- och 1940-talen*. Stockholm: Allmänna förlaget.

Heinen, Jacqueline (1990) 'The impact of social policy on the behaviour of women workers in Poland and East Germany', *Critical Social Policy*, 10(2): 79–91.

Heitlinger, Alena (1987) 'Reproduction', in *Medicine and the Socialist State*. London: Macmillan.

Hernes, Helga M. (1984) 'Women and the welfare state. The transition from private to public dependence', in H. Holter (ed.), *Patriarchy in a Welfare Society*. Oslo: Universitetsforlaget. pp. 26–45.

Hernes, Helga (1987a) *Welfare State and Woman Power*. Oslo: Norwegian University Press.

Hernes, Helga (1987b) 'Women and the welfare state: the transition from public to private dependence', in Anne Showstack Sassoon (ed.), *Women and the State*. London: Hutchinson. pp. 72–92.

Hewitt, Christopher (1977) 'The effect of political democracy and social democracy on equality in industrial societies: a cross-national comparison', *American Sociological Review*, 42(3): 450–64.

Hicks, Alexander and Swank, Duane (1992) 'Politics, institutions and welfare spending in industrialized democracies, 1960–1982', *American Political Science Review*, 86(3): 658–74.

Hirdman, Yvonne (1989) *Att lägga livet till rätta – studier i svensk folkhemspolitik.* Stockholm: Carlssons.

Hobson, Barbara (1990) 'No exit, no voice: women's economic dependency and the welfare state', *Acta Sociologica*, 33(3): 235–50.

Hobson, Barbara (1991) 'Decommodification in gender terms: a critical analysis of Esping-Andersen's social policy regimes and women's social citizenship', paper presented at the Conference on Gender, Citizenship and Social Policy, Social Science History Association, New Orleans.

Hobson, Barbara (1993) 'Gendered discourses and feminist strategies in welfare states: the debate over married women's right to work in Sweden and the United States', in Seth Koven and Sonya Michel (eds), *Mothers of a New World: Gender and Origins of Welfare States in Western Europe and North America*. New York: Routledge.

Hofferth, Sandra and Wissoker, Douglas (1992) 'Price, quality and income in child care choice', *Journal of Human Resources*, 27(1): 70–111.

Hofferth, Sandra, Brayfield, April, Deich, Sharon and Holcomb, Pamela (1991) *National Child Care Survey, 1990*. Washington, DC: Urban Institute Press.

Holter, Harriet (1984) 'Women's research and social theory', in Harriet Holter (ed.), *Patriarchy in a Welfare Society*. Oslo: Universitetsforlaget. pp. 9–25.

Holzman, Robert (1992) 'Social policy in transition from plan to market', *Journal of Public Policy*, 12(1): 1–35.

Hubner, Sabine, Maier, Friederike and Rudolph, Hedwig (1991) *Labour Market and Social Policy Implications of Structural Change in Central and Eastern Europe'*. Paris: OECD.

Hutton, Sandra and Whiteford, Peter (1992) *Women and Social Security in Retirement: a Comparative Analysis*. Luxembourg Income Study working paper 82.

Huttunen, E. and Tamminen, M. (1989) *Day Care as Growth Environment*. Helsinki: National Board of Social Welfare in Finland.

ILO (International Labour Organization) (1988) *Yearbook*. Geneva: International Labour Organization.

ILO (International Labour Organization) (1992) *The Cost of Social Security: Thirteenth International Inquiry, 1984–1986*. Geneva: International Labour Organization.

Institut für Arbeitsmarkt- und Berufsforschung (ed.) (1981) *BeitrAB 3.1 Arbeitsmarktstatische Zahlen in Zeitreihenform*. Nürnberg: Druckhaus Nürnberg.

Institut für Arbeitsmarkt- und Berufsforschung (ed.) (1984) *BeitrAB 3.1 Arbeitsmarktstatische Zahlen in Zeitreihenform*. Nürnberg: Druckhaus Nürnberg.

ISSR (1970) 'Social security in the Netherlands', *International Social Security Review*, 23: 3–61.

Jallinoja, R. (1989) 'Women between the family and employment', in K. Boh, M. Bak, C. Clason, M. Pankratova, J. Qvortrup, G. B. Sgritta and K. Waerness (eds), *Changing Patterns of European Family Life: A Comparative Analysis of 14 European Countries*. London: Routledge.

John Paul II (1981) *On Human Work* (Laborem Exercens). Boston: St Paul Books & Media.

John Paul II (1991) *On the Hundredth Anniversary* (Centesimus Annus). Boston: St Paul Books & Media.

Jónasdóttir, Anna G. (1988) 'On the concept of interest, women's interests, and the limitations of interest theory', in Kathleen Jones and Anna G. Jónasdóttir (eds), *The Political Interests of Gender*. London: Sage. pp. 33–66.

Jónasdóttir, Anna G. (1991) *Love Power and Political Interests*. Kumla: Örebro Studies 7.

Jónasdóttir, Anna G. (1994) *Why Women Are Oppressed*. Philadelphia: Temple University Press.

Jones, Catherine (1985) 'Types of welfare capitalism', *Government and Opposition*, 20(3): 328–42.

Joshi, Heather (1990) 'Obstacles and opportunities for lone parents as breadwinners in Great Britain', in *Lone-Parent Families*. Paris: OECD.

Kaim-Caudle, P. R. (1973) *Comparative Social Policy and Social Security*. London: Martin Robertson.

Kälvemark, Ann-Sofie (1980) *More Children of Better Quality? Aspects on Swedish Population Policy in the 1930s*. Uppsala: Almqvist & Wiksell.

Kamerman, Sheila B. and Kahn, Alfred J. (1988) 'Social policy and children in the United States and Europe', in John L. Palmer, Timothy Smeeding and Barbara Boyle Torrey (eds), *The Vulnerable*. Washington, DC: Urban Institute Press.

Kamerman, Sheila B. and Kahn, Alfred (1991) *Child Care, Parental Leave, and the Under 3's. Policy Innovation in Europe*. New York: Auburn House.

Kersbergen, Kees van (1991) 'Social capitalism. A study of Christian Democracy and the post-war settlement of the welfare state'. Doctoral dissertation, European University Institute, Florence.

Kessel, Ellen van, Kuperus, Marga and Pott-Buter, Hettie (1986) 'Hoezo, gelijk belast?', in *Invloed van arbeid, belasting – en premieheffing op het leven van vrouwen*. Amsterdam: De Populier/Amazone.

Kickbusch, Ilona (1984) 'Familie als Beruf – Beruf als Familie: Der segregierte Arbeitsmarkt und die Familialisierung der weiblichen Arbeit', in I. Kickbusch and B. Riedmüller (eds), *Die armen Frauen. Frauen und Sozialpolitik*. Frankfurt am Main: Suhrkamp. pp. 163–78.

Kiss, Yudit (1991) 'The second "no": women in Hungary', *Feminist Review*, 39: 49–57.

Knijn, Trudie (1991) 'Citizenship, care, and gender in the Dutch welfare state', paper presented at the Conference on Gender, Citizenship and Social Policy, Social Science History Association, New Orleans.

Knijn, Trudie (1994) 'Fish without bikes: revision of the Dutch welfare state and its consequences for the (in)dependence of single mothers', *Social Politics: International Studies of Gender, State and Society*, 1(1): 83–106.

Koeppinghoff, Sigrid (1984) 'Endstation Sozialhilfe. Defizite der Einkommenssicherung von Frauen im Alter', in I. Kickbusch and B. Riedmüller (eds), *Die armen Frauen. Frauen und Sozialpolitik*. Frankfurt am Main: Suhrkamp. pp. 252–65.

Kohleiss, Annelies (1988) 'Frauenrechte in der gesetzlichen Krankenversicherung', in U. Gerhard, A. Schwarzer and V. Slupik (eds), *Auf Kosten der Frauen. Frauenrechte im Sozialstaat*. Weinheim and Basle: Beltz. pp. 117–72.

Kolberg, Jon E. (1991) 'The gender dimension of the welfare state', *International Journal of Sociology*, 21(2): 119–48.

Köppen, Ruth (1985) *Die Armut ist weiblich*. Berlin: Elefanten Press.

Korpi, Walter (1978) *The Working Class in Welfare Capitalism: Work, Unions and Politics in Sweden*. London: Routledge & Kegan Paul.

Korpi, Walter (1983) *The Democratic Class Struggle*. London: Routledge & Kegan Paul.

Koven, Seth and Michel, Sonya (1990) 'Womanly duties: maternalist politics and the origins of welfare states in France, Germany, Great Britain and the United States, 1880–1920', *American Historical Review*, 95 (Autumn): 1076–108.

Księżopolski, Miroslav (1992) 'The prospects for social policy development in Poland', in Bob Deacon (ed.), *Social Policy, Social Justice and Citizenship in Eastern Europe*. Aldershot: Avebury.

Kulawik, Theresa (1989) 'Auf unsicheren Wegen. Perspektiven der sozialen Sicherung für Frauen', in B. Riedmüller and M. Rodenstein (eds), *Wie sicher ist die soziale Sicherung?* Frankfurt am Main: Suhrkamp. pp. 241–65.

Kulawik, Theresa and Riedmüller, Babara (1991) 'Institutionelle Arrangements und die Lebenssituation der alleinstehenden Frauen', in Riedmüller *et al.* (eds), *Die Lebenssituation der alleinstehenden Frauen in der Bundesrepublik Deutschland*. Stuttgart: Schriftenreihe des Bundesministerium für Frauen und Jugend, Bd. 1.

Kulcsár, Rózsa (1985) 'The socioeconomic conditions of women in Hungary', in Sharon Wolchik and Alfred Meyer (eds), *Women, State, and Party in Eastern Europe*. Durham, NC: Duke University Press.

Ladó, Mária (1991) 'Hungary', in *The Impact of Economic and Political Reform on the Status of Women in Eastern Europe*, Proceedings of a United Nations Regional Seminar, Vienna.

Land, Hilary (1978) 'Who cares for the family?', *Journal of Social Policy*, 7(3): 257–84.

Land, Hilary (1983) 'Poverty and gender: the distribution of resources within the family', in M. Brown (ed.), *The Structure of Disadvantage*. London: Heinemann.

Land, Hilary (1985) 'Who still cares for the family? Recent developments in income maintenance, taxation and family law', in Clare Ungerson (ed.), *Women and Social Policy: A Reader*. London: Macmillan.

Land, Hilary and Parker, Roy (1978) 'United Kingdom', in Sheila B. Kamerman and Alfred J. Kahn (eds), *Family Policy: Government and Families in Fourteen Countries*. New York: Columbia University Press.

Langan, Mary and Ostner, Ilona (1991) 'Geschlechterpolitik im Wohlfahrsstaat: Aspekte im internationalen Vergleich', *Kritische Justiz*, 24(3): 302–17.

Leibfried, Stephan (1990a) 'Sozialstaat Europa? Integrationsperspektiven europäischer Armutsregimes', *Nachrichtendienst des deutschen Vereins für offentliche und privat Fürsorge*, 70(9): 295–305.

Leibfried, Stephan (1990b) 'Income transfers and poverty in EC perspective. On Europe's slipping into Anglo-American welfare models', paper presented at the EC seminar Poverty, Marginalisation and Social Exclusion in the Europe of the 90s, Alghero, Italy.

Leibowitz, Arleen, Klerman, Jacob, Alex and Waite, Linda J. (1992) 'Employment of new mothers and child care choice', *Journal of Human Resources*, 27(1): 127.

Leira, Arnlaug (1989) *Models of Motherhood*, Report 89/7. Oslo: Institute of Social Research.

Leira, Arnlaug (1992) *Welfare States and Working Mothers. The Scandinavian Experience*. Cambridge: Cambridge University Press.

Lenoir, Remi (1991) 'Family policy in France since 1938', in John S. Ambler (ed.), *The French Welfare State: Surviving Social and Ideological Change*. New York: New York University Press.

Leo XIII (1942[1891]) *On the Conditions of the Working Classes* (Rerum Novarum). Boston: St Paul Editions.

Leon, Carol Boyd (1981) 'The employment–population ratio: its value in labor force analysis', *Monthly Labor Review*, 104(2): 36–45.

Lévai, J. (1985) 'Adalékok az idskorúak, nyugdíjasok helyzetének megismeréséhez. Munkavállalás, foglalkoztatás, szociális ellátás' (Data on the situation of the elderly and pensioners. Employment, welfare care), in J. Széman (ed.) Idsekrl különféle megközelítésben (On the elderly, in different approaches), MTA Szociológiai Kutató Intézet, *Szociápolitikai Értesit*, 1985, no. 3, Budapest.

Lewis, Jane (ed.) (1983) *Women's Welfare, Women's Rights*. London: Croom Helm.

Lewis, Jane (1991a) *Women and Social Action in Late Victorian and Edwardian Britain*. Stanford: Stanford University Press.

Lewis, Jane (1991b) 'Models of equality for women: the case of state support for children in twentieth-century Britain', in Gisela Bock and Pat Thane (eds), *Maternity and Gender Policies: Women and the Rise of European Welfare States, 1880–1950*. London: Routledge. pp. 73–93.

Lewis, Jane (1992a) 'Gender and the development of welfare regimes', *Journal of European Social Policy*, 2(3): 159–73.

Lewis, Jane (1992b) *Women in Britain since 1945*. Oxford: Blackwell.

Lewis, Jane (1993) *Women and Social Policies in Europe. Work, Family and the State*. Aldershot: Edward Elgar.

Lewis, Jane and Ostner, Ilona (1991) 'Gender and the evolution of European social policies', paper presented at the CES Workshop on Emergent Supranational Social Policy: The EC's Social Dimension in Comparative Perspective, Center for European Studies, Harvard University.

Lister, Ruth (1994) 'The Child Support Act: shifting family financial obligations in the United Kingdom', *Social Politics: International Studies of Gender, State and Society*, 1(2): 211–22.

Lofström, Åsa and Gustafsson, Siv (1991) 'Policy changes and women's wages in Sweden', in Steven L. Willborn (ed.), *Stability and Change in Six Industrialized Countries: International Review of Comparative Public Policy*, Vol. 3.

Lopata, Helana Znaniecka and Brehm, Henry P. (1986) *Widows and Dependent Wives. From Social Problem to Federal Program*. New York: Praeger.

Lupri, Eugen (1983) 'The changing positions of women and men in comparative perspectives', in Eugen Lupri (ed.), *The Changing Position of Women in Family and Society*. Leiden: E. J. Brill.

Maassen van den Brink, Henriëtte (1994) *Female Labor Supply, Childcare and Marital Conflict*. Amsterdam: Amsterdam University Press.

McIntosh, C. Alison (1983) *Populaton Policy in Western Europe. Responses to Low Fertility in France, Sweden and West Germany*. Armonk: Sharpe.

McIntosh, Mary (1978) 'The state and the oppression of women', in A. Kuhn and R. M. Wolpe (eds), *Feminism and Materialism*. London: Routledge & Kegan Paul.

McIntyre, Robert (1985) 'Demographic policy and sexual equality: value conflicts and policy appraisal in Hungary and Romania', in Sharon Wolchik and Alfred Meyer (eds), *Women, State, and Party in Eastern Europe*. Durham, NC: Duke University Press.

Mackie, Thomas and Rose, Richard (1991) *The International Almanac of Electoral History*, 3rd edn. London: Macmillan.

Maier, Friederike (1992) 'The regulation of part-time work: a comparative study of six EC countries', discussion paper of the Science Center, Berlin.

Marshall, T. H. (1950) *Citizenship and Social Class*. Cambridge: Cambridge University Press.

Marshall, T. H.(1964) *Class, Citizenship and Social Development*. Garden City, NY: Doubleday.

Mennel, Annemarie (1988) 'Frauen, Steuern, Staatsausgaben, Subventionen für das Patriarchat', in U. Gerhard, A. Schwarzer and V. Slupik (eds), *Auf Kosten der Frauen. Frauenrechte im Sozialstaat*. Weinheim and Basle: Beltz. pp. 79–116.

Meyer, Alfred (1985) 'Feminism, socialism, and nationalism', in Sharon Wolchik and Alfred Meyer (eds), *Women, State, and Party in Eastern Europe*. Durham, NC: Duke University Press.

Michalopoulos, Charles, Robins, Philip K. and Garfinkel, Irwin (1992) 'A structural model of labor supply and child care demand', *Journal of Human Resources*, 27(1): 166–203.

Mieczkowski, Bogdan (1985) 'Social services for women and childcare facilities in Eastern Europe', in Sharon Wolchik and Alfred Meyer (eds), *Women, State, and Party in Eastern Europe*. Durham, NC: Duke University Press.

Milanović, Branko (1992) 'Income distribution in late socialism: Poland, Hungary, Czechoslavakia, Yugoslavia and Bulgaria compared', paper 1, Socialist Economies Reform Unit, Country Economics Department, World Bank.

Millard, Frances (1992) 'Social policy in Poland', in Bob Deacon (ed.), *The New Eastern Europe: Social Policy, Past, Present and Future*. London: Sage.

Miller, Dorothy C. (1990) *Women and Social Welfare*. New York: Praeger.

Mincer, Jacob and Polachek, Solomon (1974) 'Family investment in human capital: the earnings of women', *Journal of Political Economy*, 81(2): 76–108.

Mink, Gwendolyn (1990) 'The lady and the tramp: gender, race and the origins of the American welfare state', in Linda Gordon (ed.), *Women, the State and Welfare*. Madison: University of Wisconsin Press. pp. 92–122.

Mishra, Ramesh, (1977) *Society and Social Policy*. London: Macmillan.

Mishra, Ramesh (1990) *The Welfare State in Capitalist Society*. Brighton: Wheatsheaf Books.

Morris, Lydia (1987) 'Constraints and gender', *Work, Employment, and Society*. 1: 85–106.

Myrdal, Alva and Myrdal, Gunnar (1934) *Kris i befolkningsfrågan*. Stockholm: Bonniers.

Nelson, Barbara (1990) 'The origins of the two-channel welfare state: workmen's compensation and mothers' aid', in Linda Gordon (ed.), *Women, the State and Welfare*. Madison: University of Wisconsin Press. pp. 123–57.

Neusüss, Christel (1985) *Die Kopfgeburten der Arbeiterbewegung*. Hamburg and Zürich: Rasch & Röhrig.

Niemi, I. and Paakkonen, H. (1990) *Time Use Changes in Finland in the 1980s*. Helsinki: Central Statistical Office of Finland.

Nordic Statistical Secretariat (1990) *Social Security in the Nordic Countries: Scope, Expenditure and Financing 1987*, Statistical Reports of the Nordic Countries 51. Copenhagen: Nordic Statistical Secretariat.

Norris, Pippa (1987) *Politics and Sexual Equality: The Comparative Position of Women in Western Democracies*. Brighton: Wheatsheaf Books.

O'Connor, Julia S. (1993) 'Gender, class and citizenship in the comparative analysis of welfare state regimes: theoretical and methodological issues', *British Journal of Sociology*, 44(3): 501–18.

OECD (1984) *Labour Force Statistics 1962–82*. Paris: OECD.

OECD (1990) *Employment Outlook*. Paris: OECD.

OECD (1992) *Historical Statistics 1960–1990*. Paris: OECD.

OECD (1993a) *National Accounts 1960–1991 Main Aggregates*. Paris: OECD.

OECD (1993b) *Labour Force Statistics 1971–91*. Paris: OECD.

Offe, Claus (1992a) 'Smooth consolidation in the West German welfare state: structural change, fiscal policies and populist politics', in Frances Fox Piven (ed.), *Labor Parties in Postindustrial Societies*. New York: Oxford University Press.

Offe, Claus (1992b) 'The politics of social policy in East European transitions', paper presented at the conference on Comparative Studies in Welfare State Development: Quantitative and Qualitative Dimensions, Centre for Social Policy Research, University of Bremen.

O'Higgins, Michael (1987) 'Lone-parent families in the European Community: numbers and social economic characteristics', Working Paper 23 of the European Programme to Combat Poverty, Bath.

Okin, Susan Moller (1989) *Gender, Justice, and the Family*. New York: Basic Books.

Ólafsson, Stefán (1993) 'Variations within the Scandinavian model', in Erik Jørgen Hansen, Stein Ringen, Hannu Uusitalo and Robert Erikson (eds), *Welfare Trends in the Scandinavian Countries*. Armonk: Sharpe.

Orloff, Ann Shola (1992) 'Gender and the social rights of citizenship: state policies and gender relations in comparative perspective', paper presented at the conference on Comparative Studies of Welfare State Development, Bremen.

Orloff, Ann Shola (1993) 'Gender and the social rights of citizenship: state policies and gender relations in comparative research', *American Sociological Review*, 58(3): 303–28.

Ostner, Ilona (1989) 'Frauen und "Community Care" – Das Beispiel Grossbritannien', *Zeitschrift für Sozialreform*. 11/12: 751–62.

Ostner, Ilona (1993) 'Slow motion: women, work and the family in Germany', in Jane Lewis (ed.), *Women and Social Policies in Europe. Work, Family and the State*. Aldershot: Edward Elgar. pp. 92–115.

Pahl, Jan (1988) 'Earning, sharing, spending: married couples and their money', in Robert Walker and Gillian Parker (eds), *Money Matters: Income, Wealth, and Financial Welfare*. London: Sage.

Palme, Joakim (1990) *Pension Rights in Welfare Capitalism: the Development of Old Age Pensions in 18 OECD Countries 1930–85*. Swedish Institute for Social Research, 14. Stockholm: University of Stockholm.

Palme, Joakim (1992) 'Nations of welfare: comparing income inequalities among pre-retirement elderly', paper presented at the Department of Sociology, University of Stockholm.

Pascall, Gillian (1986) *Social Policy. A Feminist Analysis*. London: Tavistock.

Pateman, Carole (1988) 'The patriarchal welfare state', in A. Gutmann (ed.), *Democracy and the Welfare State*. Princeton: Princeton University Press. pp. 231–60.

Pateman, Carole (1989a) *The Disorder of Women: Democracy, Feminism, and Political Theory*. Stanford: Stanford University Press.

Pateman, Carole (1989b) 'Feminist critiques of the public/private dichotomy', in Carole Pateman, *The Disorder of Women*. Cambridge: Polity Press.

Pension Report (1989) Bundestags-Drucksache 11/3735.

Pension Report (1993) Bundestags-Drucksache 530/93.

Petersen, Hanne (1989) 'Lovgivning i EF inden for arbejdsmarked/ligestilling', in *Det indre markeds indflydelse på kvinders beskæftigelse*, Copenhagen: Dansk Kvindesamfund.

Pierson, Christopher (1991) *Beyond the Welfare State? The New Political Economy of Welfare*. Cambridge: Polity Press.

Pieters, D. C. H. M., Oomen, C. J. C. M. and van Rooij, J. W. T. M. (1992) *Lone Parent Families in the European Community: Summary and Conclusions*. S-Gravenhagen: Vuga.

Pius XI (1931) *On Social Reconstruction* (Quadragesimo Anno). Boston: St Paul Editions.

Plantenga, Janneke (1993) *Een afwijkend patroon. Honderd jaar vrowenarbeid in Nederland en (West) Duitsland*. Amsterdam: SUA.

Polinsky, Ella (1969) 'The position of women in the social security system', *Social Security Bulletin*, 32(7): 3–33.

Popenoe, David (1988) *Disturbing the Nest: Family Change and Decline in Modern Societies*. New York: Aldine de Ruyter.

Pott-Buter, Hettie (1993) *Facts and Fairy Tales about Female Labor, Family and Fertility. A Seven-country Comparison 1850–1990*. Amsterdam: Amsterdam University Press.

Quadagno, Jill (1987) 'Theories of the welfare state', *Annual Review of Sociology*, 13: 109–28.

Quadagno, Jill (1988) 'Women's access to pensions and the structure of eligibility rules: systems of production and reproduction', *Sociological Quarterly*, 29(4): 541–58.

Qvist, Gunnar (1975) 'Landsorganisationen i Sverige och kvinnorna på arbetsmarknaden (1898–1973)', in Eva Karlsson (ed.), *Kvinnor i arbetarrörelsen – hågkomster och intervjuer*. Stockholm: Prisma.

Rainwater, Lee (1979) 'Mothers' contributions to the family money economy in Europe and the United States', *Journal of Family History*, 4: 198–211.

Rainwater, Lee, Rein, Martin and Schwartz, Joseph (1986) *Income Packaging in the Welfare State: A Comparative Study of Family Income*. Oxford: Clarendon Press.

Rein, Martin (1985) 'Women in the social welfare labour market'. Berlin, Wissenschaftscentrum discussion paper 85–18.

Rhein-Kress, Gaby von (1993) 'Coping with economic crisis: labour supply as a policy instrument', in Francis G. Castles (ed.), *Families of Nations: Patterns of Public Policy in Western Democracies*. Aldershot: Dartmouth.

Riedmüller, Barbara (1984) 'Frauen haben keine Rechte. Zur Stellung der Frau im System der sozialen Sicherheit', in I. Kickbusch and B. Riedmüller (eds), *Die armen Frauen. Frauen und Sozialpolitik*. Frankfurt am Main: Suhrkamp. pp. 46–72.

Riedmüller, Barbara (1988) 'Geschlechtsspezifische Wirkung der Sozialpolitik. Eine Analyse der Rolle der Frau in der Sozialpolitik', in Rolf G. Heinze, Bodo Hombach and Henning Scherf (eds), *Sozialstaat 2000. Auf dem Weg zu neuen Grundlagen der sozialen Sicherung*. Bonn: Verlag Neue Gesellschaft. pp. 95–104.

Rijswijk-Clerkx, Lily van (1981) *Moeders, kinderen en kinderopvang. Veranderingen in de kinderopvang in Nederland*. Nijmegen: Socialistische Uitgeverij.

Ritter, Gerhard A. (1989) *Der Sozialstaat. Entstehung und Entwicklung im internationalen Vergleich*. Munich: Oldenbourg Verlag.

Roebroek, Joop and Berben, T. (1987) 'Netherlands', in Peter Flora (ed.), *Growth to Limits*, Vol. 4. Berlin: De Gruyter.

Rolf, Gabriele (1991) 'Ideologiekritik am Rentenrecht und ein Reformvorschlag zur eigenständigen Alterssicherung von Frauen', in Claudia Gather *et al.* (eds), *Frauenalterssicherung. Lebensläufe von Frauen und ihre Benachteiligung im Alter*. Berlin: sigma. pp. 179–94.

Rolf, Gabriele and Wagner, Gert (1992) 'Erwerbstätigkeit von Frauen und Alterssicherung', in Karl Schwarz (ed.), *Frauenerwerbstätigkeit-Demographische, soziologische, ökonomische und familienpolitische Aspekte*. Wiesbaden: Bundesinstitut für Berufsbildung, Materialien zur Bevölkerungswissenschaft 77. pp. 133–49.

Rose, Hilary (1984) 'Wohlfahrt ohne Frauen. Neubetrachtung einer klassischen Sozialpolitiktheorie', in I. Kickbusch and B. Riedmüller (eds), *Die armen Frauen. Frauen und Sozialpolitk*. Frankfurt am Main: Suhrkamp. pp. 15–45.

Rose, Richard (1991) 'Between state and market: key indicators of transition in Eastern Europe', *Studies in Public Policy*, 196, CSPP, University of Strathclyde, Glasgow.

Rose, Richard (1992a) 'Divisions and contradictions in economies in transition: household portfolios in Russia, Bulgaria and Czechoslovakia', *Studies in Public Policy*, 206, CSPP, University of Strathclyde, Glasgow.

Rose, Richard (1992b) 'Making progress and catching up: a time-space analysis of social welfare in Europe', paper presented at the European Centre for Social Welfare Policy and Research Workshop, Vienna.

Rose, Richard, Boeva, Irina and Shironin (1993) 'How Russians are coping with transition: new Russian Barometer II', *Studies in Public Policy*, 216, CSPP, University of Strathclyde, Glasgow.

Ruggie, Mary (1984) *The State and Working Women*. Princeton: Princeton University Press.

Sacks, Michael Paul (1978) 'Women in the industrial labour force', in Dorothy Atkinson, Alexander Dallin and Gail Warshofsky Lapidus (eds), *Women in Russia*. Hassocks: Harvester.

Sainsbury, Diane (1990) 'Gender and comparative analysis: welfare states, state theories, and social policies', paper presented at the ECPR planning session on Requirements for the Comparative Study of Women in European Politics: Theories, Methodologies, Data and Resources, Bochum, Germany.

Sainsbury, Diane (1991) 'Analysing welfare state variations: the merits and limitations of models based on the residual-institutional distinction', *Scandinavian Political Studies*, 14(1): 1–30.

Sainsbury, Diane (1993a) 'Dual welfare and sex segregation of access to social benefits: income maintenance policies in the UK, the US, the Netherlands and Sweden', *Journal of Social Policy*, 22(1): 69–98.

Sainsbury, Diane (1993b) 'Welfare state restructuring? Gender equality reforms and their impact', paper presented at the ECPR workshop on Welfare States and Gender, Leiden.

Sainsbury, Diane (1994) 'Social policy and the influence of familial ideology', in Marianne Githens, Joni Lovenduski and Pippa Norris (eds), *Different Roles, Different Voices: Women and Politics in the United States and Europe*. New York: HarperCollins.

Sapiro, Virginia (1986) 'The gender basis of American social policy', *Political Science Quarterly*, 101(2): 221–38.

Saraceno, Chiara (1994) 'The ambivalent familism of the Italian welfare state', *Social Politics: International Studies of Gender, State and Society*, 1(1): 60–83.

Schallhöfer, Petra (1988) 'Frauen als Sozialhilfeempfängerinnen', in U. Gerhard, A. Schwarzer and V. Slupik (eds), *Auf Kosten der Frauen. Frauenrechte im Sozialstaat*. Weinheim and Basle: Beltz. pp. 231–78.

Scharpf, Fritz W. (1986) 'Strukturen der post-industriellen Gesellschaft, oder: Verschwindet die Massenarbeitslosigkeit in der Dienstleistungs- und Informationsökonomie?', *Soziale Welt*, 37: 3–24.

Scheiwe, Kirsten (1991) 'Male times and female times in the law. Normative models of time in labour law, social security law and family law, and their impact on the gendered division of labour'. Doctoral dissertation, European University Institute, Florence.

Scheiwe, Kirsten (1993) *Männerzeiten und Frauenzeiten im Recht*. Berlin: Duncker & Humblot.

Scheiwe, Kirsten (forthcoming) 'The gender dimension in German labour law – time revisited', in Yota Kravaritou (ed.), *Le sexe du droit du travail en Europe*. Dordrecht, Boston and London: Martinus Nijhoff.

Schmähl, Winfried (1993) 'The "1992 reform" of public pensions in Germany: main elements and some effects', *Journal of European Social Policy*, 3(1): 39–51.

Schmidt, Manfred G. (1985) *Der schweizerishe Weg zur Vollbeschäftigung*. Frankfurt and New York: Campus Verlag.

Schmidt, Manfred G. (1988) *Sozialpolitik: Historische Entwicklung und internationaler Vergleich*. Opladen: Leske & Budrich.

Schmidt, Manfred G. (1993a) 'Erwerbsbeteiligung und Politik: Internationaler Vergleich der Frauen- und Männererwerbsquoten', in Roland Czada and Manfred G. Schmidt (eds), *Verhandlungsdemokratie, Interessenvermittlung, Regierbarkeit. (Festschrift für Gerhard Lehmbruch)*. Opladen: Westdeutscher Verlag.

Schmidt, Manfred G. (1993b) 'Gendered labour force participation', in Francis G. Castles (ed.), *Families of Nations: Patterns of Public Policy in Western Democracies*. Aldershot: Dartmouth.

Schultz, T. Paul (1981) *Economics of Population*. Reading, MA: Addison-Wesley.

Schunter-Kleemann, Suzanne (ed.) (1990) *EG-Binnenmarket – EuroPatriarchat oder Aufbruck der Frauen?*. Bremen: Wissenschaftlichen Einheit Frauenstudien und Frauenforschung.

Schwencke, Tine (1992) *Kvinner og det Europæiske felleskap. Rammebetingelser for EFs likestillingspolitikk*, Universitetet i Bergen: Institutt for sammenliknende politikk.

Scott, Joan W. (1986) 'Gender: a useful category of historical analysis', *American Historical Review*, 91(5): 1053–75.

Scott, Joan W. (1988) 'Deconstructing equality versus difference: or, the uses of post-structuralist theory for feminism', *Feminist Studies*, 14(1): 33–50.

SCP (1993) *Sociale Atlas van de Vrouw*. The Hague: Social en Cultured Planbureau.

Shalev, Michael (1983) 'The social democratic model and beyond: two generations of comparative research on the welfare state', *Comparative Social Research*, 6: 315–51.

Shaver, Sheila (1991) 'Gender, class and the welfare state: the case of income security in Australia', in Michael Adler, C. Bell and A. Sinfield (eds), *The Sociology of Social Security*. Edinburgh: Edinburgh University Press. pp. 145–63.

Shaver, Sheila (1992) 'Body rights, social rights and the liberal welfare state'. SPRC Discussion Paper 38, University of New South Wales, Sydney.

Shaver, Sheila and Bradshaw, Jonathan (1993) 'The recognition of wifely labour by welfare states'. Discussion Paper 44, Social Policy Research Centre, University of New South Wales.

Siemieńska, Renata (1983) 'Women and the family in Poland', in Eugen Lupri (ed.), *The Changing Position of Women in Family and Society*. Leiden: E. J. Brill.

Siemieńska, Renata (1985) 'Women, work, and gender equality in Poland: reality and its social perception', in Sharon Wolchik and Alfred Meyer (eds), *Women, State, and Party in Eastern Europe*. Durham, NC: Duke University Press.

Siim, Birte (1987a) 'A comparative perspective on the organization of care work in Denmark and Britain', paper presented at the ECPR workshop on Women and Democratic Citizenship, Amsterdam.

Siim, Birte (1987b) 'The Scandinavian welfare states – towards sexual equality or a new kind of male domination?', *Acta Sociologica*, 30(3/4): 255–70.

Siim Birte (1988) 'Towards a feminist rethinking of the welfare state', in K. B. Jones and A. G. Jónasdóttir (eds), *The Political Interests of Gender*. London: Sage. pp. 160–86.

Siim, Birte (1990) 'Women and the welfare state: between private and public dependence. A comparative approach to care work in Denmark and Britain', in Clare Ungerson (ed.), *Gender and Caring. Work and Welfare in Britain and Scandinavia*. Hemel Hempstead: Harvester Wheatsheaf. pp. 80–109.

Siim, Birte (1993a) 'The gendered Scandinavian welfare states: the interplay between women's roles as mothers, workers and citizens in Denmark', in Jane Leiws (ed.), *Women and Social Policies in Europe*. Aldershot: Edward Elgar.

Siim, Birte (1993b) 'Gender, citizenship, and political participation in the Scandinavian welfare states', paper presented in the ECPR Joint Sessions of Workshops, Leiden.

Sik, Endre (1992) 'From the second economy to the informal economy', *Studies in Public Policy* 207, CSPP, University of Strathclyde, Glasgow.

Simonen, Leila (1990) *Contradictions in the Welfare State. Women and Caring*. Tampere: University of Tampere.

SIT (1968) *Report of the Task Force on Social Insurance and Taxes to the Citizens' Advisory Council on the Status of Women*. Washington, DC: US Government Printing Office.

Skocpol, Theda (1992) *Protecting Soldiers and Mothers. The Political Origins of Social Policy in the United States*. Cambridge: Belknap Press of Harvard University Press.

Skocpol, Theda and Amenta, Edwin (1986) 'States and social policies', *Annual Review of Sociology*, 12: 131–57.

Skocpol, Theda and Ritter, Gretchen (1991) 'Gender and the origins of modern social policies in Britain and the US', *Studies in American Political Development*, 5: 36–93.

Slupik, Vera (1988) '"Kinder kosten aber auch Geld." Dis Diskriminierung von

Frauen im Kindergeldrecht', in U. Gerhard, A. Schwarzer and V. Slupik (eds), *Auf Kosten der Frauen. Frauenrechte im Sozialstaat*. Weinheim and Basle: Beltz. pp. 193–212.

Smeeding, Timothy (1991) 'Gold mines and mine fields', LIS-CEPS Working Paper 68.

Sørensen, Annemette (1992) 'Zur geschlechtsspezifischen Struktur von Armut', *Kölner Zeitschrift für Soziologie und Sozialpyschologie*, special issue 32 on 'Poverty in the Welfare State', ed. Stephan Liebfried: 345–66.

Sørensen, Annemette and McLanahan, Sara (1987) 'Married women's economic dependency, 1940–1980', *American Journal of Sociology*, 93: 659–87.

Sørensen, Bjørg Aase (1984) 'The organizational woman and the Trojan-horse effect', in Harriet Holter (ed.), *Patriarchy in a Welfare Society*. Oslo: Universitetsforlaget, pp. 88–105.

SOU 1935: 6 *Arbetslöshetsutredningens betänkande*. Stockholm: Ministry of Internal Affairs.

SOU 1964: 25 *Nytt skattesystem*. Stockholm: Ministry of Finance.

SOU 1990: 44 'Genussystemet', *Demokrati och makt i Sverige*. Stockholm: Office of the Cabinet.

Stark, David (1992) 'The great transformation? Social change in Eastern Europe', *Contemporary Sociology*, 21: 299–304.

Statistics Sweden (1989) 'Barns levnadsvillkor', *Living Conditions Report No. 62*. Stockholm: Central Bureau of Statistics.

Statistisches Bundesamt (1980–91), *Statistisches Jahrbuch*. Stuttgart and Mainz: Kolhammer.

Statistisches Bundesamt (1993) *Statistisches Jahrbuch für die Bundesrepublik Deutschland 1993*. Wiesbaden.

Stephens, John D. (1979) *The Transition from Capitalism to Socialism*. London: Macmillan.

Stuurman, Siep (1993) *Verzuiling, kapitalisme en patriarchaat. Aspecten van de ontwikkeling van de moderne staat in Nederland*. Nijmegen: Socialistiese Uitgeverij Nijmegen.

Swain, Nigel (1992) *Hungary: The Rise and Fall of Feasible Socialism*. London: Verso.

SYN. *Statistical Yearbook of the Netherlands*, Selected years. The Hague: Central Bureau of Statistics.

Szalai, Júlia (1991) 'Some aspects of the changing situation of women in Hungary', *Signs*, 17(1): 152–70.

Szeman, Zsuzsa (1992) 'New policy for the old', in Bob Deacon (ed.), *Social Policy, Social Justice and Citizenship in Eastern Europe*. Aldershot: Avebury.

SZW (1982) *Social Security in the Netherlands*. The Hague: Ministry of Social Affairs and Employment.

Taira, Koji (1983) 'Japan's low unemployment: economic miracle or statistical artifact?', *Monthly Labour Review*, 106((7): 3–10.

Tausz, Katalin (1992) 'Reforming the Hungarian welfare state', paper presented at the conference on Comparative Studies in Welfare State Development: Quantitative and Qualitative Dimensions, Centre for Social Policy Research, University of Bremen.

Therborn, Göran (1987) 'Welfare states and capitalist markets', *Acta Sociologica*, 30(3/4): 237–54.

Therborn, Göran (1989) 'Pillarization and popular movements; two variants of welfare state capitalism: the Netherlands and Sweden', in Francis G. Castles (ed.), *The Comparative History of Public Policy*. Cambridge: Polity Press.

Tijdens, Kea and Lieon, Saskia (eds) (1993) *Kinderopvang in Nederland, Organisatie en financiering*. Utrecht: Jan van Arkel.

Titmuss, Richard (1963) *Essays on the Welfare State*, 2nd edn. London: Allen & Unwin.

Tracy, Martin B. (1988) 'Equal treatment and pension systems: a comparative study', in International Social Security Association (ed.), *Equal Treatment in Social Security*, Studies and research 27. Geneva: ISSA. pp. 37–48.

Ulc, O. (1974) *Politics in Czechoslovakia*. New York: W. H. Freeman.

Ungerson, Clare (ed.) (1990) *Gender and Caring: Work and Welfare in Britain and Scandinavia*. New York: Harvester Wheatsheaf.

UN (United Nations) (1991a) *The World's Women 1970–1990: Trends and Statistics*. New York: United Nations.

UN (1991b) *Human Development Report 1990*. New York: Oxford University Press for United Nations Development Programme.

Veil, Mechthild, Prinz, Karin and Gerhard, Ute (eds) (1992) *Am modernen Frauenleben vorbei. Verliereinnen und Gewinnerinnen der Rentenreform 1992*. Berlin: sigma.

Waerness, Kari (1990) 'The rationality of caring', in Clare Ungerson (ed.), *Gender and Caring: Work and Welfare in Britain and Scandinavia*. New York: Harvester Wheatsheaf.

Wagnerová, Alena (1983) 'Women in Czechoslovakia', in Eugen Lupri (ed.), *The Changing Position of Women in Family and Society*. Leiden: E. J. Brill.

Waring, Marilyn (1988) *Counting for Nothing: What Men Value and What Women Are Worth*. Wellington, NZ: Allen & Unwin.

Watson, Peggy (1993) 'Eastern Europe's silent revolution: gender', *Sociology*, 27(3): 471–87.

Wennemo, Irene (1992) 'The development of family policy: a comparison of family benefits and tax reductions for families in 18 OECD countries', *Acta Sociologica*, 35(3): 201–17.

Wennemo, Irene (1994) *Sharing the Costs of Children: Studies on the Development of Family Support in the OECD Countries*. Swedish Institute for Social Research, 25. Stockholm: University of Stockholm.

Wilensky, Harold L. (1990) 'Common problems, divergent policies: an 18-nation study of family policy', *Public Affairs Report*, 31: 3, Institute of Governmental Studies, University of California at Berkeley.

Wilensky, Harold L. and Lebeaux, Charles N. (1965) *Industrial Society and Social Welfare*. New York: The Free Press.

Wilensky, Harold L., Luebbert, G., Hahn, S. and Jamieson, A. (1987) 'Comparative social policy: theory, methods, findings', in M. Dierkes *et al.* (eds), *Comparative Policy Research*. Aldershot: Gower. pp. 381–457.

Wilkinson, Margaret (1982) 'The discriminatory system of personal taxation', *Journal of Social Policy*, 11: 307–34.

Wilson, Elizabeth (1977) *Women and the Welfare State*. London: Tavistock.

Wnuk-Lipinski, Edmund (1992) 'Freedom or quality: an old dilemma in a new context', in Bob Deacon (ed.), *Social Policy, Social Justice and Citizenship in Eastern Europe*. Aldershot: Avebury.

Wolcott, Irene (1986) *Work and Well-being: Satisfaction, Strains and Strategies*. Melbourne: Australian Institute of Family Studies.

WRR (1991) *Een werkend perspectief: Arbeidsparticipatie in de jaren 90*. Den Haag: Wetenschappelijke Raad voor het Regeringsbeleid.

Zaretsky, Eli (1986) 'Rethinking the welfare state: dependence, economic individualism and the family', in J. Dickinson and B. Russell (eds), *Family, Economy and State: The Social Reproduction Process under Capitalism*. London: Croom Helm.

Index